Planning Safer Communities

Communities

Edited by
Alan Marlow & John Pitts

 RHP

Russell House Publishing

First published in 1998 by

Russell House Publishing Limited
4 St. George's House
Uplyme Road Business Park
Lyme Regis
Dorset
DT7 3LS

British Library Cataloguing-in-Publication Data:
A catalogue record for this book is available from the British Library.

ISBN: 1-898924-18-X

Typeset by: Exe Valley Dataset, Exeter, Devon

Printed by: Short Run Press, Exeter, Devon

This book is dedicated to the memory of Gill Blowers (1944–1994) the first co-ordinator of the Luton Crime Reduction Programme who showed that community safety is an achievable aspiration

Foreword

We should like to thank the Gill Blowers Trust for their support for the *Planning Safer Communities* symposium upon which this book is based. The Economic and Social Research Council's *Crime and Public Order Programme*, under the directorship of Tim Hope, has played a central role in both the symposium and the book, as has the extensive professional and academic network which developed around the programme. Mike Ashley at the Local Government Association offered support and useful advice, as did Judy Renshaw and John Tench of the Audit Commission. We also appreciated the support of *Community Care's* marketing department. Geoffrey Mann of Russell House Publishing has, as usual been good humoured, appreciative and flexible, in fact, everything one wants in a publisher. Ultimately, however, a symposium or a book is only as good as its contributors. In this we have been very fortunate since, as you will discover, the contributors to this book are amongst the most eminent in this rapidly expanding field.

Alan Marlow and John Pitts, February 1998

Contents

Notes on the Contributors   vii

Section One: The Development of Community Safety Strategies

Introduction Law and Order, Crime Control   *Alan Marlow and*
and Community Safety   *John Pitts*   1

Chapter 1.   Planning for Safer Communities   *Helen Edwards*   11

Chapter 2.   Tackling Social Exclusion:
The Work of NACRO   *Frank Warburton*   15

Chapter 3.   'From Stranger to Servant':   *Andrew Elvin and*
A Durable Model of a   *Alan Marlow*   23
Community Safety Partnership

Chapter 4.   Putting the Community into
Community Safety   *Usman Khan*   33

Chapter 5.   Evaluating Community Safety
Initiatives   *Steve Osborn*   42

Chapter 6.   Policing in an Uncertain World   *Michael O'Byrne*   53

Chapter 7.   Zero Tolerance: Back to the
Future   *Jock Young*   60

Section Two: Children, Young People and Community Safety

Chapter 8.   Young People, Crime and
Citizenship   *John Pitts*   84

Chapter 9.   Preventive Work With Children
and Young People at Risk
of Offending   *John Graham*   98

Chapter 10. Youth Justice Services and   *Mike Thomas and*
Community Safety Strategies   *Peter Ashplant*   116

Chapter 11. School Exclusion, Risk and
Community Safety   *Isabelle Brodie*   121

Chapter 12. Young People's Experience of
Crime and Violence: Findings
from a Survey of School Pupils   *David Porteous*   130

Chapter 13. Youth Conflict in a London
Neighbourhood   *Philly Desai*   140

Chapter 14. Youth Prostitution and Planning   *Lana Burroughs and*
for Safer Communities   *David Barrett*   158

Section Three: Community Safety, the Messages From the Research

Chapter 15. Community Safety, Crime and
Disorder   *Tim Hope*   168

Chapter 16. Community Safety in High Crime
Neighbourhoods: A View from
the Street   *Karen Evans*   181

Chapter 17. Monitoring, Measuring and   *Alexander Hirschfield*
Mapping Community Safety   *and Kate Bowers*   189

Chapter 18. Delivering Multi-agency
Partnerships in Community Safety *Adam Crawford*   213

Chapter 19. The French Social Prevention
Initiative   *John Pitts*   223

Notes on the Contributors

Peter Ashplant   Community Safety Co-ordinator, Solihull. Member of the National Association for Youth Justice

David Barrett   Head of the Department of Applied Social Studies, University of Luton

Kate Bowers   Research Student, Urban Research and Policy Evaluation Regional Research Laboratory, University of Liverpool

Isabelle Brodie   Research Associate, University of Luton

Lana Burroughs   Senior Lecturer in Social Work, University of Luton

Adam Crawford   Deputy Director, Centre for Criminal Justice Studies, University of Leeds

Philly Desai   Freelance Researcher and Youth Worker

Helen Edwards   Chief Executive, NACRO

Andrew Elvin   Co-ordinator, Luton Crime Reduction Partnership

Karen Evans   Institute for Social Research University of Salford. Community Safety Co-ordinator, Manchester City Council

John Graham   Principal Research Officer, the Home Office

Alexander Hirschfield   Research Co-ordinator, Urban Research and Policy Evaluation Regional Research Laboratory, University of Liverpool

Tim Hope   Professor of Criminology, Keele University, Visiting Professor of Criminology, University of Luton.

Director, ESRC Crime and Public Order Programme

Usman Khan   Senior Lecturer in Politics, University of Luton

Alan Marlow   Development Fellow, Joint Director, Vauxhall Centre for the Study of Crime, University of Luton

Michael O'Byrne   Chief Constable of Bedfordshire

Steve Osborn   Director, Safe Neighbourhoods Unit

John Pitts   Professor of Socio-Legal Studies, Joint Director, Vauxhall Centre for the Study of Crime University of Luton

David Porteous   Research Associate, Vauxhall Centre for the Study of Crime University of Luton

Mike Thomas   Chair, National Association for Youth Justice, Principal Youth Justice Officer, Luton Borough Council

Frank Warburton NACRO Social Exclusion Unit

Jock Young   Professor of Sociology, Director of the Centre for Criminology, University of Middlesex

Section One
The Development of
Community Safety Strategies

INTRODUCTION

Law and Order, Crime Control and Community Safety

Alan Marlow and John Pitts

1979 and all that: rhetoric, riots and rethinks

It was in 1979 that the issue of law and order was dragged to the centre of the political stage in the UK. However, the prototype for this electoral strategy was originally fashioned by Richard Nixon's 1968 presidential campaign team. In a now familiar phrase, Nixon declaimed that the police should be armed with the 'tough but fair' powers which would enable them to 'take off their gloves and get on with the job' (Downes and Morgan 1994).

True to their election pledge, the new Conservative Government of 1979 increased, substantially, expenditure on criminal justice in general and policing in particular. What they were paying for, they said, was certainty of detection and enforcement and the routine imposition of deterrent penalties upon wrongdoers. However, within two years, events out in the world had forced a change of policy. The urban riots of the early 1980s gave weight to the argument that detection and enforcement alone were unlikely to be successful, at least in the sphere of public order. Lord Scarman, in his influential report, indicated that preventing further major disorder required not merely an adjustment of prevalent policing styles, but a radical rethink about the nature and purpose of policing in a modern, multi-cultural society.

1

"Any attempt to resolve the circumstances from which the disorders this year sprang cannot be limited to recommendations about
policing but must embrace the wider social context in which policing
is carried out"   (Scarman 1982 p 203)

Although the government responded positively to some of Scarman's
specific recommendations for change, it appeared reluctant to address the
wider questions, of social change, social inequality and racial discrimination which Scarman had suggested, were at the root of the disturbances
(see Raison, in Benyon 1984).

Sleeping policemen and wide awake janitors

Lord Scarman identified a profound sense of injustice as the motor of the
urban riots in the UK of the early 1980s. Meanwhile, at the Home Office, a
new crime prevention strategy, one which edited out the motivation of the
offender, was being devised (Clarke and Mayhew 1980). At the core of
'situational', or 'environmental', crime prevention was the belief that crime
could be effectively reduced by eliminating or reducing opportunities for its
commission, rather than intervening to change the attitudes, values or
social circumstances of perpetrators (Clarke and Mayhew 1980). The logic
of this approach was that a far broader range of organisations, groups and
individuals should be involved in crime control than had previously been
the case. Thus 'social intervention' and more narrowly focused 'criminal
justice' approaches to crime prevention were supplanted by one in which
alliances were forged between, for example, local authority housing,
planning and amenities departments, the police, local businesses and transport authorities, to devise strategies for reducing the vulnerability of the
physical environment through 'target hardening', the application of better
locks, and better lighting, and the introduction of concierge systems,
janitorial patrols, and 'sleeping policemen'. One commentator (Young
1994) observed, somewhat ironically, that we were witnessing the
emergence of a 'dimmer switch' theory of crime in which, if the lights went
up crime went down and vice versa, but such criticisms did nothing to slow
the apparently inexorable rise of situational crime prevention in the 1980s.

Working together: the advent of 'community safety'

This changed direction in crime prevention was first signalled by a Home
Office inter-departmental circular endorsing and promoting the concept of
'inter-agency co-operation' in tackling problems of crime and victimisation
(Home Office Circular 8/84). This was an influential document which
appeared to release hitherto repressed energies and, before long, inter-
agency projects began to multiply as did research projects which strove to

evaluate their effectiveness. For its part, the government supported the *Five Towns Initiative* in 1986 and the *Safer Cities Programme* in 1988. In 1990 the government issued a further interdepartmental circular (Liddle and Gelsthorpe 1994) and in 1991, the Home Office Standing Conference on Crime Prevention published *Safer Communities; The Local Delivery of Crime Prevention Through the Partnership Approach*, better known as the *Morgan Report* after its chairman James Morgan. The Report recommended that:

- local authorities, working in conjunction with the police, should have responsibility for the development and stimulation of community safety

- the development of a community safety strategy should take place at the highest tier of local government

- local multi-agency partnerships should give particular attention to the issue of young people and crime in preparing a portfolio of crime prevention activities

- wherever possible a co-ordinator with administrative support should be appointed in each unitary or county-level local authority

- central government should provide a community safety impact statement for all new legislation and major policy initiatives

There were nineteen recommendations in all, including others concerning central government funding of key activities and the drafting of codes of practice. The Report also gave currency to the term 'community safety':

> "The term 'crime prevention' is often narrowly interpreted and this reinforces the view that it is solely the responsibility of the police. On the other hand, the term 'community safety' is open to wider interpretation and could encourage greater participation from all sections of the community in the fight against crime"　　　(para 3.6)

Voluntarism preferred

In its response to the *Morgan Report* the government made it clear that it did not share the authors' enthusiasm for a disseminated system of 'community safety' led by local authorities. And, in a dismissive response, the Home Secretary of the day rejected its key recommendations. It seems evident that Morgan had inadvertently triggered the government's two major domestic phobias, public spending and local authorities.

What was left was a patchy mix of initiatives which depended largely on voluntarism, local political will and a perpetual hunt for resources for their realisation. Although the government was a signatory to the United Nations' 1990 resolution on crime prevention and urban safety, it appeared to be:

> "attempting to tackle a multi-billion pound problem with an under-resourced package of voluntary action, multi-agency co-operation and short-term, centrally controlled projects"   (Bright 1991 p 81)

As a result, much of what was passed for crime prevention in the early 1990s was merely public relations whose impact, if any, was upon the fear of crime rather than crime itself (Bright 1991). While selected initiatives were praised and community safety continued to infuse political rhetoric, the major thrust in crime control concerned the development of an increasingly punitive criminal justice apparatus and an increasingly retributive criminal justice policy. In their study of the development of the government's community safety strategy, Liddle and Gelsthorpe (1994) concluded that.

> "Progress being made in the delivery of multi-agency crime prevention has been patchy across the country, and successful work can variously be attributed to combinations of local factors such as the presence of key individuals who are dedicated to crime prevention, a particular agency having adopted a strong crime prevention focus for one reason or another, or the involvement of an external group"   (p 31)

Criminal motivation revisited

In their report, *Misspent Youth: Young People and Crime*, the Audit Commission (1996) argued for forms of crime prevention which focused upon the behaviour, attitudes and social circumstances of young people in trouble. This was a response to their finding that very little work was done with most young offenders in the early stages of their criminal careers and the inordinate costs of processing them through the youth justice system. However, it also marked an acknowledgement of a broader disenchantment with situational crime prevention strategies. While, on the one hand, situational crime prevention had revealed a tendency to displace crime into other forms of offending or other neighbourhoods, on the other it had made little apparent impact upon the rapidly rising crime rate in the 1980s.

The Audit Commission's principle recommendation was that resources should be shifted from the processing of young offenders towards effective prevention and timely intervention with adjudicated young offenders. Like the *Morgan Report*, *Misspent Youth* recommended that government should require local authorities to convene inter-agency groups and that agencies should be given a duty to co-operate with such groups. As with the *Morgan Report*, the Conservative Government duly dismissed *Misspent Youth*.

New Labour, new responsibilities

In the campaign which preceded the 1997 general election, the Labour Party indicated that if it were to form the next government, it would bring forward proposals for community safety which accorded with the recommendations in the *Morgan Report*. True to this manifesto pledge, in September 1997, the government circulated a consultation document which indicated that the future administrative arrangements for community safety would form part of the Crime and Disorder Bill to be presented to parliament at the end of 1997. The consultation document proposed that:

- Local authorities and the police service will be given new duties to develop statutory partnerships to prevent, and help reduce, crime.

- The implications of all decisions by local authorities, for the reduction of crime and disorder, should be considered by elected members and council officials in the same way that the financial or equal opportunities implications of decisions are presently considered.

- This new duty should rest jointly on the district/unitary authority (or London Borough), the chief officer of police and, where the two tier structure still exists, the county council, and that the key partners are to have an equal stake.

- This duty will require these bodies to form a leadership group and jointly conduct an audit of crime and disorder in their area, consult collectively with local agencies on targets and timescales for reducing crime and publish a local community safety strategy.

- The Home Secretary will be given a reserve power to call for a report from the leadership group on its discharge of any of these duties.

- The Government will also specify agencies which must be involved in the audit, planning and delivery process.

- There will be a legal obligation on the leadership group to produce targets, publish them and report the outcome. (Home Office 1997)

There is, we feel, much to applaud in these proposals, and although not all of Morgan's recommendations are adopted, where responsibility for community safety should rest is clear. It is also a fairly clear expression of political will and indicates the direction in which we should move which, as Michael O'Byrne points out in Chapter 7, is an essential pre-condition for rational action. The requirement to produce explicit targets within a corporate strategy will stimulate performance in agencies which have, thus far, been reluctant to become involved, while central government's new power to designate the agencies which must be involved will reduce the hiding places for the apathetic. The establishment of community safety as a focus for resource allocation decisions marks the achievement of a goal which those in the van of community safety have pursued for years. As a result, the task of the community safety professional is likely to become clearer, if not necessarily easier.

New Labour new money?

The rather worse news in the consultative document concerns the assertion that the proposals do not amount to the delivery of a new service but are, rather, a matter of 'putting crime and disorder considerations at the heart of decision making' (p11). As to the costs of this endeavour, the paper suggests that 'there will be no additional money from central Government for these new duties.' but that substantial savings should result from these new arrangements. Although perfectly predictable, the lack of new funding means that many of community safety's present weaknesses will be perpetuated. Most project funding is volatile. It usually takes the form of short-term, 'pump-priming' or 'seed corn' money which evaporates as projects become established. If, as the Audit Commission suggests, a combination of greater efficiency and effective youth crime prevention will generate significant savings in the one billion pound youth justice budget, these savings might usefully be redirected towards community safety. At present, however, there are no plans to effect such a transfer. As Adam Crawford notes in Chapter 18:

> "The question of the relationship between designated crime prevention funding and wider mainstream social and criminal justice funding is a particularly vexed one . . . there is little point in setting up pilot or demonstration projects if they collapse at the end of the funding period due to lack of mainstream support."

It is to be hoped, therefore that experience and a properly evaluated practice will allow community safety to develop from its present base in time-limited 'experimental' or 'developmental' projects, to become a central feature of local provision supported by stable funding regimes. Yet, even if this should happen, we will still have to confront the fact that good community safety practice alone cannot solve the problem of crime and social disorder. There are, as both Jock Young (Chapter 1) and Adam

Crawford (Chapter 18) point out in this volume, limits to what can be achieved because community safety strategies may only be able to address surface manifestations of more profound social and economic dislocations which generate crime and disorder in our society. Nonetheless, its seems that after nearly twenty years of unrealised promises, disappointments and fitful accomplishments, the time of 'community safety' and the 'community safety professional' has finally arrived.

The structure of this book

Planning Safer Communities is divided into three sections. In the first section, *The Development of Community Safety Strategies,* contributors address the question of how the community safety strategies which local authorities will be required to produce can be realised. In Chapter 1, Helen Edwards enjoins us to look beyond strategies which merely strive to change the attitudes, beliefs and behaviour of offenders and recognise the evident links between crime, unemployment and social exclusion. Like Jock Young (Ch. 7) she asks us not to lose a sense of the social context of crime in our enthusiasm to develop strategies and projects. In Chapter 2, Frank Warburton, who like Helen Edwards works in NACRO, offers practical examples of how concerns about the changing socio-economic predicament of young people can be translated into a practice which strives to reduce 'social exclusion' at local level. In Chapter 3 Alan Marlow and Andrew Elvin offer a potted history of the development of one of the UK's most successful crime reduction partnership. In it they highlight the importance of the political commitment of local politicians and the enthusiasm of senior officers in the key services. This points up the reality that, often, the processes whereby the partnership is constructed, and the quality of the relationship between key players, are as important, if not more so, than the nature of the partnership which eventually emerges. Whereas Andrew Elvin and Alan Marlow explore the political and professional relationships which facilitate effective community safety partnerships, in Chapter 4, Usman Khan explores the ways in which the 'public' might be involved in the development of community safety strategies. Like Jock Young he highlights the danger that while we may achieve a high level of public participation, if we do this by raising false expectations, our initial success will be short-lived. The *Safe Neighbourhoods Unit* (SNU) has more experience in the development and evaluation of neighbourhood community safety strategies than virtually any other organisation in this country. In Chapter 5 SNU's director, Steve Osborn, spells out the criteria, developed by SNU over the period, by which community safety initiatives might be evaluated. In Chapter 6 Michael O'Byrne, Chief Constable of Bedfordshire, asks how we can gauge the extent of political will underlying any particular central government initiative. Using the example of drugs, he charts the waxing and waning of political will in this area and sketches out a legislative framework and a direction for preventive practice, commensurate with the present government's stated priorities in the areas of drugs and community safety. In Chapter 7 Jock Young offers a chastening account of recent developments in the policy and practice of crime control and its tenuous relationship with the changing shape of crime and disorder in a world characterised by growing social and economic polarisation. He points to the need for those concerned with community safety to focus on the broader socio-structural origins of crime and not merely their local manifestations.

Section Two, *Children, Young People and Community Safety*, concerns a group of people who will constitute a major target for any community safety initiative. In Chapter 8 John Pitts argues that the rights and obligations of citizenship, if they were to be extended to socially excluded children and young people would, of themselves, contribute significantly to the reduction of youth crime. In developing this thesis he offers examples from action research undertaken at the Vauxhall Centre for the Study of Crime at the University of Luton in neighbourhoods in France and the UK characterised by high levels of youth crime and youth victimisation. John Graham has brought together the major findings of studies of early intervention with crime prone children and young people (the Crime and Public Order Bill 1998 provides the legal frameworks for such effective early intervention). In Chapter 9 he argues that the new youth justice legislation offers us the means to operationalise these insights. Mike Thomas is chair of the National Association for Youth Justice and in Chapter 10 he makes a plea to both community safety and youth justice professionals to put the youth justice service and its expertise at the centre of community safety initiatives and points to the dangers of the continued marginality of youth justice in the community safety debate. All the evidence we have suggests that strong links exist between school exclusion and youth crime. Thus, as school exclusion grows we can anticipate a parallel growth in youth crime. In Chapter 11 Isabelle Brodie offers a review of all that is currently known about school exclusion. The message is clear. Intervention after a child is excluded is far too late. The answer lies in prevention and the challenge concerns the development of effective preventive interventions by the educational and welfare services working in partnership. It is still only rarely acknowledged that children and young people are the most heavily victimised social group. In Chapter 12 David Porteous reports on his research in a North London secondary school which aimed to quantify and explain the nature and level of youth victimisation. He notes that victimisation is structured by age, race, gender and geography and that an effective intervention strategy must be sufficiently sophisticated to match the complexity of the reality of youth victimisation. Philly Desai is a youth worker with, and researcher of the lives of Bengali young people. In Chapter 13 he presents a report he wrote about a violent episode which unfolded around two North London schools and the responses of the schools, the police and other agencies to this conflict. Thus far, child and youth prostitution have received relatively little attention in the debate about community safety. Yet there is growing evidence that this is a problem which affects most urban areas of any size and that it not only has a deleterious effect upon the young people involved but also serves to attract crime to neighbourhoods. In Chapter 14 Lana Burroughs and David Barrett argue forcefully for child and youth prostitution to be placed within the purview of the child protection services and for the law to be targeted at 'punters' rather than the youngsters who are prostituting themselves.

Section 3, *Community Safety, the Messages from the Research*, as its title suggests, brings together chapters written by participants in the Economic and Social Research Council's Crime and Social Order research programme which was headed by Tim Hope. In Chapter 15 Tim traces the recent history of crime control and community safety in this country. He argues that the main message from the research is that there is no 'quick fix' or 'magic bullet' which we can simply fire at problems of community safety in the expectation of a bullseye. We must, he argues, always be aware that whatever it is that works, does so because it interacts creatively with the environment in which it is applied. This is not particularly bad news since we are developing a far clearer understanding of the factors at work in this encounter between technique and social context and, in a growing number of instances, this is leading to a more sensitive and flexible practice. Karen Evans offers an useful example of this point in her discussion of patterns of victimisation in Oldtown and Bankhill. Oldtown she characterises as a 'defended community' while Bankhill is a 'frightened community'. She attributes these differences to quite different local histories and patterns of relationships in the two adjacent areas. Whereas Karen Evans offers us a 'view from the street', Alexander Hirschfield and Kate Bowers in Chapter 17 offer us a view from high above the street or, more specifically, an account of their investigation of the contribution of the monitoring and mapping of threats to community safety on the basis of telephone calls to the police and the fire brigade in Merseyside. From this data they have been able to develop profiles of particularly vulnerable groups and the nature of the risks posed to them. This typology has offered an important base from which local community safety strategies can be devised. Adam Crawford is concerned with the administrative and financial basis of community safety, arguing that the 'new public management' paradigm which has had an important impact on public services in the UK in the 1980s and 1990s may not be the most useful model upon which to develop community safety. Echoing themes raised in Chapter 3 by Andrew Elvin and Alan Marlow he argues that 'trust', not merely revised performance indicators, is a precondition for success in inter-agency collaboration. In the final chapter, John Pitts offers an account of his comparative study of the responses of local politicians and public professionals to youth crime in two high crime neighbourhoods, one in London and the other in Paris. Raising similar questions about political will to those posed by Michael O'Byrne in Chapter 6 he points to the different possibilities opened up by policies which proceed from the assumption that youth crime and disorder is essentially a problem of discipline, and those which view it as a breakdown of social cohesion and social solidarity.

Bibliography

Audit Commission (1996) *Misspent Youth: Young People and Crime*, London, Audit Commission

Benyon J. (ed.) (1984) *Scarman and After*, Oxford, Pergamon

Bright J. (1991) *Crime Prevention: The British Experience,* in Stenson K. and Cowell D. (eds.) (1991) The Politics of Crime Control, London, Sage

Clarke R. and Mayhew P. (eds.) (1980) *Designing Out Crime*, London, HMSO

Downes D. and Morgan R. (1994) *Hostages to Fortune? The Politics of Law & Order in Post-War Britain* in Maguire M. Morgan R. and Reiner R. (1994) The Oxford Handbook of Criminology, Oxford, Oxford University Press

Farrington D. (1996) *Understanding and Preventing Youth Crime,* York, Rowntree Foundation

Home Office (1984) *Interdepartmental Circular 8/84*, London, HMSO

Home Office (1997) *Getting to Grips with Crime: A New Framework for Local Action* London, HMSO

Home Office (1991) *Safer Communities: The Local Delivery of Crime Prevention Through the Partnership Approach* (The Morgan Report), London, Home Office

Liddle M. and Gelsthorpe L. (1994) *Inter-Agency Crime Prevention: Organising Local Delivery*, Crime Prevention Unit Series Paper 52, London, Home Office

Scarman L. (1982) *The Scarman Report: The Brixton Disorders 10–12 April 1981*, Harmondsworth, Pelican

Young J (1994) *Incessant Chatter: Recent Paradigms in Criminology* in Maguire M. Morgan R. and Reiner R. (1994) The Oxford Handbook of Criminology, Oxford, Oxford University Press

CHAPTER 1

Planning for Safer Communities

Helen Edwards

When we started work on the Morgan Committee in 1990 one local authority person said 'I don't know why I am here – it seems to me that crime is a police responsibility.' We travelled a long road to reach our recommendation – which was unanimous – that it was local authorities which should have a clear statutory responsibility for the development and stimulation of community safety. In effect we were putting local authorities in the lead. Seven years later the reasons for that recommendation will be clear to most people.

The responsibilities of local authorities and the services they run not only to maintain the physical fabric of towns and cities but to ensure the well-being of the people who live there are critical to the prevention of crime. Our view was that local authorities had two clear tasks – firstly to ensure that crime prevention/community safety was reflected in the activities of all its departments and secondly to co-ordinate its activities with all the other main players, in particular the police. We are now at the point where a new statutory duty is being drafted although I suspect it will be drafted as a shared responsibility between the police and local authorities. But I don't see that necessarily as a problem. The central point has been established that local authorities have a lead role in preventing crime.

So seven years after Morgan what impact is that duty likely to have? First we must recognise that substantial progress has been made since the Morgan Committee did its work. There are now thriving partnerships up and down the country, an impressive range of initiatives being pursued and an impact which is starting to show through. If the claim that crime is falling has any substance it seems to me to be much more likely to be because of the impact of crime prevention than anything to do with prisons. How much more we achieve will depend on how the statutory duty is translated into action.

I would like to suggest three things which should be taken into account:

1.   Get the range of activities right
In much crime prevention activity, there is still an over-emphasis on technical devices and opportunity reduction. Schemes to address the causes of crime have developed but not as much as they need to. And one

aspect that is often not addressed is the economic circumstances of high crime neighbourhoods. In particular the employment prospects of marginalised, disaffected and disadvantaged young men. Research has been telling us about the importance of this for years and it is now generally accepted that the disappearance of unskilled and semi-skilled work opportunities for young men has been one of the driving forces pushing up crime rates. This has been particularly apparent in those neighbourhoods and communities where a potent mixture of market forces and social and economic policies have brought together those most vulnerable to crime with those most likely to commit crime. This has created deep pockets of social exclusion, deprivation and instability, the like of which I certainly have not seen before.

Community safety strategies already focus on such communities but the recently published Joseph Rowntree report by Anne Power and Rebecca Tunstall on riots and violent disturbances underlines, amongst other things, the importance of changing the long-term economic prospects of young men. Otherwise money invested will not achieve the desired results. All the areas studied had had significant amounts of public money invested in them. Yet, if anything, developments had served to further exclude the young men who were involved in the disturbances.

Often the question of jobs and economic regeneration are not addressed because the answers are not easy or because they are seen as falling beyond the remit of community safety. But we shall not get far if we continue to ignore them. There may be opportunities which could be grasped. For example the Government's New Deal for the under 25s could be deployed to change a situation where young people in such neighbourhoods have been progressively excluded from the job and training opportunities which do exist. And perhaps to examine much more creatively the possibilities for creating real and lasting work opportunities.

So in determining the range of activities we must not be narrow in our approach. Nor must we fail to make the links with other programmes and initiatives. Community safety is a distinct discipline but if it does not make the links, opportunities to reduce crime will be missed. Apart from links with the New Deal others which spring to mind include:

- children's service plans
- SRB programmes
- youth justice strategies

2. Avoid the superficial attractions of quick-fix solutions

In terms of protecting people from the impact of crime this can result in over-reliance on technical solutions. In terms of dealing with the people who commit it, it can boost the crack-down approach where crime is seen to be a problem committed by a few criminals and undesirables who deliberately set out to make life difficult for the rest of us. The answer is therefore to get the criminals and undesirables off the streets, off the housing estates and ideally into the prisons.

I am not trying to say that technical inputs to community safety are not important – clearly they are – or that ridding long suffering people of neighbours who make their lives a misery is not necessary on occasions. But it has become fashionable in some quarters to present such approaches as solutions. They are not. You can't deal with social problems by trying to sweep them away and pretending they don't exist. However attractive prison or injunctions or 'zero tolerance' may seem as a way of getting rid of problems they are, at most, a temporary respite.

Prisoners are released and in large return to the same high crime communities, they came from often more racially intolerant, resentful and ill-equipped than when they went in. People who are evicted or moved on do not disappear. Neither do their problems. Sooner or later we need to start designing strategies for re-integration rather than relying on the quick-fix solutions which, longer-term, can lead to further exclusion. We have to begin to tackle some of the root causes.

3. Sell and market community safety

In the public mind the answer to crime is tougher laws, more prison. Most people have only the vaguest notion of crime prevention. Tougher laws and more prison will not produce greater safety (although it does fulfill a desire to punish) but in the absence of any other solutions being put to them the public will continue to look in this direction. Then, when the criminal justice system disappoints them, which it will given their unrealistic expectations, the disappointing results will simply fuel the demand, robustly informed and fortified by the media, for even tougher penalties. The assumption will be that society is not getting safer because we have not been tough enough.

We have to put the other options before them and break out of this circle. Otherwise solutions, such as crime prevention, which really will reduce crime, will continue to be marginal, under-funded activities squeezed by the huge expenditure on the criminal justice system. As part of this we have to engage the media with crime prevention, which will not be easy given the preoccupation with violent crime and sensational stories. But it can be done. There are success stories to tell and interesting ways of telling them. We need to improve our communication; stop talking in jargon or using obscure terms, e.g. target hardening, repeat victimisation. We have to explain what 'community safety' is, most people will have only the haziest notion that it is anything to do with crime.

If we are to sell crime prevention to people we have to make clear what it is:

- in language people can understand
- in the context of their concerns about crime and
- in ways which are interesting and grab peoples attention.

In conclusion, we have a real opportunity to put crime prevention on the map. There is enthusiasm and commitment by the new administration and we must make the most of it. The price of not doing so will be very high. Not least an ever-rising prison population, already at record levels, which will take resources and attention away from the very things which could actually reduce crime.

CHAPTER 2

Tackling Social Exclusion: The Work of NACRO

Frank Warburton

Introduction

The tackling of social exclusion is both an important precondition for community safety and part of the process of responding to offending behaviour. This view underpins NACRO's approach to crime prevention. NACRO manages a range of services which engage with, support and work to integrate those at-risk of crime and those who have already been in trouble. It has also developed a number of new approaches to crime prevention and worked at local level to help shape the action of other agencies also concerned to reduce crime. This broad experience provides a number of examples of what works, both in terms of project delivery and the processes involved in implementing crime prevention strategies. As importantly, it provides a picture of the context within which such work takes place, the obstacles to more generally deploying what works and what is necessary to overcome such obstacles.

A partnership approach to tackling social exclusion represents one of the greatest challenges on the partnership agenda. All community safety partnerships are advised to have certain processes – multi-agency committees, joint information systems, shared planning and there can be difficulties with implementing these, but if social exclusion is included in the equation there is a much greater need to examine carefully the culture, the practice and the priorities within local services to see how they affect or fail to affect excluded groups; in particular young men, from disadvantaged communities.

To date, criminologists and others whose main interest has been the prevention of crime have tended to view from a distance other agents of social policy, such as the school system, the youth service, training and employment bodies and housing authorities and tried to persuade them to realise their full preventive potential. There has been limited success in getting an authoritative response from those involved. The arguments don't appear to have carried enough weight to take hold if they have appeared to detract from the overall priorities of each department or agency. In recent years those priorities have been shaped by other, much more powerful external forces – funding crises, re-organisations, and fragmentation, and radical reappraisals of the main thrust and purpose of particular services.

This chapter deals with the main issues that NACRO has encountered in promoting an emphasis on social exclusion within crime prevention both within its projects and its more strategic work and suggests ways in which such difficulties can be overcome.

What is 'social exclusion'?

Although the term exclusion arose as a term to describe lack of involvement with the labour market it has come to have a much broader meaning. This is indicated in the 1994 European Social Policy White Paper.

Exclusion processes are dynamic and multi-dimensional in nature. They are linked not only to unemployment and/or to low incomes but also to housing conditions, levels of education and opportunities, health, discrimination, citizenship and integration in the local community.

Unsurprisingly, the social factors to which exclusion is linked are broadly similar to the risk factors associated with offending. These have been set out recently by NACRO in *Getting Serious About Youth Crime* – a ten point plan prepared for the incoming Labour Government. Similar lists have been drawn up by the Audit Commission, The Joseph Rowntree Foundation and others. Risk factors include:

- families where parents need assistance
- truancy or exclusion from school
- a lack of opportunity for constructive leisure activity
- being without a job or training
- alcohol and drugs misuse
- being involved in nuisance and anti-social behaviour
- being sent to prison

The extent of social exclusion

Social exclusion is a growing problem. According to the European Social Policy White Paper 'Social exclusion is a endemic phenomenon . . . It threatens the social cohesion of each member state and of the union as a whole'.

In the UK exclusion refers to a number of things for many people. It can refer to the 250,000 plus people aged 18–25 who are long term unemployed (Misspent Youth). It can refer to the 13,419 children permanently excluded from school in 1995/96 (DfEE). It can refer to 60 per cent of 16 and 17 year old offenders who are unemployed when sentenced (Basic Skills Agency). It can also mean disappearance. In 1994, 76,000 16 and 17 year olds were missing from the work force, full-time education or youth training schemes according to a study by the Royal Philanthropic Society and the Trust for the Study of Adolescence. This trend is confirmed by a more recent study commissioned by Fairbridge which suggested that more than 105,000 18–20 year olds are currently outside education, employment and training networks.

Examples from NACRO's work

Three examples of NACRO's work show aspects of successful practice in tackling social exclusion but also point to a number of conclusions about what needs to happen for such approaches to be more routinely applied at local level and what the main obstacles are for successful corporate action.

Tackling exclusion from training, employment and further education – The work of NACRO Youth Choices
NACRO has managed a number of 'youth choices' projects which are detached youth projects linked to training and employment schemes. They are a means of engaging with and holding on to young people in order to give them increased opportunities to acquire skills and obtain work. NACRO set up its first youth choices project in Newcastle in 1991. The aims of the initiative were to identify and work with young people aged 16 and 17 who did not appear on careers service records, were not in employment or further education, nor on youth training schemes. This group of 'missing' young people comprising 6–9 per cent of the target age group, were considered to be the most vulnerable and the most at risk of crime.

NACRO worked in partnership with Tyneside Training and Enterprise Council, the careers service and many other local organisations to make contact with these young people, to find out their reasons for non-participation in training and to help them find and take up suitable opportunities. In its first year of operation over 200 young people were contacted. 80 were homeless, many had been in care or custody and a high proportion had been persistent absentees from school. Of the 200, 88 took up youth training or education and a further 56 were actively considering training. Subsequent youth choices initiatives have focused on related problems such as homelessness and a number of other projects were set up by NACRO elsewhere.

Detached work is not a startling new idea and is used by many other agencies principally by the local authority youth service to encourage participation in youth centres. Although detached youth work is now carried out to a greater extent compared to centre-based work than it used to be, the shift in emphasis has occurred at the same time as an overall decline in local authority provision. The experience of youth choices suggests two questions for local partnerships.

First, youth choices staff naturally came across a range of problems over and above the need for training which they themselves cannot resolve. Such work therefore needs an integrated system where young people can access the appropriate advice and support.

Second, unemployment continues at a high level and while youth training remains underfunded there will be a danger that current levels of young people will carry on slipping through the training net. Some of the need could be met by an extra service to engage such young people but it is equally important that there is improved co-ordination between schools, career services, training providers and job centres to ensure that records are adequately maintained and passed on and individual cases are checked and if necessary followed up.

This kind of co-ordination requires underpinning by an integrated policy linked to a community safety strategy which is prepared to target resources at those who are excluded and at greater risk of crime.

An integrated approach to exclusion from leisure – The Salford Football Community Link Project
Launched in 1994, the project works with local communities to set up and run football clubs for young people aged 8 to 16. With one paid staff member acting as co-ordinator, volunteers – local residents – take the lead role in organising and running the clubs, organised by the project which provide coaching and take part in tournaments throughout the city.

The aims of the project are to enable local communities to develop activities which benefit the young people who participate, the adults who set them up and run them, the communities themselves and the agencies which serve these communities. Ultimately, the project promotes community-based initiatives as a means of tackling anti-social, self-destructive and criminal behaviour amongst young people.

Salford has high levels of social and economic deprivation: the local authority covers an area which is the ninth most disadvantaged in the country in terms of poverty. Young people in Salford have had few opportunities to take part in recreational activities. Some of those on local housing estates have had none.

In consequence problems of vandalism and anti-social behaviour by teenagers at local facilities were common. Some of the young people who could afford to use them found themselves barred from the local recreation centres because of their behaviour, and centre staff were ill-equipped to deal with them. The centres had lost out on custom as customers felt intimidated or had their cars damaged by young people.

The socio-economic conditions have been a significant barrier to the development of local activities: lack of funds, few resources, poor access to training and support all militate against community-led initiatives being developed and sustained. Unemployment or living on a low income can prevent people from taking part in those activities which do exist.

The project developed out of a neighbourhood football scheme established in 1991. Some of the 16 to 19 year old participants entered a team in the Salford Sunday League and became division champions at the end of the first season. Motivated by their success, the players volunteered to run weekly football training sessions for younger boys. This led to a local tournament, subsequently held every summer for three years with over 70 adults and young people taking part each time. Setting up the tournament required careful negotiation with recreation centre staff as a number of them had been intimidated by participants or had their cars vandalised. Despite this, centre staff took an active part in organising the tournaments because they recognised the positive nature of the activities

The success of the scheme on the estate suggested that it could be expanded to cover the whole of Salford. In 1994, after an enthusiastic response to a consultation exercise with the young people, parents, volunteers, community groups and local statutory agencies, work started on setting up a city-wide project. By the end of the first season, nine clubs had been established with over 300 participants; 18 clubs were running 50 weeks of the year by the end of 1996.

Despite the simplicity of the project, its successes are considerable. At any one time, up to 1,000 young people and 130 volunteers are taking part in the project, which works with a range of local authority departments, the local probation service, the police and diverse community groups and individuals. It has attracted energetic and committed volunteers in an area where severe disadvantage has often led to residents' apathy. The project and its volunteers have worked with some very difficult young people with great success.

Activities based around football coaching, games and tournaments are easily replicable and with only a minimum of resources, local communities can take the lead themselves. The question then is why isn't this kind of scheme more common and in other areas where something similar is taking place are the implications for crime and social exclusion fully appreciated.

Has the problem arisen chiefly because the schools and the Sunday leagues which traditionally would have met this kind of need can no longer do so or is there now the need for some kind of bridging mechanism for excluded young people to school and Sunday league provision.

Safer cities: moving from project work to policy and practice within local agencies

NACRO has managed on behalf of the government 15 of the 32 Safer Cities projects in England and Wales under phase two of the programme. Each project has a small team and access to a grant fund of £100,000 a year.

Each project has assisted local community safety schemes with grant aid and works towards a clear joint strategy for crime prevention guided by steering committees representing local organisations concerned with crime prevention.

NACRO has provided advice to each project steering committee about how best to carry out its strategic plan and good practice in community safety. Each project took a number of steps to try and ensure that features of social exclusion were considered by local partnerships.

Each project carried out a crime and community profile rather than a crime audit of the local area to ensure that information on social conditions such as unemployment and poverty were considered alongside crime data. In each of the projects young people were identified as a priority for action within strategic plans not only in terms of offending but victimisation and disaffection as well. In the Leeds project Safer Cities funding was used to commission research into diverting young people from crime by evaluating the work of the SPACE (Positive Alternatives to Crime) project. The research, carried out by Leeds Metropolitan University found that youth work methods can be successful in tackling offending behaviour.

Careful consideration was given to how each three year project could make maximum long-term impact. For, although the Safer Cities grant monies provided a useful focal point for each partnership the yearly grant fund of £100,000 represented a tiny amount compared with the overall spending of local agencies. The Sheffield Project was disbursing its grant in a city where the combined budget for education and social services in 1995/96 was £272 million. It was therefore important to devote time to drawing mainstream services into the community safety arena. In Sheffield seminars were organised for officers and members from relevant local authority departments and each agency represented on the steering committee prepared a policy statement detailing its own contribution to community safety.

Issues

Although NACRO phase two Safer Cities projects can show progress in the development of local partnerships and supporting a number of targeted and innovative schemes to deal with actual or potential offending behaviour there remains much to be done in moving from time-limited demonstration projects to a process that is central to the policy and practice of local agencies. There is a lot of good work taking place up and down the country within the local authorities, within other local agencies and within the voluntary sector. However there are still marked variations in practice and security measures still dominate the measures perceived by local authorities to be preventive. According to the 1996 survey of local authorities carried out by the (then) three local government associations the most commonly undertaken community safety activities were:- CCTV 83 per cent, housing estate improvements 72.8 per cent, diversionary holiday schemes for young people 66.7 per cent, door entry schemes for housing estates 66 per cent, car park security 63.6 per cent. Only one of these activities can be described as contributing directly to dealing with social exclusion.

A broad approach to community safety has not been reflected strongly in regeneration strategy within the Single Regeneration Budget Challenge round two – a minority of successful projects have community safety as one of the main listed objectives.

There have been other significant developments within local authorities such as the use of increased powers by housing departments consolidated by part V. of the Housing Act 1996 to take action against anti-social tenants. In many areas these developments have taken place without the active involvement of community safety partnerships. Many community safety partnerships will be created or reviewed as a result of the statutory duties being placed on local authorities. A number of key points need to be considered by local partnerships.

They need some clear definitions about what constitutes crime prevention. For example when is youth provision 'youth diversion'? It would be of limited use to define all youth work as diversionary yet the literature on what works in this field contains many examples where it is difficult to distinguish between what is cited as preventive and good youth work practice. Partnerships need to incorporate measures to tackle social exclusion into a wide vision for community safety and more specifically:

- target effort and resources toward excluded groups
- build community capacity and involve young people
- invest in young people generally

A good test of whether tackling social exclusion and community safety have genuinely become an integral part of local agency work, is when issues facing local authorities in general start applying to community safety.

This would mean that community safety would be fully integrated with other local strategies such as anti-poverty; that the operations of community safety partnerships become more transparent and that community consultation becomes a matter of routine rather than a subsection of the crime audit and that the focus of activity shifts from short-term projects to mainstream services.

Conclusion

NACRO can claim some successes in its work to reduce social exclusion as a means of reducing crime. It is by no means alone in being able to make these claims. Other voluntary sector organisations and local authorities can provide many similar examples. The question still remains why is such success still comparatively rare and why can it be such a struggle to implement a successful partnership response to social exclusion? Security measures usually require, at the most, bilateral co-operation and the use of punishment in the criminal justice system requires very little co-operation at all.

The fact that security measures are tangible, are measures associated in the public mind with what prevention is about and are less problematic to implement provides much of the explanation for their prevalence on many local community safety agendas.

Nonetheless there are powerful arguments for making the effort to develop partnerships to tackle social exclusion not just as a means of ensuring joint investment in our disadvantaged communities but as a means of preventing crime.

CHAPTER 3

'From Stranger to Servant': A Durable Model of a Community Safety Partnership

Andrew Elvin and Alan Marlow

Introduction

Whenever there is a television programme on the subject of football hooliganism, the producers usually include recordings of a horde of young men charging police across a football pitch and throwing plastic seats that had been wrenched from the terraces. These were scenes from an FA Cup quarter final between Luton Town Football Club and Millwall in 1985. The incident proved to be something of a watershed as it stimulated a radical approach to the control of football hooliganism – a supporters membership scheme and a total prohibition on the attendance of away team supporters at Luton Town home matches. These initiatives were deeply unpopular with the football authorities and those who studied the phenomenon of violence at football matches warned that there would be a displacement of football related conflict and that rival supporters would seek to attend in any case.

The results were, however, remarkable. No longer was the town under siege every time there was a home match. The football ground is situated in the main area of minority ethnic group settlement and the racist incidents that attended football matches simply disappeared. There were only one or two arrests per season and the numbers of police necessary on match days was the lowest in the old first or second divisions of the league. Despite the loss of away supporters, numbers attending matches increased as more families felt able to come. There was no displacement effect and very few examples of away supporters attempting to enter the ground.

This effective solution to a problem that had been a running sore for years was the product of co-operation between the football club, the borough council and the police and it gave powerful testimony to the fact that original and effective solutions could emerge from a multi-agency focus on a pernicious problem. The scheme lasted five years before new

owners re-admitted away supporters but it allowed the football establishment time to improve control and local youth gangs to grow out of
football violence. It also stimulated a realisation that more of the town's
problems might be solved by similar approaches. Out of that, the Luton
Crime Reduction Programme emerged.

During the mid to late 1980s, a number of models began to emerge
nationally that sought to combine local agencies, energies and initiatives to
focus on the goal of crime reduction or what the Morgan Report was later
to term 'community safety'. The structures varied according to local conditions and political possibilities. According to the Morgan Report which
was published in 1991, five models for the delivery of crime prevention at
local level could be discerned:

1. The independent model
2. The local authority based model
3. The police controlled local model
4. The police centred headquarters model
5. The indeterminate model

This chapter describes the evolution and durability of the Luton
partnership approach which fits Morgan's independent model. The
distinguishing features of the model include a co-ordinator who is not part
of any of the local agencies, an area wide committee chaired by an eminent
local person and funding from a variety of sources. The programme was
initiated in 1989 and is still functioning as a high profile feature of the
town. It has been visited at various times by the Princess Royal, the Home
Secretary and the Shadow Home Secretary. An examination will also be
made of the reasons for its longevity, its strengths and its weaknesses.

The Setting

Luton occupies the south-eastern tip of the county of Bedfordshire. Its
population is presently 181,000 – which is probably an under-estimate.
Since the last century its growth has been rapid – a ten fold increase in
population since 1876 and a three fold increase since 1914.

The job opportunities and prosperity that attracted its new citizens
resulted from the establishment of manufacturing industries, notably
motor vehicle construction, chemicals and engineering. Companies came
to the town to take advantage of good communications, cheap land, low
rates and a labour force with few union restrictions. The abundance of
semi-skilled jobs in earlier years provided the pull for this immigration and
created a richly diverse, cosmopolitan population. Many Lutonians trace
their ancestry to Ireland, Scotland and Wales, whilst about 20 per cent have
their origins in the Indian sub-continent or the Caribbean.

Unusually for its location, Luton is a working class industrial town and despite a general decline in manufacturing, that sector still employs 30 per cent of the workforce.

As Luton matured, high profile companies became linked to the town's identity. They have an interest in promoting a positive image of the town to attract and retain employees. A strong civic tradition exists with a fierce sense of independence. The town enjoyed Borough status from 1876. In 1964, having fought for the status for decades it became a County Borough. This status was lost in 1974 when it became a District Authority. In April 1997, it was granted unitary status

The need

Luton has always experienced a high level of crime although this has stabilised in recent years. In surrounding areas, crime has increased at a faster rate. The chances of a Luton resident being a victim of crime in the late 1980s was about twice the national average (British Crime Survey data). The proportion of crimes that can be categorised as serious or 'fear-generating' is significantly higher than the expected level when compared with adjacent or similar areas.

It was also clear that the high rate of victimisation was correlated to indicators of social deprivation. Unemployment is a persistent feature at around 10 per cent of the work force. In 1994, 41 per cent of the total had been unemployed for one year or more and 26 per cent of the unemployed were in the 18–24 age group. In the late fifties, motor manufacturing absorbed a labour force of more than 30,000 people. That demand for labour has now reduced to 6,000 people and yet Vauxhall Motors produces more vehicles than ever.

Unsurprisingly, indicators demonstrated that deprivation was most keenly felt by minority groups, predominantly South Asian, who are concentrated in the two most deprived wards of the town. The unemployment rate for the wards is 21 per cent and some of the enumeration districts in these wards are amongst the most deprived in England. The population of the town is relatively young with 36.8 per cent under the age of 24. The profile of the minority groups is even younger with 54 per cent under the age of 24.

Coupled with the actuality of crime, town surveys indicated that the fear of crime was a real issue and far exceeded the actuality, albeit that the latter was relatively high (Luton Initiative Survey 1989, Comedia Research 1990, Crime Reduction Programme Survey 1991 – all unpublished).

Development

A number of elements combined to determine the form of the programme.

For some time, there had been liaison meetings between the police and council officers. Both the Chief Executive and the Divisional Police Commander had a strong commitment to the notion of co-operative crime reduction. A number of projects had been jointly developed. At about the same time, the Home Office announced the Safer Cities Programme. A proposal to place Luton in the programme was rejected as it did not meet the criteria.

Luton's crime level was of real concern to local politicians and leaders from all parties were persuaded to fund an initiative to tackle crime in the town. It was agreed that the council would provide core funding to allow the appointment of a co-ordinator. A steering committee was created comprising senior representatives of business, statutory agencies, the voluntary sector and others with specialist abilities. It was chaired by a prominent local citizen. Finance was attracted from the private sector and other sources. The timing of the events also coincided with the establishment of Crime Concern. Its Chairman played a prominent part in 'selling' the idea to local businesses. Additionally, Crime Concern agreed that the Co-ordinator would be their employee to signify independence from the local authority.

Structure

A structure was devised that would allow prioritisation of problems and a strategic approach to action planning. Key focus areas were identified as 'youth', 'the town centre', 'residential burglary', 'autocrime' and 'vulnerable persons'. A task group known as a target group was created for each of these areas, headed by a senior professional with some commitment to the issue or an appropriate expertise and a membership drawn from practitioners from a range of agencies within the town. A crime profile group was formed to assess needs and priorities and to inform, receive information from the target groups and act as an executive tier. The steering group, as a policy group, headed the structure.

Demographic and crime data was synthesised to provide a crime profile upon which logical decision making could be based. Machinery was therefore in place for a cool assessment of need, the assessment of priorities, the formulation of action plans, project development and evaluation. Whilst the model has coherence and functions reasonably well, it is not the whole story. Many of the initiatives are not driven by strictly applied logic but by chance, networking and opportunity. Often, projects occur not because of 'what should be done' but 'what can be done'.

The programme was initially funded for three years but there has been sequential extensions from its core funding bodies, the Borough Council and Business.

A model for assessing development and progress

Tilley (1992) evaluated Safer Cities and Community Safety strategies that prevailed at that time. He devised a model to make sense of the roles performed by such strategies by drawing on George Simmel's notion of the 'stranger'. He points out that the "Safer Cities projects could be understood as stranger institutions, and their staff as embodiments of stranger status." (Tilley 1992 p 5) Using a modified form of Simmel's model to assess the effectiveness of the strategies. The model has five stages:

Phase one: The suspicious incomer – Problem: Building trust

Phase two: The honest broker – Problem: Building motivation and capacity

Phase three: The necessary catalyst – Problem: Getting strategy developing structure built

Phase four: The faithful servant – Problem: Nurturing structure and strategy

Phase five: The guest who stayed too long – Problem: Exiting

This model provides a useful perspective for analysing status and effectiveness of the Luton Crime Reduction Programme.

Phase one: The suspicious incomer
The programme represented a new structure within which a number of agencies were being invited or even urged to work. At a time of constraint in public expenditure what was, in effect, a new form of service, was likely to be treated with caution and concern. Without drive from policy makers, the incomer may have withered as a seedling. The key elements for the transcendence of this phase were the personal commitment of the Chief Executive of the Council and the Divisional Police Commander. There was also strong political support. The main political groups within the Council were persuaded of the need and voted to core fund the programme for three years. It was also noticeable that whilst those agencies that lay outside the influence of the council or the police expressed willing support, real commitment to action was often lacking.

The steering group often simply 'nods through' policy which has been decided elsewhere. For that reason, it is often accused of being merely a constitutional device. However, its prime function is that it enlists and embraces powerful local individuals and links them to the programme.

Phase two: The honest broker
The honest broker, according to Tilley, seeks to bring together those who might usefully complement each other and enable them to act synergistically. The best way of achieving such a state is an early demonstration of success – a tangible project, based upon a multi-agency approach in which the gains exceed expectations. By good fortune, an opportunity arose in the early life of the Programme through what became known as the Hockwell Ring Project.

The Project had a number of elements:-

- target hardening of council property on the estate
- concierge systems and CCTV in blocks of council flats
- nursery provision in a block mainly occupied by single mothers
- community facilities in the tower blocks
- the community centre to be a community resource for youth, the unemployed and the elderly
- a responsive system of local policing

Funding was provided by the Borough Council and County Council, but a number of fortuitous elements combined to help shape the Project.

1. The council had refurbishment planned for the estate and key politicians and officers were persuaded of the need for a community safety focus and committed considerable extra expenditure as a result

2. Links with the county council allowed revenue funding for the appointment of workers and nursery staff

3. A raid by Customs and Excise on the club that occupied the community centre freed it for extension, refurbishment and managed programmes that supported local people. The extension was paid for out of conditional funds available from a building contract with a firm which was constructing houses on the estate.

The pre-condition for the success of the project was the willingness of powerful local politicians and council officers as resource providers to view local needs from a community safety perspective. This was achieved by the programme co-ordinator who had the skills to lobby and persuade. The Project was managed by a committee of residents and councillors. These arrangements are in place several years later and as one resident commented – "There are still problems on the estate, but we now feel they are manageable and no longer is there a sense of impotence and despair."

The timing of the project was fortunate. It gave the Crime Reduction Programme a high profile both locally and nationally. It was visited by prominent political figures and prompted press articles. "Luton is sending pulses racing as it bucks the trend of rising crime" (*The Times* 15.10.93)

Such publicity gave the Programme a local acceptance. Crime on the estate was reduced by 50 per cent and nuisances by nearly 70 per cent.

These benefits were clear, not only to residents but also to politicians whose support was crucial.

Phase three: The necessary catalyst
> 'Where confidence that partnerships can create useful outcomes for agents has been built, and there is a shared desire to see them persist, a phase of structure building for the development of strategy and its implementation becomes possible' (ibid. p 9)

The early high profile successes gave the programme a firm base within the often difficult terrain of inter-agency cooperation. A habit of analysis was developed through the production of crime profiles of the town. It was always intended that projects should be linked to a clear identification of priorities and to a certain extent this was achieved. However, there were and are limitations to this approach. It is one thing to identify a need but it quite another to implement a remedy. Reform and changes in education policy led to an increase in school exclusions. It was also clear that many of the excluded were engaged in offending. The two factors were probably symptoms of the same circumstances of disadvantage. The most positive achievement was to address the issue with the agencies concerned. To implement solutions on the meagre resources available was not an option.

Equally, projects were often dictated not necessarily by strategic priorities but by funding sources or other opportunities that emerged at a particular time. The reduction of business crime became a priority as a result of an unsuccessful funding bid, subsequent interest from the Economic Regeneration Unit of the borough council and the possibility of Single Regeneration Budget funding linked to projects based upon economic regeneration.

The coordinator has become expert at the preparation of funding proposals and this skill has become a valuable asset to the programme and its constituent agencies.

Strategy formulation also suffers from the fact that analysis and evaluation is expensive and time consuming. Often the expertise is simply not available and in the early years, projects tended not to be effectively evaluated. That has been overcome by forming a partnership with the University of Luton's Vauxhall Centre for the Study of Crime. The outcomes of projects are now routinely measured and funding bids include a contingency for evaluation. Most funding bodies recognise the value of such expenditure and are prepared to provide it.

Phase four: The faithful servant
> "The fourth phase describes the period during which the stranger
> ceases to be an outsider leading and provoking action, but instead
> becomes the servant" (ibid. p 10)

There is some evidence of this phase. The multi-agency approach, though
not entirely a product of the programme, has become a habit. Individual
members bring ideas to the group. Its resources and expertise are shared
and used. Nevertheless, the programme remains the fulcrum for community safety activity and it is difficult to conceive of a self-sustaining
focus without it.

Its initial three year life has been continually extended and after eight
years, it is fairly firmly embedded. Without the core funding from the
Council, it is unlikely that it would have lasted. Whilst the core funding has
been more that matched from other sources, the additional finance has
been project based and therefore short term and uncertain. Since its formation in September 1989, the programme has received funding of £419,000
from its principal sponsors, Luton Borough Council and local business.
This has been more than matched by grants trusts, charities and government agencies amounting to £421,000.

Phase five: The guest who stayed too long
> "During this, the final stage, the existence of a replicating and,
> perhaps, confusing external body, adding nothing more than money
> to what can be done locally, becomes an irritant" (ibid. p 10)

The original philosophy underpinning the Safer Cities Projects was that
they would have a limited life after the encouragement and teaching of the
habits and techniques of community safety. It was hoped, to borrow a
phrase from elsewhere, that they would 'wither away' having nurtured and
facilitated. Perhaps because the Luton Crime Reduction Programme was
local in origin and whilst a 'stranger' it was implanted by its own
participants and beneficiaries rather than by central government. It might
now be seen as the centre of a network rather than a stranger. Two factors
are likely to contribute to its continuance – the recent achievement of
unitary status by the borough council and the government's intentions for
promoting community safety.

Marlow et al. (1993) identified the four key factors which have sustained
the programme:

- Although there is a strong underpinning from the police and the
  local authority it has its own corporate identity. Independence is
  important as potential sponsors are not deterred by it appearing
  to be a 'town hall' or 'police' run initiative.

- A strong and continuing commitment from the Chief Executive of the Council and the Divisional Police Commander. That commitment encourages the delivery of resources from their respective organisations.

- A co-ordinator with appropriate skills and energies. Remuneration must be at a sufficient level to attract an individual of the right calibre.

- Whilst independence is a virtue, the programme would not survive without a willingness of the council to provide core funding. Almost all other sources of finance are project linked. Sponsors require a high profile linkage with positive acts in return for their support.

That analysis still applies. Bright (1991) is critical of the lack of clarity and guidance given by government, perhaps wary of increasing local authority power and conflicts with police autonomy, on the issue of leadership. The Luton Programme has not solved that problem but has shown how the power to get things done can operate through shared aims within a nominally independent structure.

Concluding remarks

The programme has continued to flourish whilst initiatives elsewhere have foundered. There are a number of reasons for that relative longevity:

Continued political support – local councillors of all hues have continued to support and willingly core fund the programme. At the same time however, it is prudent to continue to develop a public relations strategy that publicises achievements. The programme has to continually market itself and develop contacts, channels and cheap graphic designers to do so.

Impetus from the powerful – Chief executives and divisional commanders, have, through the life of the programme, continued to give it priority and to ensure that subordinates contribute to it. Unitary status makes this task much easier as former county agencies become part of the Borough.

The nature of the town – Luton is fairly compact without the sprawling nature of big cities. It is also of value that it contains large concerns such as Whitbread and Vauxhall which have a commercial interest in promoting projects that improve Luton's image.

However, the obverse of the factors that have sustained the programme are also those that indicate fragility. The support at political level and at the executive level could drain at any time. As already indicated, the programme could not survive in its present form without the core funding from the council. It is only possible to attract funding if linked to finite projects or where there are commercial benefits accruing for commercial sponsorship. It is perhaps unrealistic to expect durable programmes based on the whim of sponsorship or the vagaries of project funding.

It seems that the government may lay some responsibility on local authorities and if this extends only to ensuring that plans or strategies are in place, then the implications for this type of structure are positive. However, if community safety were to become a primary responsibility for the local authority to deliver, then it is unlikely that the programme would survive – at least in its present form. Community safety would be seen as a problem for local government and the corporacy and breadth that exists would be threatened. Commercial interests may not be quite so ready to be linked to local authority departments.

Finally, the obvious question is 'has it worked?' Crime in Luton has increased at a much lower rate that in the rest of the country. In particular, between 1991 and 1995, crime increased by 12.6 per cent nationally, in Luton it decreased by 7.7 per cent. The victimisation rate was by 1995 1.5 times rather than double the national average. Clearly, something was happening but whilst it would be folly to claim a direct causal link with community safety projects, it is also impossible to deny their influence. Such helpful statistics were allies for seeking support and sponsorship.

References

Bright J (1991) Crime Prevention: The British Experience in Stenson K & Cowell D (Eds.)(1991) *The Politics of Crime Control.* Sage. London

Home Office (1991) *Safer Communities: The Local Delivery of Crime Prevention Through the Partnership Approach.* The Morgan Report. London. Home Office

Hough M and Mayhew P (1985) *Taking Account of Crime: Key Findings from the 1984 British Crime Survey.* Home Office Research Study No 85. London. HMSO

Marlow A, Blowers G, and Southwell J C (1993) *Harnessing Energy for Crime Reduction. Police Journal* Vol LXVI No 1 (1993)

Tilley N (1992) *Safer Cities and Community Safety Strategies.* Police Research Group. Crime Prevention Unit Series Paper 38. Home Office

Times, The (15.10.93) *Prevention Proves Better Than Cure in Crime Town.*

CHAPTER 4

Putting the Community into Community Safety

Usman Khan

Introduction

Community safety is a term which defines a new area of urban policy where local policy makers, working alongside local communities, seek to tackle crime, the fear of crime and its underlying causes. Crime in this sense most commonly refers to specific areas such as vandalism, drug trafficking, theft, violence to the person and street disorder; crime that affects the community as much as it does the person. Community safety has in practice been a top-down policy, representing an attempt by a number of state agencies which include the police, central government, local government, the probation service, and TECS to bring together policy relating to crime under a single generic term. This has not always meant single co-ordinating bodies or even single strategies, although it has increasingly seen local authorities taking a lead with respect to policy co-ordination. Yet if the reality of community safety has been the often *ad hoc* co-ordination of a series of crime-oriented policies, implicit within the term itself is the idea that local people could and should be involved in the policy process as a whole. This reflects upon the nature of the policy area as well as the broader climate of public policy making, where public involvement has become an important watchword.

The aim of this chapter is to examine the relationship between community safety and strategies to involve the public in the local policy process. In doing so, the chapter will seek to establish how those working in the area of community safety can best utilise existing models of good practice in the field of public participation. The underlying aim is to ensure that local communities themselves are involved in, and consequently develop ownership over, the policies which are seeking to make their communities safer and more pleasant places to live.

The chapter itself is divided into three distinct parts. The first of these presents a discussion of community safety in relation to public participation, highlighting in particular the challenges and opportunities that a policy area such as this presents. The second section goes on to discuss six central questions which any organisation should ask itself, prior to embarking on an exercise in public involvement. In the third section a brief overview is presented of current methods for public involvement, and a discussion on which are likely to be best suited to the needs of community safety.

Community safety in context

Attempting to introduce structures for public consultation within the sphere of community safety offers up a number of unique challenges. These relate to the definition of the field of community safety, the nature of the subject area and the operation of the broader policy process.

As has been mentioned, community safety does not represent an agreed field of urban policy. It may include elements of policing, crime prevention, and education. Community safety policies can encompass the eviction of 'problem' families from estates, the introduction of CCTV, Neighbourhood Watch schemes, 'designing out' crime in city centres, as well as broader policies relating to the treatment of offenders. This is in itself not necessarily a problem, but it does demonstrate that establishing a structured 'voice' for the public is likely to be a complicated process.

One problem relates to the location of many community safety initiatives. With the exception of the Neighbourhood Watch scheme, a majority of community safety initiatives are based in urban areas, most notably in city centres and areas of high crime. This leaves the community safety professional facing the problem of defining what constitutes a 'community' in a city centre which may have little or no residential population, or establishing the best way to canvas the opinions of a community which has a number of crime-related problems and where there will be a number of distinct and often transient groupings, high levels of material deprivation and some distrust of police and related state agencies.

The third and final aspect which those working in the field of community safety need to face is the nature of the existing policy process. As was mentioned earlier, community safety commonly operates on the basis of a multi-agency concern, with a top-down decision making structure. Establishing the framework for and gaining political approval over, a programme of public participation can be problematic enough in what may be termed more straightforward policy areas such as housing or education. Where public organisations are finding it difficult to agree or co-ordinate policy within and between themselves, the problems that this can present for a public involvement strategy will be magnified greatly.

Guidelines for involving the public

On one level, the decision to involve the public in a policy process appears a simple one. However the adage that poor public involvement is worse than no public involvement has more than a grain of truth to it. As a consequence, if a public body is seeking to implement a consultation strategy, or is merely trying to gauge public sentiment with respect to a single issue, a series of questions needs to be asked of the organisation or organisations contemplating such a course of action.

What are your aims and what are you prepared to give in order to achieve them?

It may be stating the obvious but not all public involvement is the same. Yet while academics such as Arnstein (1971), Gyford (1991) and Burns et al. (1994) have always proved keen to classify and categorise, those who have actually developed public involvement strategies have written little in this important area. The importance of establishing at the outset whether one's primary aim is to inform the public, consult with the public or empower the public, cannot be underestimated. Having said this, making such a judgement can be a problematic exercise, all the more so given the implicit normative underpinning of such a judgement. Handing over power is seldom viewed to be anything other than a good thing to do. But power at the local level forms a complex matrix and this needs to be considered before embarking on a public involvement exercise. The question needs to be asked as to whether the local authority or whichever body it is, has the appropriate powers in the first place and if so to what extent is control over that power already vested in others, be they elected members or boards of quangos? The watchword must be honesty. Honesty with the public as to what powers are available and honesty with regard to what power or authority the organisation is prepared to relinquish or share. False expectations are the bane of many a public consultation exercise.

Why do you want to consult in the first place?

Again this might appear a straightforward question, yet the answer might not be as simple as it first appears. The most common answer may be that the aim of involving the public is to enable a better policy outcome in terms of the service or services provided. This in turn may be linked to the generation of what is termed 'ownership' over the policy. But ownership is rarely achieved over a policy that has already been agreed in all but detail. Ownership, which is often seen as the key to successful policy implementation, is most likely to be gained in circumstances where people have had an opportunity to discuss and alter policy at an early stage in the policy process. At the same time a comprehensive and open system of communication, while not offering the public any control over the decision making process itself, may be welcomed more readily than a façade of a consultation exercise which seeks only to legitimate a *fait accompli.*

At what stage in the policy process do you want to consult?

This question can be divided into 'the strategic' where broad aims are established, 'the developmental' where those aims are put in more concrete terms, and finally 'implementational' which is concerned with policy implementation rather than policy making. Quite often a public body will begin a consultation exercise at the point where a policy goal has already been agreed and are often surprised at the lack of community interest in their forum or public meeting. Why consult over the type of entrance for a new swimming pool when the people you are consulting were not directly asked whether they wanted a new swimming pool in the first place and if they did, where they would have preferred it to be. While it may often be the case that strategic and policy development issues are and should remain the principal responsibility of elected representatives, the greater the level of public involvement in these issues the greater the level of commitment that will be evident in relation to implementational issues.

Who do you intend to consult?

When considering a strategy for public involvement, the 'public' can quite easily be viewed as an amorphous whole. Yet establishing who the public are, is another important stage in the consultation process. One may firstly think of the users of a service and then of the groups which seek to represent them. This then can be expanded to include voluntary and community groups, associated either directly or indirectly with a particular service. Finally, one needs to consider the wider public be that for a ward, constituency or a particular community for whom a service is to be provided. Selective consultation can not only leave one open to the charge of not having effectively consulted, but it can also have a detrimental effect on policy outcomes.

This issue is subject to further complication, most particularly in areas such as community safety, when thought has to be given to the other side of the policy equation. In most cases there will be a number of agencies that are involved in setting the policy agenda, with little more than a steering group to bring these together. In addition to this, within each agency there will be the views of officers, members and front-line staff to consider. Gaining agreement on a broad policy platform can in these circumstances be difficult, gaining their support for a programme of public involvement even more so.

What methods for public involvement will be utilised?
Having established a position in relation to each of the prior four points it is then possible to move on to examine the best method or methods for involving the public. Over a dozen distinct methods can be identified and the most straightforward way to present these is to cluster them into three broad groupings. First, there are the wide ranging community centred mechanisms which would include neighbourhood forums, parish councils and latterly electronic town meetings. The second set are also group based, but their focus is on a particular issue. Citizen juries and study groups are both examples of this. Finally, there are the mechanisms which are focused on the individual rather than the group. Opinion polls and comments and complaints systems are two such examples.

Community forums

Establishing forums or councils has become one of the most popular methods for involving the public in the local policy process. Typically, these bodies are established by a local council, health authority, or other such organisation, in order to encourage local participation in the management and organisation of a particular area, or a specific project. Forum or council members are in the main self-selecting, although a number of councils are now attempting to introduce some form of electoral process. They have the advantage that they are relatively cheap to set up, are flexible in relation to how they can be used, and can fit easily into the existing policy process.

Forums and councils can and do provide a useful means to incorporate local concerns into the policy process, and in areas such as Islington in North London where the local authority has introduced forums on a borough wide basis, they have established an important role for themselves. However, forums have been dogged by a number of common failings. The most often cited of these relates to poor levels of representation, whereby not only do forums fail to reflect the make-up of the community that they represent, but many of those who do become involved are established activists rather than 'ordinary' members of the public. A second problem relates to the role played by these bodies, with the exception of parish councils, these forums cannot legally be given any statutory powers and their advisory roles often lead to the accusation that they are primarily just talking shops. However, these problems are not insurmountable and forums can and do offer an important means to develop a more decentralised policy process.

Deliberate issue based groups

Drawing heavily on developments in both marketing and political theory, this group of initiatives have at their core two basic principles. Firstly, in order to counter the perceived limitations of activist dominated structures, citizen's juries, deliberative panels and other similar developments have utilised market research based random sampling techniques, in order to get to what are often termed the 'real' people. Secondly, these mechanisms have built into them a level of deliberation, the premise underpinning this being that if people are presented with adequate information and are given the time to ask questions, debate, and reflect, then the solutions produced will be more robust or rational, a better reflection of their 'real' beliefs.

Mechanisms such as these are viewed by many academics and practitioners alike to represent a significant breakthrough and few would deny that they have given a new impetus to the movement to increase public involvement in the local policy process. The drawbacks of mechanisms such as these, are still the subject of debate. Aside from cost, a single citizen's jury can cost upwards of £15,000 to organise and run. Concerns have been raised in relation to the status of the findings of these panels plus juries. In most cases these bodies have dealt with substantive issues such as drugs policy or health care funding. As such they are commenting on policy areas which have historically been the preserve of elected counsellors and nominated board members. This begs the question as to whether these bodies are simply advisory and if so what guarantees are there that their views will be taken into account. Concerns have also been raised in relation to the information that is given to these groups, with questions being raised as to whether juries or panels could be presented with biased information and as such be open to manipulation.

Mechanisms based on the individual

Mechanisms which are centred on the individual rather than the group, whilst having a history which dates back to the 1970s, came to the fore in the 1980s and early 1990s. Focusing on the individual as citizen or more particularly as service user, they fitted in well with the prevailing ethos of new public managerialism with its commitment to service responsiveness. The idea that underpins this is that service providers must be aware of the views of their users, or they risk losing or alienating them. As such they are not directly concerned with empowerment, and these market research techniques can be best placed at the passive end of the spectrum of consultation. However, this should not lead to an underestimation of their value in generating meaningful public feedback to the policy process. With mechanisms such as the choice questionnaire, where respondents are given a greater level of background material as well as time to think through issues, a participation technique with significant potential exists.

Strategies for public consultation

Although the field of community safety presents a number of distinct challenges, it would not be true to say that these were insurmountable and a number of public bodies have already taken a lead.

In the London Borough of Lambeth the local authority successfully ran a citizen's jury which examined the issue of drugs. The social and criminal effects of drugs as a community safety issue is of particular concern to inner city areas such as Lambeth and the council's aim was to establish the public's view of the existing multi-agency approach. The jury was deemed to have been a success by both the council and the jury members themselves. A number of recommendations were put forward which recognised the difficulties involved in this complex area of policy and which in essence broadly followed existing council policy.

Citizen's juries are then a useful technique for establishing what a considered public view about an issue is, but they also have a number of drawbacks. These relate to cost, the possibility that jury members can be 'blinded by science', and the lack of a substantive position for juries in the policy making process. On a broader level too, there is the possibility that where jury members come out with conclusions which are very different from the views of the communities from which they are drawn and most particularly where these coincide with existing 'professional' opinion, that the wider community may have some difficulty accepting their legitimacy.

The forum may also be a good option for the field of community safety, as it fits well into the geographic orientation of many community safety initiatives and is able to involve people over the longer term. Such forums can seek to target the general public, or can be utilised as an umbrella body in order to bring together a range of community and voluntary organisations. Who sits on these forums and what powers they have will remain a central question to be addressed. The experience from forums in Islington and Sheffield showed that while more traditional and homogeneous communities were willing to engage with issues relating to vandalism, theft and drugs their views were at times motivated more by 'nimbyism' than anything else and some of the views expressed would be considered by many to be quite reactionary. However, experience does point to the value in allowing communities to give vent to their anger and frustration. Unlike the format of the public meeting, where such responses are all that is likely to be generated, the forum does offer the opportunity to move on from that initial response to a more considered opinion where a broader range of policy alternatives can be discussed.

One of the newer methods which has become an increasing focus of attention is the public or consumer panel. Successfully operated by a number of local authorities including Kirklees and Bradford, the panel works on the basis of an extended market research programme. Communities are invited to join a panel, most commonly through a mailshot, and the host organisation then selects a broad cross section of around 5,000 members from this initial group. These people then provide continuing resources which can be used to assess public views on a range of issues, as well as providing a network to pass information back to their community. In the first instance panels have been used primarily to complete postal questionnaires, although it is now being realised that the potential is far greater. Panels offer a much cheaper and more flexible means to run citizens juries and they can also be utilised to establish how opinions change over time or in the light of more reflective forms of public involvement. And in addition to being cheaper to run than traditional market research, panels are also more likely to generate a greater sense of ownership over the policies they consider. In a medium sized conurbation of around 250,000, with a panel size of 2,500, one percent of the population will be immediately involved in the policy making process and with friends and family often likely to become aware of what a panel member is doing, that figure could reach 10 per cent of the population. No other form of public participation can expect to involve so many people so closely in the policy making process.

Due to their relatively high costs and the need to use them to the maximum, panels are best suited to multi-agency work. It is also important to remember that, as with all of the methods that have been considered in this chapter, panels will only be effective if they are given the necessary support and if the agencies using them commit themselves to listening to what they hear. The panel system does have an advantage here over most other methods. It is likely to be far more difficult to ignore with over two thousand people chosen to be an accurate reflection of their local community, than would be the case with a single citizen's jury for instance. Yet it would also be wrong to get carried away with the potential of the panel system. Even where panels have been successfully developed, they have not been allowed to undermine either the existing representative systems or the established roles of pre-existing community and voluntary sector groups. As such they should be seen in terms of their potential to augment existing structures and networks.

Conclusions

Having examined both the challenges with which community safety is presented as an area of urban policy in seeking to involve the public and a number of possible solutions, what final conclusions can be drawn? Firstly, it seems apparent that public involvement in community safety initiatives should be seen to be a necessity and not a luxury. This relates firstly to the issue of service efficiency. No one knows their community better than the community itself and their involvement in issues of implementation are likely to make any policy more successful. The second reason why greater levels of community involvement would be beneficial, relates to broader issues of policy development. Circumstantial evidence points to the idea that community safety is often viewed to be so valuable that it does not require public debate. Yet to look at schemes such as the introduction of area-wide CCTV is to see something which will have a profound and long term impact on the communities in which they are established. As such the public have both a right and a need to be involved in the development of community safety policy from an early stage.

Finally, underpinning all aspects of public participation should be comprehensive and accurate information. Community safety is an area where poor quality or misleading information can have a marked effect on peoples perceptions and behaviour. Increasing fear of crime is one such example. Thought must be given to how best to combine structures for increasing public involvement with methods for ensuring that the resulting debate is based on good quality information.

Which particular public involvement mechanisms will prove to be of greatest benefit will, as has already been discussed, depend on circumstances. Whatever choice or choices are made it is important not to forget that, as with all forms of participation, there is a risk of raising public expectations beyond that which can be achieved.

Finally, much that has been said in this chapter has been concerned with a discussion of how organisations can engage with the community. Yet if expectations are not to be falsely raised and if there is going to be a meaningful debate about the way in which government and community can help create safer communities, it needs to be remembered that public consultation should be a two-way process, a partnership for safer communities.

CHAPTER 5

Evaluating Community Safety Initiatives

Steve Osborn

Evaluation framework

It is necessary to develop a set of standard criteria against which to assess the impact of community safety initiatives. In developing the evaluation criteria we need to be guided by practical considerations and, in particular, we need to be confident that it is feasible to collect the data required to satisfy the criteria.

A number of questions need to be asked about the initiatives. Not only do we want to know whether they are 'successful', we also want to know whether the effects are likely to last and if the lessons learned are generalisable.

The evaluation framework could involve the following basic structure.

1. **Evidence of change**
   We are interested in evidence presented in a variety of forms, both quantitative and qualitative, from a variety of sources. One important issue to address is the length of time prior to implementation for which evidence is to be collected. It may be that the period immediately preceding the initiative implementation is 'abnormal' in some respects. For instance, in relation to a housing focused initiative, communal repairs may be neglected in anticipation of refurbishment or flats may be allowed to remain void in anticipation of new allocation procedures. It may be necessary, therefore, to compare the situation after implementation with an earlier pre-implementation period.

2. **Evidence of the scheme's effect**
   We need to know whether the scheme is responsible for the observed changes or whether they merely reflected general trends in the area (for instance, crime rates may be falling generally in the area), changes in the make up of the target population unrelated to the initiative or other co-terminus but unrelated local initiatives. We need to collect

'control' data and demographic information and to document other local initiatives.

3. **Evidence of the effect of individual measures**
We are interested in evidence that any individual measure, within the overall package, accounts for the changes. It is often difficult to disentangle elements of a package, but it may be possible to do so through careful and precise documentation of the implementation of measures.

4. **Evidence of permanence**
Judgements are often made on the success of initiatives on the basis of data collected shortly after implementation. In our view, a minimum three year follow up period is required to be confident about the permanence of changes and evidence from shorter follow up periods needs to be treated more cautiously.

5. **Evidence of replicability**
A judgement needs to be made on whether there are any particular features of an initiative or the local context which might reduce its potential for implementation elsewhere. For example, the costs of the scheme may be prohibitive or a scheme may rely heavily on special local circumstances.

Cost benefit assessment and cost-effectiveness are key replicability issues. We need to assess the net financial cost of a scheme (i.e. we need to take into account savings which accrue from the scheme) and we need to take into account unquantifiable or difficult to quantify benefits such as increased resident satisfaction and reductions in the fear of crime. We also need to assess whether the scheme is cost effective, i.e. whether similar outcomes could have been achieved at a lower cost. These judgements are difficult to make, of course.

The development of performance indicators

Three questions need to be asked. What phenomena are we going to be measuring? How are we going to measure those phenomena? And how are we to isolate the impact of initiatives from other influences?

We want to find out whether crime problems are reduced as a result of the initiative. Apart from changes in the overall level of crime, we should also look at:

- Changes in the levels of particular crimes, paying attention to the trends in violent crime as well as in property crimes such as burglary. Changes in the overall crime level will largely reflect property crime trends but changes in overall perceptions of safety may equally reflect violent crime trends. Offence displacement may also be an issue, particularly if there is displacement to more *serious* crime.

- Changes in levels of concern and fear, which may reflect changes in crime levels but may equally relate to individual incidents rather than to the totality and may relate to 'incivilities' or antisocial behaviour rather than to officially defined crime.

- Changes in the impact of crime, in terms of the seriousness of incidents (individual offence categories often cover a wide spectrum of incidents) and in terms of victim profiles (the same kind of incident can have very different effects on different victims).

- Changes in the levels of 'quasi' crimes, which residents often describe as crimes but which are not officially defined or are rarely treated as such – noise nuisance, littering and fouling, loitering, antisocial behaviour (from youths in particular) etc.

- Changes in 'intervening variables' shown to be associated with delinquency (e.g. educational attainment), particularly important for initiatives such as pre-school schemes where the crime outcomes are likely to be long-term.

Of course, we should not expect initiatives to have an impact on all types of crime. For example, can we expect autocrime to be affected if a housing initiative does not extend its coverage to the parking areas?

Key indicators and what they tell us:

Recorded crime levels
These represent a partial record of crimes dependent on public reporting and police recording practices – unlikely to be adequate on their own to judge whether actual crime levels have changed. Breakdowns by offence category are required to derive trends for individual categories.

Residents' survey crime levels
These also represent a partial record of crimes committed in the area as crimes committed against non-residents (visitors, staff, etc.) are not included. Also, it is not feasible to build up a picture of trends over a number of previous years in this way (as it may be possible to do through police records), not only because of the problem of obtaining accurate information from residents about long past events but also because of the constant turnover of residents. Demographic data will enable us to obtain information on which categories of resident are victimised and whether there are any changes to the picture over time.

Residents' survey fear/concern levels
Levels of fear and concern about crime can be measured over time. These may not necessarily be related to actual crime levels. The survey will identify which crimes are causing most fear or concern and to whom, and will measure the extent of avoidance behaviour generated. It may be possible to derive a single 'quality of safety' measure from the combined responses to questions.

Levels of 'quasicrime' or 'incivilities'
Information can be obtained from a number of sources to give a picture of the extent of incidents which are on the margins of being officially recorded as crime. Condition surveys can provide quantifiable environmental monitoring data on littering, fouling, graffiti and deliberate damage (although the latter may be difficult to define). Quantifiable noise nuisance data can be sought from Environmental Health Departments, although we may have to rely on residents perceptions of the problem from residents' surveys. Residents' surveys will also provide data on residents' perceptions of environmental conditions and antisocial behaviour in their neighbourhoods.

Cost of crime data
The extent of crime can also be measured on the basis of cost. It may be possible to obtain information on the costs of criminal damage to the local authority. However, there are difficulties in obtaining such data (local authorities do not normally collect this kind of information) and in interpreting the trends (fluctuations in costs may reflect the authorities' preparedness to repair damage rather changes in the level of damage).

Other crime related data
It may also be possible to collect crime related data from other sources, although we cannot rely on being able to do so. For example, information can be sought from the police on call outs to respond to incidents, such as antisocial behaviour, which do not lead to a crime being recorded and from the fire brigade on call outs (including false alarms) to deal with arson. In addition, local authorities can utilise any special monitoring data they are collecting, for example, on racial harassment or domestic violence.

Intervening variables
A range of factors have been associated with delinquency. These 'intervening variables' such as school attendance and achievement may be useful measures where longer term outcomes are anticipated. A discussion of the problems associated with obtaining measures in this way is included in the final section of this chapter Some Problems of Evaluation.

Evaluating effectiveness

In determining the effectiveness of initiatives, it is important to separate out and take account of those effects which are part of some wider or unrelated trends. For this purpose, local trends in crime levels need to be monitored. We are interested in changes which are additional to trends elsewhere.

Measuring change
A number of key performance indicators need to be selected to measure the extent of any improvements in respect of each initiative. The performance indicators should not be framed in terms of a uniform scale of performance. For instance, changes in key indicators such as recorded crime levels and survey victimisations data cannot be combined to produce a single measure of safety. Of course it is possible by means of standardisation devices, to create scales for each indicator and scores which can be combined to create a single measure. However, this technique can produce very misleading results.

Measuring achievement
To identify achievement we need to show that improvements in the target area are attributable to the initiative rather than other external factors, such as changes in authority-wide policy. One approach is to monitor trends for the performance indicators at the borough-wide (or other appropriate) level. Improvements at the initiative level need to be additional to any identified at the wider level to show achievement.

Attention needs to be paid, however, to the possibility of the initiative having an impact beyond the level of the targeted areas. It may be that the lessons of the initiative, if it is well-regarded are part of a broader programme, will influence or amend practice more generally. This 'ripple effect' is unlikely to be substantial but may be a factor where an authority has embarked on a large programme of similar initiatives.

There is also a possibility that a failure to secure improvements may be regarded as achievement. Absence of change, or even some deterioration, on the initiative site may contrast with substantial deterioration elsewhere. For instance, there may be no reduction in crime problems on the initiative site at the same time as local trends indicate substantial increases in crime elsewhere. However, it is difficult to conceive of circumstances in which this form of achievement would be recognised as meaningful from the resident or authority perspective.

Evaluating costs and benefits

A comprehensive economic evaluation could be undertaken. This should not be a narrowly based financial appraisal concentrating on the financial costs and benefits alone. Our view is that such approaches, which make relatively 'broad brush' assumptions about the prospective lifetime of assets, can distort the evaluation by assuming that the financial cost of capital-intensive schemes can be spread over an extended period in contrast to ongoing revenue costs of less capital-intensive schemes. Where the effective life of assets is less than assumed (through obsolescence, wear and tear or other factors), simple financial appraisal may be unsuitable. Our view is that these circumstances are likely to apply.

An economic evaluation aims to capture both financial and non-financial costs and benefits associated with initiatives. These need to be considered separately in terms of data generation. Inevitably, the availability of appropriate data constrains the evaluation, but here we focus on the principles of evaluation, recognising that some modification may be required to reflect practicalities.

Appraisal of financial costs and benefits
The underlying principle relating to the financial aspects of the appraisal is the use of discounted cash flow (DCF) and net present value (NPV) to assess the totality of costs and benefits. Given that the aim is to assess the impact of initiatives on a 'before and after' basis, this is reflected in the approach to data collection and use.

The basic assumption of the exercise must be that, overall, costs associated with the initiative are lower after implementation than before. The aim of this part of the exercise must therefore be to identify/estimate costs:

- prior to the scheme being introduced
- after scheme implementation

DCF can then be applied to the stream of presumed savings and, together with the initial capital outlay, a NPV associated with the scheme can be generated.

Obviously, the task is more complex than this, even when considering only the principles involved. In order to estimate savings, it is of course necessary to obtain some indication of the scale of costs which would have been incurred in the absence of any new scheme. There are three ways of doing this.

One way of achieving this is simply to generate trend information in respect of past costs and project this into the post-implementation period.

A second approach is to use the relationship between average and actual management costs in the past to project post-implementation costs and to estimate notional savings in this way.

A third alternative takes account of the fact that it is possible that costs prior to scheme implementation are lower than might be expected or seem appropriate. It might be appropriate to gauge the extent to which particular areas are being *under-managed* in the pre-implementation period compared with appropriate performance standards and to make some adjustment to actual management costs to reflect or compensate for this.

Whatever approach is adopted, it may be necessary to use cross-sectional data from the authority.

Non-financial costs and benefits
The significance of these costs and benefits increases greatly in circumstances where the economic appraisal suggests a negative present value, i.e. where there is no evidence from that part of the appraisal of overall benefits from the investment.

In these circumstances the significance of the non-financial element is the extent to which the negative present value can be seen as justified in the light of any non-financial benefits. It has to be accepted that this is ultimately a matter of judgement – in particular the judgement of the residents and the authority. This is made more difficult by the fact that, unlike financial/economic benefits, there is no means of cumulating the non-financial benefits into a single measure (positive or a negative).

Some problems of evaluation

Key measurement issues

The obvious objectives of a community safety initiative are to reduce crime and fear of crime. The less obvious, linked objectives include reducing the impact of crime and the cost of crime.

Ways of measuring effectiveness appear straightforward:

- reduced crime levels – measured by police/victimisation survey data

- reduced fear levels – measured by victimisation survey data

- reduced costs – measured by, for example, vandalism cost centres

There are problems in measuring effectiveness in this way, however:

- It will not be possible to collect survey data for every scheme or initiative (and one cannot rely on police data, even if it is available).

- Cost measurement is notoriously difficult because of the problems of attributing costs to crime.

There are also other kinds of objectives which are valid but do not fit into the reduced crime perspective. Most obviously, action may be directed at increasing the observed/known incidence of particular crimes – for instance child abuse, domestic violence and racial harassment – to ensure that perpetrators are identified and the appropriate measures taken to deal with them. Clearly the intention here is to unearth hidden crime in an effort to reduce its incidence, but the short term observed effect may well be an increase in reported cases.

Evaluating crime related effects of council practices

Data collection issues
It is important to have a clear idea of what is wanted from data collection exercises and to limit the data requirements to those which are both essential and practical. Also given that it will not always (or even generally) be possible to collect data which directly measures impact on crime/fear of crime, decisions will have to be made about what can be considered *indicative* measures (i.e. measures which can be associated with broader effects), *associated* measures (i.e. measures which can be associated with reduced crime) or *intervening* variables (i.e. variables which are early indicators of reduced delinquency). The distinctions become clearer in the following discussion.

Selection of key measures, by department
The starting point is to get individual departments to agree on their crime prevention objectives. This means departments looking at their services and deciding how their work impacts on crime and then how best to measure that impact. There are problems to be overcome. Firstly, it will not be clear to all departments how their work impacts on crime, even indirectly. Secondly, it will be difficult to collect data which paints the whole picture.

The crime prevention activities of some services are easier to measure than others. In many respects, housing departments are in the best position to measure the impact of their work on crime. Where there are estate initiatives, there is often a requirement to undertake evaluation, including utilising residents' surveys. The following are examples of housing department objectives and how they could be measured in the absence of police or survey data:

Reduced burglary
– indicative measures – numbers of repair orders attributable to burglary (if it is possible to attribute repairs in this way), where reduced repair orders could be judged as 'indicative' of reduced burglary:

- associated measures – numbers of homes secured, where increased home security is judged to lead to less burglary (or is this an act of faith?).

Reduced vandalism on estates

This is a difficult area because:

- the easiest way to reduce vandalism may be to leave damaged fittings unrepaired

- it is difficult to separate out repairs attributable to vandalism from repairs attributable to wear and tear or accidents.

In our view housing departments should concentrate on communal damage and should pick out one or two elements as indicative of the general pattern. On flatted estates, the best measure might be changes in lift down time (on the basis that lift repairs are emergencies and there is no discretion over leaving lifts unrepaired). For cottage estates the issue is obviously more difficult and it may be impossible to select a measure which is both robust and possible to collate.

Reduced racial harassment of tenants

In relation to hidden crimes such as racial harassment where it is very difficult to persuade victims to report incidents either to the police or the council, the key objective, at least in the short term, must be to increase reporting rates amongst victims and to identify and take action against perpetrators.

It is important to establish a mechanism whereby police and council figures are brought together. There are also arguments for broadening out this monitoring to include all forms of harassment, not least because the perpetrators of racial harassment may very well be engaged in other forms of harassment and information on the latter can help to build up more substantial cases against perpetrators.

The same kind of issues apply to other services which deal with the built environment, particularly as their work overlaps with the housing department in many cases. There may be a case however, for the crime prevention activity of design and planning services to be measured in a rather different way. It may be possible to evaluate their effectiveness in terms of the attention paid to crime in their design/planning processes.

The problem services

There are clearly greater problems of evaluating education, youth, leisure and social services activity which can impact, directly or indirectly, on delinquency. Activities such as family support schemes, pre-school projects and outreach youth work often make little reference to delinquency but may very well have an impact on factors associated with delinquency. These are factors which are correlated with delinquency in that their presence makes people more prone to committing criminal acts and becoming delinquent. A whole range of studies from the early work by Glueck and Glueck (1950) in the United States to the Cambridge study in *Delinquent Development* (e.g. Farrington and West, 1973) identified a range of factors associated with delinquency – so-called 'intervening variables' such as:

- individual factors – such as coping behaviour, social skills and cognitive skills;

- family factors – such as parental supervision and control;

- peer factors – such as identification and involvement with same-sex groups and sexual/romantic relationships;

- neighbourhood factors – such as social networks and involvement in formal community organisations;

- school factors – such as attendance, achievement and behaviour;

- economic factors – such as income, welfare dependency and tenure.

Social work, youth work and educational practice could be said to address most of these factors – as a general rule, the exception would be economic factors.

The problem presented by these areas of activity is that evaluation is not normally built in, in terms of measuring their impact on these factors 'intervening variables'. There are strong arguments for persuading these services to adopt formal evaluations.

If these areas of activity can be shown to have an impact on 'intervening variables' then there is a case for judging that they are contributing to delinquency prevention, if only in the longer term.

There are also areas of social services involvement which can be associated with the likelihood of individuals offending or re-offending. Most obviously, alternatives to care and custody can be judged to reduce delinquency and recidivism – on the grounds that incarceration is associated with increased chances of re-offending. By implication, reduced care or custody could be viewed as a measure of crime prevention effectiveness.

The reality is that, in terms of evaluation, it might be possible to identify some measures of general effectiveness – e.g. for education (truancy rates), social services (care and custody rates) – but for the most part it will be necessary to develop an evaluation framework tailored to a specific initiative, for example:

- pre-school schemes: measures of educational attainment at primary school;

- family support schemes: measures of parenting skills, children's social skills;

- outreach youth work: numbers of contacts with police, self-report behaviour.

CHAPTER 6

Policing in an Uncertain World

Michael O'Byrne

Police officers have always been faced with the problem of policing a changing and uncertain world. This has been the case since the middle of the last century when most forces were established. At that time the issues were the massive expansion of industrialisation and urbanisation and the growth of the Chartist movement which sought to increase the voting franchise. Indeed even in the supposed halcyon days of the 30s and 50s whilst society appeared to remain relatively stable in terms of crime, that stability existed in a context of mass unemployment, the recovery from one war and the preparation for another in the 20s and 30s. In the 50s the seeds were being sown for the changes which would become apparent and accelerate during the 60s.

I have approached my subject on the basis of what causes uncertainty and against that examined what has happened in a particular problem for police – how we are tackling drugs.

There are two aspects, in my view, to the factors which create uncertainty. The first factor is change itself. As a bureaucratic organisation and a part of the establishment the police always tends to be behind change in society and can often be caught out by the fact that its view of accepted norms is no longer that of society. Classic examples of this were the 'OZ' magazine and Lady Chatterley's Lover trials of the sixties where the official views on obscenity were clearly very different from those of the majority of people. The second element which, in my view, creates uncertainty is that of the presence or absence of political will or support for the actions which the police are carrying out. The situation here is further complicated in policing by the fact that the government will often pass a new law apparently aimed at the control of a current problem with 'much ado' whilst at the same time hoping that the police will exercise their unique powers of discretion and by doing so make a poor law workable whilst allowing the politicians to assert that they have done their part and it is now up to the police, and other agencies, to do theirs. There are many examples of legislation being passed in a hurry with the expectation that the way that we would enforce it would make good practice out of bad law. A classic example of this is Section 39 of the Public Order Act which gives the police the power to remove travellers from land on which they are trespassing. When it was passed, as always in a hurry, it allowed the government to say that they had given the police adequate powers to deal with the problem of travellers trespassing. In a parallel debate it was made clear to the police that they should not normally use the power to deal with gypsies and that, even when dealing with new age travellers, they should only use the power when there was a serious threat to public order. This left police as the jam in the sandwich between local authorities and the travellers.

However to return to the issue of change. As in any situation concerning change the key to success is to introduce as much certainty into the process as possible. This can be done by using this model, which looks at four aspects of change. These are:

- the direction of change;

- the pace of change;

- the ability of those involved to anticipate what will happen in the future in both of these factors;

- the willingness of those involved either to live with what they antici- pate will happen or to do enough to change either the anticipated direction or pace.

I propose to examine briefly the approach to drugs against this model and then comment on what they indicate should happen against what is actually happening.

Drugs and the direction of change in use

The direction of change is clear. More and more young people are experimenting at earlier and earlier ages with 'soft' or 'leisure' drugs.

The range of drugs of abuse has also increased going from the tradi- tional opiates through to adulterated and adapted prescription drugs and ending at the point where any aerosol-based product is at least worth trying once and there is clear evidence of a significant increase in the use of heroin and its acceptance by some young people as a 'recreational' drug.

The pace of change of use

Empirical evidence is hard to come by in this area due to the need to use 'self-report' surveys as the main source of information. Hard evidence such as the use of needle exchanges, hospitalisation and deaths can be affected by the change of use of the drug; for example the current change from injecting to inhaling heroin reduces the need for needles and reduces the danger of overdosing and injection-related infection. The problem is compounded by the degree of hype that the issue attracts in the media. That said there does appear to be a general consensus that the rate of increase in the use of drugs is becoming faster. This appears to be true for both soft and hard drugs. In the 'soft' drugs the use of cannabis appears to be pervasive and all of the evidence is that amphetamines, in their many forms, appear to now be a commonplace part of the lifestyle of a significant proportion of young people.

The immediate and short term future?

From the trends that are evident to date I think it would be reasonable to state that if we only continue to do what we have been doing to date then the use of both soft and narcotic drugs will continue to increase, that the age of introduction to them will continue to fall and that the levels of narcotic use will continue to rise.

All of this must be seen against the background of the fact that the drugs market is exactly that – a market, with all of the features of a market. In this market there are three interacting factors. They are price, supply, and demand. Whilst a change in one will effect the others it must be remembered that the model will continually try to achieve balance. At the end of the day it must be accepted that no matter what is done to reduce the supply, as long as demand exists new players will continually enter the market to try to satisfy that demand and the only real effect will be short-term variations of price. From this it is clear that the only worthwhile long-term strategy is one which seeks to reduce or eliminate demand. Anything else will merely change the level and cost of supply.

That then is the situation and prognosis on drugs, what of the other factor which creates uncertainty in policing: that of political will? Political will makes itself felt in my view through two channels. The first is the clear support given to police, and other agencies, when they are carrying out tasks which are manifestly unpopular with a significant section of society but which clearly support the line that the government wishes to pursue. The second way that political will makes itself manifest is in the provision of resources.

Probably best the best example of a comparison of situations where the political will was made clear was that of the 1974 and 1985 miners' strikes. In 1974 the police failed to contain the miners' picket and this failure led to the successful conclusion of the strike from the miners' perspective. In my view part of the reason for this was the fact that the police did not have in place the right tactics but the main reason for failure was that there was no clear political direction given nor was there any guarantee that adequate resources would be made available to ensure that the police would have the capability of controlling the unlawful picketing. Compare that with 1985. The strike came at the end of a period of significant change in the freedoms which unions had to enforce strike action. The will of the elected government could not have been clearer. At the appropriate points in the dispute it was made clear to chief constables that the resources necessary to ensure police capability would be made available. The result was that the law on picketing was strictly enforced and the rights of individuals were protected regardless of the cost. My point here is not to state that what was done was right rather it is to illustrate the difference in dealing with difficult issues when the political declaration is accompanied by real support both in public statements and in terms of resources.

How does the current approach to the drugs problem look in the light of this model? It has already been established that if we continue to do only what we do already it does not appear likely that we will contain, never mind reduce, the amount of drug taking in society. Either the analysis at government level is faulty or there is a lack of political will to do something meaningful to affect the problem. It is clear that the only way to contain or reduce the problem is to achieve success on two fronts at the same time. The first front is to stop young people becoming involved in drug taking of any kind; the second front is to develop an effective system of containing drug use once someone becomes addicted and to develop approaches to treatment which have some probability of success in getting addicts off the habit.

This would indicate that if the political will was there we should expect to see a powerful and focused strategy aimed at effecting both of these elements. We do have drugs action teams and we have the outward appearance of having a strategy, if you like a clear statement of intent, but when we look at the key issue of resources then in my view the position looks entirely different.

In education if prevention is the objective then the target groups will be between the ages of 8 and 14. These are children who are still attending school and are thus a captive audience for any education programme. In almost every county in England in the last several years the education budget has been reduced year on year whilst at the same time the emphasis has been put very clearly on improving performance in those subjects which are tested. This has led to inexorable pressures on time and materials to ensure that tested subjects are those which are best supported even if that is at the expense of subjects which are considered to be important.

The effect of this is then compounded by the effect that these cuts have had on the youth service. The service, in my view, is vital to any drugs education programme in two ways. Firstly, it has the ability to reach young people in situations where they are more likely to take on the message being delivered and secondly it can reach those young people who are poor school attenders or, even more important these days, those who have been excluded. This service has been reduced almost to the point where it is non-existent in this county (Bedfordshire) and I cannot believe that it is all that different elsewhere. If the political will reflected the political propaganda there would be adequate dedicated resources available to ensure that an effective drugs education programme could be delivered and there would be in place properly funded and focused research to establish exactly what does work.

The same position exists regarding treatment. The approach to treatment has varied in a confusing way over the years. In the seventies the subject of addiction was treated with sympathy and the main approach was to contain the addict's problem whilst at the same time maintaining contact so as to grab any window of opportunity which presented itself to reduce dosage and get the addict onto a detoxification programme. That was replaced in the 80s with a more hard-nosed approach where no treatment was offered unless the addict made a commitment to reduce dosage and eventually come off the drug. We are gradually returning to the more sane seventies approach however if we look at the issue of political will again we find the same situation as in education in that treatment centres are critically dependent on funding from local health authorities. Performance in drug treatment is not seen to be important. I say that because it is not measured and whilst other areas are, then they will always be more important. It is commonly accepted that there are far more potential customers or clients for treatment centres then those centres have funds to cater for. So again we have a situation where drugs are at the fag-end of the budgetary provision.

What do I think should happen if the government was to remove uncertainty in this area? Firstly, it would fund serious and extensive research into what works in drugs education. The difficulty in establishing this should not be underestimated. The programme must be such that it can provide information about the safe use of drugs whilst at the same time both reflecting young people's experience of the drug scene and doing enough to persuade them that they should not get involved. We must move away from the current situation where there are a rag-bag of schemes grabbed from goodness-knows-where but usually America and implemented by a variety of agencies with highly varied levels of expertise and where there has been, at best, inadequate evaluation of their effectiveness.

Having established what works we then need to fund its delivery so as to make it effective. In Bedfordshire I have just agreed to two officers being dedicated to a drug education programme. With salaries and on-costs this amounts to an investment of between £75,000 and £90,000 per year. If that was done by every force in the country on the same scale it would amount to an additional four to five million pounds on drugs education just by one agency – if that is compared with what is actually spent nationally it gives an idea of the scale of resources needed to increase the probability of having a significant impact on the problem.

So much for education what about enforcement?

In my view if we are serious about containing the problem we must reverse the current trend of decriminalisation. Whilst I recognise all of the benefits that the cautioning approach produces I do not believe that it is possible to carry out an effective drugs education programme when it is seriously undermined not only by the need to show young people how to use drugs safely if they must use them at all; but also by the fact that the low probability of arrest and the fact that the initial response is only a caution has effectively decriminalised their use. The need to reduce harm is an accepted imperative. I cannot see the same imperative being necessary for dealing with offenders found in possession. I believe that it is essential to make the position as clear as possible by stigmatising drugs use as an unacceptable and criminal activity.

If that is all that we do, however, we will fail and fail mightily. Again we come to the issue of political will and resources. A change in prosecution policy such as this must be accompanied by significant changes in the whole prosecution process. Firstly, we must change the law so that it is easier to convict traffickers and to seize their profits. A major change in approach would be to introduce a system of rebuttable presumptions, e.g. where possession of more than a stated amount of a drug raised the presumption that the possessor was trafficking thus transferring the burden of proof to the offender. The same could be done regarding any property owned by a convicted trafficker.

In addition it is essential that we set up as soon as possible a system of drugs courts where the magistrates and judges have in-depth knowledge both of the drugs scene and of the range of disposals which are most likely to be successful in any particular circumstance. For that to be effective there must be adequate support and treatment available to users. This will mean a significant increase in the number and range of treatment centres and in the staffing of those support services which are most likely to both contain drugs use and to improve the probability of the effectiveness of the treatment. As in education it is also essential that this change is accompanied by adequately funded and focused research aimed at establishing what does work in this area. It is time that we stopped exchanging views and opinions based on inadequate research evidence and that we moved on to a more robust and effective platform. In this resources are the key to success.

Following the change model I spelt out, the prognosis if we continue as we are is clear. Only one of the factors that show that the political will needed to improve the chances of success appears to be present, that is the public statements. It is time that the propaganda stopped and the will to succeed was adequately reflected in the provision of resources and the funding of research into what works. The current government has the sort of massive majority which should enable it to take the political hype and hyperbole out of the debate and allow the development, at last, of a rational and properly funded approach to this overwhelmingly important problem. It seems to me that there is still time for the policy of containment to work – if we do not use it properly then we may have to deal with drugs in the same way that our forebears had to deal with alcohol when it reached the scale depicted by Hogarth and move from criminalisation to legalisation and regulation.

CHAPTER 7

Zero Tolerance: Back to the Future

Jock Young

"In the book I wrote some time ago with George Erdos, *Families Without Fatherhood*, we tell a story about zero-tolerance, confident, policing in Sunderland in 1941. Three boys were sharing a Woodbine one Sunday morning in the loading bay of a town-centre store. A policeman appeared at one end of the short back lane, another at the other. The boys were marched home to their parents. (The boys and the policemen both walked a mile.) Their fathers smoked. The policemen smoked. But boys of twelve were not allowed to smoke. They certainly could not thumb their noses at generalized adult authority by smoking in public. The boys whose fathers were not away fighting in the war were in trouble with their fathers. All of them were in trouble with their mothers.

If any journalist had seen fit to write an article condemning the waste of police resources on a trivial – and victimless – offence when their fathers and brothers were being killed at the front or at sea, his editor would have wondered what on earth his point could be. If the editor had published it, the public would have had difficulty in understanding what was being proposed – that because their fathers were absent, their sons should be allowed to flout rules that they would have upheld if they had been at home?

When policing was detailed and consensual, we conclude, it was low-key, good humoured and effective. Of these three boys from working-class homes in terrace houses without gardens and opening straight onto the street, the products of depression and war, one became one of the town's best ship-yard welders, one a bank manager, and one the head of a polytechnic."

Norman Dennis, *Zero Tolerance: Policing a Free Society*, 1977, p 2

The diversity of late modernity evokes a nostalgia for the inclusive, secure world of the past; the rise in crime and disorder characteristic of the period creates the demand for a quick fix, a panacea, in order to conjure back the secure streets and backyards of childhood memories. Father is at work (or at war) mother at home, the Bobby is on the beat, mischief is caught in the bud, and ill-doing firmly dealt with. Put the film on fast rewind: back to the future . . .

The last third of the Twentieth Century witnessed a rise in crime in all advanced industrial countries with the possible exception of Japan. The increase occurred early in some countries, such as the United States, later in others, such as The Netherlands, but it seemed for a long time remorseless and inevitable. It occurred through periods of full employment and in the recession of the Eighties, sometimes its force was dramatic, in one year alone in England and Wales (1991) the rise in the recorded crime rate was one and a quarter times that of the total crime rate in 1950. Often its impact was gradual but far-reaching in its eventual consequence. It occurred despite massive rises in living standards, expenditure in the criminal justice system and on crime prevention and measures of personal security. Experience of crime moved from the exceptional in every life to become part of normal everyday life (Lea and Young, 1993; Garland, 1997) and the precautions against it seemed at times like some ghastly Maginot Line of colossal cost and minimal effectiveness. For a time the slogan became 'nothing works' and the crime statistics were awaited with apprehension: as one Metropolitan Police Commissioner put it, they became like "the sins of the community . . . annually visited upon the police", noting that "the 'figures' beast has the strength of years in its veins and is an unconscionable time dying" (Newman, 1985, pp 14–15)

Indeed by 1986 the London police, always traditionally eager to claim crime as 'their' problem, were only too ready to issue disclaimers, witness the bitterness of this Metropolitan Police document:

> "It also seems wrong in principle that some of our more vociferous critics are allowed to enjoy multiple bites at the same cherry. On the one hand the Left argues that government policy has spread and intensified relative deprivation which they argue is crimogenic. At the same time they vilify the Force for failing to stem rising recorded crime rates and protect vulnerable Londoners. The government, on the other hand, pursues an economic policy, which includes a treasury driven social policy, that has one goal – the reduction of inflation. Any adverse social by-products are accepted as necessary casualties in the pursuit of the overall objective.
> It might be more constructive to judge Force performance against a forecast that had taken account of extrinsic social and economic factors." 　　　　　(Metropolitan Police, 1986, pp 115–116)

Yet at long last the tide seems to have turned (or at least halted). Between 1993 and 1995 the crime rate in twelve of seventeen advanced industrial countries declined (Home Office, 1996) and various agencies of crime control began, once more, to claim the crime rate for themselves. No more so than in New York City, where the crime rate plummeted by 36 per cent in three years (1993/96) and where some are claiming a 'miracle'. Indeed "police leaders and consultants travel around the country preaching the new science of crime reduction and seeking miracles of their own" (Lardner, 1997, p 54) while Police Commissioner Bratton presides over the big change. Meanwhile George Kelling has embarked on a world tour expounding the 'Broken Windows' philosophy which supposedly informed these miraculous events (Kelling and Cole, 1997) in which over a short period of time the NYPD has become the most visited and researched police department in the world.

It comes as no surprise, therefore, that our own Home Secretary, Jack Straw, can announce in the first speech to a Party Conference since the Labour Party came to power, that he wanted "zero tolerance of crime and disorder in our neighbourhoods" (September 1997), whilst the incoming Prime Minister of Ireland, Bertie Ahern, in May 1997 pledged himself to zero tolerance with the Bratton's Irish-born deputy John Timoney at his side (Shapiro, 1997).

A Seminar in Westminster: the miracle revealed

On an afternoon in July 1997 I attended a seminar of the right wing tank, the Institute for Economic Affairs. It was the day after the launch of the book *Zero Tolerance: Policing a Free Society* and was to be addressed by William J Bratton, the ex-Commissioner of Police in New York City. The audience was a collection of distinguished right wing columnists, a few academics, someone from Conservative Central Office and the odd television journalist. They were looking for something that would quickly and dramatically solve the crime problem, that would set the world alight and reverse the processes of disorder that had beset the cities in the span of their lifetime. Here was a success story, New York City transformed from 'the crime capital of the world' to 'one of the safest big cities in the world': within a space of three years the crime rate dropping by 37 per cent and homicide by over 50 per cent. The title of William Bratton's leading article said it all, "Crime is Down in New York City: Blame the Police" (1997).

On the way to the seminar I armed myself with doubt: had not zero-tolerance in Brixton, South London, led to the riots in 1981? How could Bratton possibly know that it was his policies and the rule of force which had reduced the crime rate? Hadn't precisely the opposite methods been tried in San Diego with just as good results?

But before I turn to the revelations of the seminar, let us look at the concept itself. Zero tolerance has become a buzz word in community safety in the last few years. Its aim on a policing level is to flag up an intolerance of incivilities, of sweeping the streets clean of deviance and disorder, of dealing with aggressive beggars, squeegee merchants, loiterers, drunks and prostitutes. Its aim is to reverse the tendency to "define deviance down" (Moynihan, 1992; Krauthammer, 1993). In penology, it is represented by 'the three strikes and you're out' policies, and the 'war against drugs' which have contributed to the steep rise in the US incarceration rate and in the demand for a reversal of the decline in the rates of imprisonment. Thus Charles Murray (1997) has pointed to the tendency for the chances of going to prison for committing a serious crime going down in many industrial countries and the need to follow the US lead in reversing this trend (for a critique see Young, 1997).

The concept of zero tolerance would seem to have five key components:

1 a lowering of tolerance to crime and deviance
2 the use of punitive, sometimes drastic, measures to achieve this
3 a return to perceived past levels of respectability, order and civility
4 the awareness of the continuum between incivilities and crime with both low spectrum 'quality of life' rule breaking and serious crimes being considered problems
5 the belief that there is a relationship between crime and incivilities in that incivilities left unchecked give rise to crime

The key text repeatedly mentioned as the inspiration for this approach is Wilson and Kelling's classic 1982 article in *Atlantic Monthly*, entitled *Broken Windows*.

But more of this later, let us return to the seminar where the audience, suitably refreshed with white wine and canapés, were looking forward to hearing from the Commissioner something dramatic: a get tough policy that had worked. William Bratton was a bit of a revelation. He started by totally distancing himself from the concept of zero tolerance: he thought that the notion was inadmissible in police work, the only exceptions, perhaps, being drug use and corruption within the police force. Discretion was a vital part of policing and this involved working out a joint plan with the communities concerned and taking note of their priorities and preferences. He agreed that action must occur against the broad spectrum of crime and incivilities, he had read the Wilson and Kelling article in his previous job as police chief of Boston and it had confirmed his already held beliefs. But to deal with crime did not involve a rigid imposition of police control, furthermore, policing itself was only the first step, a holding operation, before the social changes which would engender a more stable society would hopefully be instituted. Finally, he had during his visit (which included a trip to Brixton) been impressed by the tranquil and relatively civil nature of London and warned of the problem of transposing techniques which work in one context too easily to another.

The audience was, to say the least, disappointed: they had come to hear that the simple and the dramatic would work but had heard largely a story of common sense laced with self-congratulation.

False claims and confused categories
It is time we examined the claims and disassembled the categories. The simple equation is that zero tolerance, based on the philosophy of 'Broken Windows', was tried out in New York City and led to a reduction in crime. All of these links are, in fact, false: they are rhetoric substituting itself for reason, fiction blinding reason. Let us look at the links one by one:

1. **Crime was dramatically reduced in New York City in the period 1993–1996**
   This is the only part of the equation that is true: it is the bedrock of truth to which the false series of linkages are hitched. The homicide figures which are recognised as the most reliable of criminal statistics reduced by a remarkable 49.5 per cent in this period (the lowest since 1968), the gunshot wound victims treated by New York City Health and Hospital Corporation data showed a drop of 56.3 per cent over these years (Jacobson, 1997). Both of these figures are extremely unlikely to be falsified whatever pressures undoubtedly occurred on the NYPD to produce the 'best' statistics over this period of intense departmental and political agitation.

2. **That the decrease was due to the specific innovative police practices of the New York Police Department**
   Here we encounter the first of the false links. Most obviously such a claim is unreasonable because the decline in crime occurred in 17 of 25 of the largest US cities in the period 1993–1996. It occurred in those cities which had explicitly adopted less aggressive policies (e.g. Los Angeles in the wake of the riots), in cities which utilise community-oriented policing such as Boston and San Diego (Pollard, 1997; Currie, 1997). It occurred where no change had occurred in policing (e.g. Oakland) and indeed in some cases where there was a reduction in police officers. Indeed differing police methods seemed to be associated with a drop in serious crime (Shapiro, 1997) and the crime rate in New York City had begun to drop *before* the new policing methods of Commissioner Bratton were instituted. Furthermore, as we have seen, the decline in crime occurred in cities across the industrialised world, long before zero-tolerance had become an international buzz word.

3. **Zero-tolerance was tried out in New York City**

Commissioner Bratton, as we have seen, explicitly denied to our disappointed seminar that he had implemented a zero tolerance policy. Such a notion of applying a blanket no tolerance policy disallows police discretion and is well nigh impossible in a modern disorderly city. To apply every letter of the law in say Harlem day in and day out would stretch the resources of any foreseeable police budget. Indeed, the movement in police focus from minor to more serious crimes (so lamented by Wilson and Kelling in *Broken Windows*) is very largely a function of the rise in crime – that is, the movement in police tolerance is not a mere function of lowering standards but of the necessity of the pressure of demand on resources. What he did was shift the focus so crimes of disorder would have a greater demand on police resources. And he also, of course, instituted a series of other policing practices which had nothing whatsoever to do with zero tolerance, e.g. use of daily computerised statistics as a guide to results.

Furthermore, not only William Bratton but George Kelling strongly deny that zero tolerance has any relationship with the philosophy of *Broken Windows*. (See B Walsh, 1997)

The links between police practice in New York City and zero tolerance and between the latter and the philosophy of 'Broken Windows' are, therefore, strongly denied and tenuous.

4. **The *Broken Windows* approach was tried out in New York City**

If zero tolerance was not attempted in New York City, was the *Broken Windows* approach implemented? Commissioner Bratton claims that this is so, indeed that as a Police chief in Boston he had come to a realisation of the effectiveness of this philosophy, so to speak, spontaneously before he had read the article. And George Kelling, the co-author, very definitely claims that the ideas he authored with James Q Wilson were the underlying philosophy. Indeed it is such a claim which underscores the triumphalism of his recent book, *Fixing Broken Windows*.

The reality of *Broken Windows*

Let us look once again at the classic article published in 1982 in *The Atlantic Monthly* and reprinted, with little change, in Wilson's best selling book *Thinking About Crime* (1985). It is perhaps the most widely cited article in the field of criminology in recent years and certainly the most influential. But like many widely claimed influences, it is rarely read and its clearly stated policy implications are simply not taken on board.

The background of the article is a disillusionment with the efficacy of normal policing methods in part based on George Kelling's pioneer study in Newark, New Jersey and numerous other studies across the United States which suggested only a limited effect of policing on crime rates (see Wilson, 1985, p 61–74; Kinsey et al., 1986, pp 77–87). Such results were backed up by international research, particularly in Britain under the auspices of The Home Office (Morris and Heal, 1981; Clarke and Hough, 1984). This position represented a sea-change in attitudes to policing and a fundamental undermining of the conventional wisdom of the police as "the thin blue line in the fight against crime". "It may be", Wilson writes:

> "that judging the police solely or even chiefly by their ability to reduce crime is a mistake. Most police work involving crime occurs after the crime is committed and reported . . . and depends crucially for its success on the subsequent actions of prosecutors and judges. The traditional function of the police – indeed, the purpose for which they were originally created about 150 years ago – was to maintain order in urban neighbourhoods. In our concern over crime, we may have mistakenly though understandably turned for help to the most visible and familiar part of the criminal justice system and thereby made the police both the object of our hopes and the target of our frustrations. Perhaps we should stand back and view the police in a broader perspective, one which assigns them an important part, to be sure in crime control, but an even more important part in the maintenance of orderly neighbourhoods."   (1985, p 74)

Indeed James Q Wilson explicitly sets himself against what he views as conservative views of policing which believe that old fashioned, no holds barred tough police tactics will solve the problem of crime. All of this is a far cry from the usual resonance of zero tolerance. The police can only have a limited purchase on the problem of crime. Wilson is especially clear about this:

> "To the extent we have learned anything at all, we have learned that the factors in our lives and history that most powerfully influence the crime rate – our commitment to liberty, our general prosperity, our childrearing methods, our popular values – are precisely the factors that are hardest or riskiest to change. Those things that can more easily and safely be changed – the behaviour of the police, the organization of neighborhoods, the management of the criminal justice system, the sentences imposed by courts – are the things that have only limited influence on the crime rate."   (ibid., p 250)

And, as we shall see later, such a reallocation of the police from a central to a more peripheral role in crime control is one which has ready agreement amongst criminologists of all theoretical persuasions.

Wilson and Kelling's insight was that the control of minor offenders, and disorderly behaviour which was not criminal was as important to a community as crime control. Incivilities, 'quality of life' crimes were a major part of the citizens' feeling of unease in the city. And to this absolutely spot-on insight they added two more contentious propositions. Namely, that the police who were ineffective at the control of serious crime would be effective against disorderly behaviour. Indeed that that was their traditional role. And that control of incivilities would, so to speak, kick start the community out of despair and disintegration and such a revitalised community, through internal controls and citizens' vigilance, would in time reverse the spiral of decay and reduce the incidence of serious crime. I do not want to enter into a critique of this philosophy, my point is that this is scarcely a programme of zero tolerance against all crime which believes that the police are the key actors in the creation of an orderly society and which views the 'sweeping up' of the streets as producing miraculous and immediate results. It is a more subtle theory, it has a more marginal role for the police and it situates the wellspring of social order in more fundamental parts of the social structure. Finally, it talks not of zero tolerance but of discretion bordering on 'realpolitik'. What police chief or politician would subscribe to the following policy nostrum?

"Therefore, each department must assign its existing officers with great care. Some neighborhoods are so demoralized and crime-ridden as to make foot patrol useless; the best the police can do with limited resources is respond to the enormous number of calls for service. Other neighborhoods are so stable and serene as to make foot patrol unnecessary. The key is to identify neighborhoods at the tipping point – where the public order is deteriorating but not unreclaimable, where the streets are used frequently but by apprehensive people, where a window is likely to be broken at any time and must quickly be fixed if all are not to be shattered.

Most police departments do not have ways of systematically identifying such areas and assigning officers to them. Officers are assigned on the basis of crime rates (meaning that marginally threatened areas are often stripped so that police can investigate crimes in areas where the situation is hopeless) or on the basis of calls for service (despite the fact that most citizens do not call the police when they are merely frightened or annoyed). To allocate patrols wisely, the department must look at the neighborhoods and decide, from first-hand evidence, where an additional officer will make the greatest difference in promoting a sense of safety."   (ibid., p 88)

Moral panics and panaceas: folk devils and fairy princesses
Why is it that such miracles are so easily propagated and dispensed across the globe? What is it that makes the notion of the quick fix, the one-off cure so attractive to wide sections of the public? To answer this I want to briefly look at the stance of the mass media, the material predicament of claim making agencies and the psychological set of people in the pluralistic world of late modernity.

1. **The mass media**
The central key to newsworthiness is as I have emphasised elsewhere the atypical: that which surprises, which is in contrast to a positive everyday 'normality' (see Young, 1971; Cohen and Young, 1981). Criminologists and students of deviance have not surprisingly concerned themselves with the negative side of the atypical: villains, serial killers, folk devils and other monsters. But the positive side, stars, heroes, fairy princesses who die in tragic circumstances, are also a site of media focus and the projection of public hopes and anxieties. And exactly the same processes of media selection, accentuation and construction of news occurs here as it does on the dark side of human existence. Thus although crime waves are a staple of news, so are 'miraculous' cures of crime (whether they be nutrition supplements, CCTV, neighbourhood watch, DNA testing or zero-tolerance in NYC). Moral panics and moral panaceas go hand in hand, and are a daily stock of news reporting just as are the repeated tragic tales of those inflicted with cancer and the regular 'revolutionary' breakthroughs in its treatment. Over and above this the backcloth of public expectancy in the Western World has been of a regular, somewhat remorseless increase in crime: the sudden decline of crime in of all places New York City, in the violent streets of Scorsese and Lumet is a miracle indeed!

This need to search for miracles and breakthroughs, institutionalised within news gathering organisations, is combined with a common objective, a drive to generate news in small, simple units which fit the insistent bitty nature of programming. The sound-bite, the fleeting picture that tells it all, combined with an underlying message which winds up the public: 'The solution is simple, why don't *they* try it out here?' is a formula for one-dimensional simplicity and the quick fix.

2. Claim-making agencies

Those which make their living from convincing government and public that they have a ready solution to the crime problem. They can be either small independent entrepreneurs (e.g. private drug clinics or crime prevention agencies) or entrepreneurial groups with large organisations (e.g. specialised police drug or burglary units). Their role is to claim and compete for the ownership of social problems (Gusfield, 1989) in contrast with the usually larger organisations which attend to the daily business of social control which more often than not adopt the role of 'disclaiming agencies'. That is their concern is more with the processing, administration and warehousing of deviance rather than the rehabilitation or cure of their subjects. It is only when the statistics go remarkably in their direction – as in the case of Commissioner Bratton and New York City, that claim-making is enthusiastically embraced. Such opportunities have been rare in the post-war period. It is scarcely surprising that the Commissioner of Police and the Mayor of New York City should believe in miracles: who after all would look a gift horse in the mouth?

3. The public

The era of late modernity brings with it a pluralism of values, a world where the embededness of the citizen in the setting of occupation, marriage and community becomes precarious and daily threatened. Such an ontological insecurity (see Giddens, 1995) has as one response a need for secure definitions of norms, coupled very often with a nostalgia: a desire to redraw the boundaries of behaviour back to an imagined past of civility and predictability. The attraction of zero tolerance policies is obvious in such a world: it defines our tolerance of deviance, back to a nostalgic past, promising a once off sweep of the disorder which confronts them. Outside of these immediate pressures, there is a general cultural predisposition to such a belief in the easy miracle and the instant cure. This lies in two basic fallacies entrenched within conventional wisdom, which I will detail below.

The cosmetic fallacy and the social as simple

The seminar was on the look-out for a quick fix, a simple solution to the problem of crime; their particular politics determined their fixation with zero tolerance, but panaceas of many varieties are on offer. More liberal audiences, for example, might have preferred the magic of Neighbourhood Watch, or of CCTV, or nutritional supplements or the treatment of offender dyslexia or psychodrama in Glendon Underwood. Take your pick, the fashions come and go – all suffer equally from the two fallacies.

The cosmetic fallacy conceives of crime as a superficial problem of society, skin deep, which can be dealt with with the appropriate ointment rather than any chronic ailment of society as a whole. It engenders a cosmetic criminology which views crime as a blemish which suitable treatment can remove from a body which is, itself, otherwise healthy and in little need of reconstruction. Such criminology distances from the core institutions and proffers technical, piecemeal solutions. It, thus, reverses causality: crime causes problems for society rather than society causes the problem of crime. Although this belief is easily held when crime is a relatively unusual behaviour, it becomes more and more difficult to hold this belief the more common it becomes without suggesting that crime itself is usually trivial in nature and impact. Such a position has its adherents although, as we shall see, the vast majority of academic criminologists, whether conservative or liberal in their disposition, do not find this logic satisfactory.

The second fallacy revolves around the remarkably widely accepted idea that the social world is a relatively simple structure in which rates of different social events (e.g. marriages, suicides, strikes, crimes) can be related to narrowly delineated changes in other parts of the structure. In fact the social world is a complex interactive entity in which any particular social intervention can only possibly have a limited effect on other social events and where the calculation of this effect is always difficult. Thus the crime rate is affected by a large number of things: by the level of deterrence exerted by the criminal justice system, to be sure, but also by the levels of informal control in the community, by patterns of employment, by types of child-rearing, by the cultural, political and moral climate, by the level of organised crime, by the patterns of illicit drug use, etc. To merely add together all these factors is complicated enough but is insufficient, for it does not allow human assessment and reflexivity – the *perceived* injustice of unemployment, for instance, or the *felt* injustices of bad policing or imprisonment. For the social is not only complex, like the natural world (who would ever think that only one factor would explain the weather?). It is even more intricate because each factor can be transformed over time by human interpretation. To take imprisonment, for example, the same sentence can be perceived by the individual as perfectly just ('I had it coming'), or as an unjust and unwarranted reaction to a petty crime which stokes up further resentment, leading to more serious crime in the future, or as a rite of passage which everyone in one's social circle goes through. Thus strange and distinctly unlinear relationships can occur. Low rates of imprisonment can act as an effective deterrent when the community is in accord as to the venality of the crime and the impartiality of the criminal justice system. In contrast, high rates of imprisonment can be counter-productive where they are seen as grossly unfair with regard to the level of gravity of the offence and the degree to which the system focuses on particular sections of the community rather than others.

It is important to stress how both the notion of the cosmetic nature of crime as a problem and its simplicity flies in the face of a consensus across the varied political and theoretical perspectives of modern criminology. James Q Wilson, as we have seen, views the source of crime as involving those basic values of liberty, childrearing, prosperity, which in his estimation we are least likely to wish to change. An impulsive, consumer oriented society with permissive childrearing habits will produce criminals – policing and prisons can only manipulate the surface of the problem. This is the basis of his 'realism'; whole areas of the city are beyond redemption, his criminology is one of the containment of crime, not of fundamental reduction, let alone elimination. Listen to Wilson, the major architect of the recent war against drugs, talk of the result of this massive and costly intervention:

> "Many people . . . think, we have lost the war on drugs. . . . [but] We did not surrender and we did not lose. We did not win, either. What the nation accomplished then was what most efforts to save people from themselves accomplished, the problem was contained and the number of victims minimized, all at considerable cost in law enforcement and increased crime." (1992, p 36)

And Wilson, the hard bitten 'realist' is perhaps the most optimistic of those on the right of the political spectrum. Travis Hirschi, the influential founder of control theory, ends *A General Theory of Crime* which he co-authored with Michael Gottfredson:

> ". . . the state is neither the cause of nor the solution to crime. In our view, the origins of criminality of low self-control are to be found in the first six or eight years of life, during which time the child remains under the control and supervision of the family or a familial institution. Apart from the limited benefits that can be achieved by making specific criminal acts more difficult, policies directed toward enhancement of the ability of familial institutions to socialize children are the only realistic long-term state policies with potential for substantial crime reduction." (1990, pp 272–3).

And in an article in *Society* they lambast American crime policy in the following terms:

> "Lacking a theory to guide it, crime policy relies on the unexamined slogans and catch phrases of an ostensibly stretched-thin and

embattled constabulary, with its emphasis on career criminals, boot camps, drug testing, 'intermediate sanctions,' gang units, and ever-increasing prison terms.

The proper response to these circumstances is to return to social theory and research. Recent events demonstrate too well that nothing is more dangerous than a policy justified only by the ambitions of politicians and bureaucrats." (1995, p 30)

Even Charles Murray, who advocates the widespread use of zero-tolerance methods together with extensive use of imprisonment, believes that these methods will not tackle the root causes, they will "contain not win the war" and that "if you are looking for a return to 1950s crime levels . . . you are going to be disappointed." (1997, p 20)

The shift into late modernity
I want to argue that both of these fallacies, the belief in the cosmetic nature of crime and the notion of the social as simple, become even more difficult to sustain as we shift into late modernity.

Let us take the cosmetic fallacy first of all. The movement from an inclusive to an exclusive society involves, as we have seen, an unravelling of the labour markets: the creation of large sectors of the population who are either economically precarious or actually excluded. Relative deprivation becomes blatant in the comparisons across such a dislocated social terrain. Meanwhile, the same market forces which transform the labour market generate a new world of lifestyle and consumerism on the back of which emerges an individualism which permeates its way throughout society (see Currie, 1997). Crime springs from this combination and becomes a normal feature of everyday life (see Lea and Young, 1993; Garland, 1997). The incidence of crime, although always much more widespread than official figures suggest, spreads palpably and obviously across the map. Criminal areas remain but there are fewer and fewer areas with low rates of conventional crime; serious, repeat offences still occur yet now there are many more of them and the casual offender is commonplace. We cease to use the word 'criminal' and substitute 'offender'; the belief in the delimited number of distinct criminals beloved by positivism becomes much less sustainable, even within their own ranks, and neo-positivism begins to conflate the rational offender with the rational citizen and indeed the opportunistic thief is cast in the same mould as the impulsive shopper (see Clarke, 1980).

In such a world it is less possible to ascribe crime to the individual criminal with a maverick dysfunctional background or to areas which 'progress' left behind. The cosmetic blemish has spread throughout society.

Let me give an example, Geoff Pearson and his associates, in their brilliant study of the British heroin epidemic of the early eighties, note that as heroin addiction is compatible with widely varying lifestyles this contradicts the 'junkie' stereotype:

> "Research has established over many years that heroin addiction is compatible with widely varying lifestyles – from stable addicts with a more-or-less normal family life and employment record, to those who live a chaotic 'junkie' lifestyle, living by crime and by doses of imprisonment. . . . Nevertheless, it is probably true that a decade ago the 'typical' heroin user would be more likely to have been someone leading a bohemian-type lifestyle, or to have been someone with some form of temperamental instability. However, as the heroin using population has steadily grown in recent years this has undoubtedly become less true, so that although some individuals are psychologically more vulnerable to opiate misuse, attempts to explain heroin use solely in terms of personality factors and psychopathology are nowadays quite inadequate." (1958, p 8)

Alan, one of their interviewees, an experienced ex-user put it nicely:

> "Oh you know how as, like. You used to be able to tell 'em a mile off, well you used to be able to . . . typical junkies, you know, scars up their arms, clapped-out hippies, that kind of thing, the whole works . . . you know what I mean . . . But now, well, I don't know about you, but I couldn't tell one if I fell over him in the street." (Alan 24 years, Manchester). (ibid. p 9)

The normalisation of drug use is parallelled by the normalisation of crime: it is no longer possible to talk of the isolated cosmetic blemishes, the spot, if you wish, has become a rash! Furthermore, it is not a great step from the normalisation of crime to the normalisation of the criminal. Such a shift involves a turning away from the modernist notion of the distinct criminal with his (sic) distinctive causality. Such a loss of the fixed locus of offenders is parallelled by the way in which the offence itself, so clear cut in neo-classicism, becomes blurred and continuous with a wide range of behaviours. In modernity positivism provided us with the notion of a small number of distinct criminals with their own individualistic aetiology: maverick characters, the product of dire and atypical situations whilst neo-classicism delineated the clear cut legal parameters of the crime. Late modernity loses both the precision of offender and offence; offenders are everywhere, offences blur together with a host of anti-social behaviours.

Let us turn now to the second fallacy: the social as simple. Here, too, the notion that the social world is simple, that intervention verges on the obvious and that measurement is easy becomes even more stretched and tenuous. If the social world has always been complex and more resilient to change than the material world – this is the more so in the late modern period. The complex becomes more complex, the intransigent more intransigent, its measurement more elusive than ever. If we think of intervention as consisting of two components, input (the variables to be changed) and output (the effect of the intervention and its measurement) it helps to look at the stages of this process in a late modern society. Here let us reiterate there is a markedly greater pluralism of value and a social system which is less inclusive and integrated.

Input

1. **Public priorities.** In a modernistic society experts proclaimed public priorities and bestowed, so to speak, problems on the public. In late modernity, experts are less able to successfully designate problems to a receptive public; 'authoritative' sources, whether it be experts in say nuclear power, food hygiene, transport, drugs or crime, are much more readily questioned. Authority is less respected and, furthermore, authority has a stranger and stranger habit of disagreeing amongst itself (Giddens, 1991; Beck, 1992). Expert opinion is less able to present itself as detached from interest groups or even worse as the objective singular pronouncement of science: experts speak with many voices and the cacophony of opinion is presented readily and competitively in the mass media. The media, themselves, have become more profligate and extensive, they constantly present a wide array of problems which differ and which change with remarkable speed and alacrity (McRobbie and Thornton, 1995). Meanwhile, the public is more heterogeneous: it shares some priorities but it disputes others and it is more frequently unclear and vacillating as to the problems of the community. What, therefore, are the problems to be tackled and which is the desirable outcome becomes contested and uncertain.

2. **The variables available.** The standard inventory of interventions to lessen crime include, in the forefront the police, the community, the family, the economy, and the educational system. All of these variables are weakened in late modernity. The community has become less cohesive, talk of reasserting community values fails to confront how we are to achieve this nostalgic dream whilst policies of rehabilitation within the community are either wishful thinking or cynical manoeuvres which leave mental patients roaming the street or ex-offenders bereft of support and sustenance. The ability to provide jobs with long-term futures and security capable of building people into the

social order depends on global forces not within the power of central, let alone local, government. Much of the fundamental repertoire of social democracy is enfeebled (see Hoffman, 1993) whilst the standard conservative options of strengthening the family and the criminal justice system are less easy to implement. As we have seen, thoughtful commentators such as James Q Wilson (1975) readily admit that the factors which have most impact upon the crime rate are hardest to change. And even those which are reasonably easy to change, such as numbers of police or prisoners, or the moral stance of schools, are grossly undermined by the weakened forces of family, community and employment.

3. **The changing values of interventions.** As society shifts into late modernity some strange things happen to variables. In a plural society the value of variables, and even the variables change themselves with increased volatility over time. Let me give two examples: a given sentence of imprisonment, say two years, will differ in meaning and impact whether one is a man or a woman, whether professional or unemployed, whether young or old. In some part of the inner city in the United States the prison sentence amongst young blacks has become so commonplace (where perhaps 1 in 4 young men are in prison at any one time) that doing time becomes 'earning your stripes' and is scarcely a negative status. In the gross context of the American penal experiment, the units of penality begin to change valence and in wide swathes of society correctional supervision (probation, parole or prison) is scarcely a stigma but rather a normal fact of life, like having your driving licence endorsed or a minor illness. Or, let us take a more positive variable, wages. An extra payment per hour offered in work (say £2 per hour) will vary in attractiveness widely through the structure. Of course it will not be noticed by those on middle income upwards, and whereas it will be seen as a welcome inducement to commit oneself to work by those on lower to middling incomes, it may well be regarded as a nonsense by those caught in the 'poverty trap'.

Output
1. **Measurement.** The problem of measurement in criminology (and indeed the social sciences in general) is that different audiences define the 'same' behaviour differently. What is violence to one person is of little or no consequence to another. The macho-adolescent gang member and the middle class professional will have totally different scales (see Young, 1988; Mooney, 1998). As pluralism increases in late modernity, the scales multiply between subsets of the population and

are volatile over time. To take another example, definitions of what is vandalism will vary from one group on the same housing estate to another (particularly by age and gender) and, even more confusingly, definitions of unsightly vandalism may change rapidly over time.

2. **Culture of congratulation.** The need to have hard headed measures of crime control interventions is paramount. A culture of congratulation permeates the crime control industry; if, for example, one tenth of the reports by practitioners working in the field of drug abuse were correct, we would have solved the drugs problem years ago. Such a problem is particularly true at a time where there are relatively frequent decreases occurring in crime rates. The temptation to claim declines for one's own agency is, as we have seen, so attractive as to undermine any professional restraint. We must replace a culture of congratulation with one of scepticism.

3. **Displacement.** Displacement is an inevitable result of any social intervention. It is not a technical problem which, with enough ingenuity, can be avoided; the question in any society is not whether but when, where and to what degree displacement occurs. A further question, less frequently asked, is to whom? 'Benign displacement', as Roger Matthews has argued, should aim

> "to limit the level and impact of victimisation by deflecting crime and incivilities away from the most vulnerable populations." (1992, p 46)

As we have seen, late modernity is characterised by a widening gap between those in the primary labour market and those in the secondary markets or out of the labour market altogether. Crime control strategies must be seen in the light of these social divisions and displacement be judged not as a mere, marginal technical problem. As it is evidence suggests that the increased social divisions within society are exacerbated by increased disparities in criminal victimisation (see Hope, 1997).

The limits of tolerance

In the above discussion, I have analysed zero tolerance in terms of its effectiveness and its degree of conceptual clarity. We have been concerned with what it is and whether it works? Let us turn finally to, perhaps the most central problem of all, the ethical and political question of tolerance. What does tolerance mean in a liberal democracy? Where should the lines of normality and deviancy be best drawn in a late modern world?

Until now we have discussed, if you want, 'the criminology of intolerance'. That is the intolerance forged of an intensive policing which focuses on marginalised people and minor infractions parallelling the intolerance of the prison system which increases its numbers every year. This recent process is in contrast to a generation of liberal opinion and scholarship whose aim was to minimise police intervention and lower police numbers. One might even say that this has been the hidden agenda of academic criminology ever since the Nineteenth Century. The implicit assumption being that a liberal democratic state implies minimal penality and, more recently, that the aim is to create a society tolerant of diversity and difference – the very *reverse* of zero tolerance.

At this juncture the easiest thing would be to close this essay with a resounding criticism of zero tolerance as part and parcel of the new penology. That is to roundly condemn it as a manoeuvre which aims to sweep the streets clean of human 'debris'; part of the process of exclusion concomitant with the emergence of a society with a large marginalised and impoverished population that has to be suppressed and contained - an actuarial processing concerned more with sanitisation than justice (Young, 1998). For the contented shoppers in the mall must not be disturbed by the antics of the dispossessed, drinking strong lager in the middle of the day. All of this is true, but such an easy conclusion is not the answer for the predicament contains a contradiction central to criminology and close to the concerns of realism.

The crux of this matter becomes evident when we turn to the other discourse of zero tolerance – that of feminism. For the feminist advocacy of zero tolerance towards violence against women clearly parallels the policing initiatives of the same name. They have their origins in the Canadian 'Family Violence Initiative' started by the Federal Government in the wake of the 'Montreal Massacre' in December 1989 of fourteen young women, mostly engineering students, by a man enraged that they were encroaching on a male preserve (Foley, 1993). The slogan was imported by Edinburgh District Council Women's Committee, who launched their famous zero tolerance of violence against women campaign in November 1992 (see Kutzinger and Hunt, 1993) and was taken up by various London Boroughs (for an evaluation, see Mooney, 1998). Here we have a campaign which advocates zero tolerance but who in their right mind would not agree that we should be intolerant of violence against women, sexual attacks and child abuse?

Not only then is there confusion about the term zero tolerance in terms of policing, but there is another contrasting usage put to good use by the women's movement. There are great differences, of course, feminist zero tolerance does not suggest that there should be any discretion in standards as do Wilson and Kelling. Violence against women is not to be tolerated anywhere in society whether amongst the rich or the poor. The same standard must be applied everywhere but there is no nostalgia, no Golden Age of the Past here. For the past for women was never 'golden', violence was always present in patriarchal society. It is not nostalgic, but progressive: it seeks to gain a world, to raise standards not resuscitate the past.

Of course the answer to the contradiction between the two discourses of zero tolerance is that we could heed one and ignore the other. That one can be zero tolerant of violence against women and tolerant about the activities of the dispossessed. This would not only violate the universalistic prescriptions of the feminist discourse (all violent behaviour against women is prescribed wherever it occurs) but would be an act of bad faith only too common in liberal circles. That is to harbour the sort of schizophrenia which was criticised in the early realist literature:

> "There was a schizophrenia about crime on the left where crimes against women and immigrant groups were quite rightly an object of concern, but other types of crime were regarded as being of little interest, or somehow excusable. Part of this mistake stems, as we have noted, from the belief that property offences are directed solely against the bourgeoisie and that violence against the person is carried out by amateur Robin Hoods in the course of their righteous attempt to redistribute wealth. All of this is, alas, untrue. Indeed, the irony is that precisely the same kids who break into the next-door neighbour's flat sit around the estates wearing British Movement badges and harassing Asians."   (Lea and Young, 1984, p 262)

Furthermore there are very significant similarities between the two discourses. Both wish, obviously, to reduce tolerance – to 'define deviancy up'. And both are concerned with the range of infractions; that is they are worried by both what are regarded by all as serious offences and by the more minor 'quality of life' crimes. Feminists, in particular, are concerned about how everyday 'normal' male incivilities such as sexual harassment at work or in the street affect the peace of mind and freedoms of women's movement through public space.

This takes us back to *Broken Windows*, Wilson and Kelling's major insight was that the cumulative effect of minor incivilities poses as much a problem to the public as crime itself. Their limitation is that they tend to hold incivilities apart from crime at times as if they were two separate problems rather than crime and deviancy being part of the same pheno-menon with the same causes. An awareness of the continuum of crime and incivilities, the importance of their overall impact and their common cause is present in both the left realist and the radical feminist literature. Witness:

"Crime is the end-point of a continuum of disorder. It is not separate from other forms of aggravation and breakdown. It is the run-down council estate where music blares out of windows early in the morning; it is the graffiti on the walls; it is aggression in the shops; it is bins that are never emptied; oil stains across the streets; it is kids that show no respect; it is large trucks racing through your roads; it is streets you do not dare walk down at night; it is always being careful; it is a symbol of a world falling apart. It is lack of respect for humanity and for fundamental human decency . . .

. . . racial harassment . . . ranges from clearly criminal offences to just plain nuisance. But they cannot be separated out, the nuisance boils over into criminal violence. The crime sticks in our mind as the most blatant example of such antisocial behaviour, but it is only the tip of the iceberg. A lot of the more frequent, everyday offences are scarcely criminal – they are 'just' kids fooling around – but they are part and parcel of the same appalling aggression towards defenceless people. It is items like this that rebuff those commentators who maintain that because most crime is 'minor', it is unimportant.

A parallel phenomenon to such racist aggression is the sexual harassment of women. Women have to take a considerable amount of sexual harassment at work and in the streets, which severely restricts their ability to move in public spaces, particularly at night. Rape is the end-point of the continuum of aggressive sexual behaviour. Its comparative rarity does not indicate the absence of antisocial behaviour towards women. On the contrary, it is a real threat which also symbolizes a massive undercurrent of harassment."

(Lea and Young, 1984, pp 55–8)

At approximately the same time feminist academics such as Liz Kelly (1987; Kelly and Radford, 1987) were developing the work of American activists (e.g. Medea and Thompson, 1972) who emphasised the continuum of violence against women.

Thus the notion of a continuum emerged in the criminological literature in the 1980s albeit in three different theoretical traditions, that of establishment criminology, that of radical feminism, and that of left realism. It is pertinent to ask what were the events exterior to the academy which called up this response in the academy. There are to my mind three main changes which relate to the emergence of a late modern world:

1. The last third of the Twentieth Century has not only been characterised by an increase in crime and disorder but by crime becoming more disorderly and disorder blurring into crime (an early sighting of this is S Cohen, 1973). Crime becomes less separate from

disorder, and poor neighbourhoods which once had select bands of professional criminals who terrorised targeted members of the public (banks, shops, clubs and each other) became racked by amateurish crime. Market individualism flourished, (see Currie, 1997) delinquency becomes more internecine and Hobbesian; disorder becomes as much of a problem as crime and is more clearly part of a continuum.

2. The development of pluralistic societies entails that there is widespread conflict between groups over what is orderly and disorderly behaviour. The need for tolerance between groups becomes a major issue whereas the limits of tolerance become increasingly disputed. One person's order is disorder for another, one group's 'normal' behaviour creates intolerable conditions for others.

3. One of the major transformations in the social structure is the changed role of women. The entry of women into the labour market has as a consequence the increased transit of women through public space both for purposes of work and leisure. The growing economic equality with men demands an equality of respect and of freedom to come and go undisturbed and unharmed within public space, at work and at home. Women are less willing to tolerate male impositions on their behaviour and security, as they enter more significantly politically and economically into public life and they bring with them much greater intolerance to violence and abuse. The feminisation of demands on law and order is a key factor in the transformation of public discourse.

The debate about tolerance, growing demands for law and order concomitant ironically with the rise in intolerable behaviour are thus central to both the public and academic discourses with regards to crime and deviancy. Indicative of this is the famous article by Daniel Patrick Moynihan, *Defining Deviancy Down* (1993). In this he suggests that a response to the rising tide of crime and disorder is to simply define less disorder whether criminality, family breakdown or mental illness as deviant. In a way zero tolerance is a response to this – it is an attempt to roll back the levels of tolerance and in its policing aspect carries with it a criticism of the liberation which it is supposed has 'allowed' this to happen. As Bruce Shapiro puts it:

> "Zero tolerance policing unquestionably makes for effective campaign rhetoric, and the original Wilson and Kelling broken window hypothesis is an easy sell to any society frightened by seemingly uncontrollable crime. On its deepest level, however, it is not about crime at all, but a vision of social order disintegrating under glassy-eyed liberal neglect. Much of Wilson and Kelling's original argument,

and Kelling and Cole's recent book, is devoted not to crime policy but to repeated attacks on civil libertarians, advocates for the homeless and social liberals. Disorder, Kelling and Cole (1997) write, 'proliferated with the growth of an ethos of individualism and increasing legislative and judicial support for protecting the fundamental rights of individuals at the expense of community interest'. Over and over, Kelling and Cole blame the 1960s for that ethos: 'The expression of virtually all forms of non-violent deviance came to be considered synonymous with the expression of individual, particularly First Amendment or speech-related rights.' Civil libertarians even get the blame for the proliferation of the homeless mentally ill in American streets – as if the Reagan administration had not cut their community support programmes and eliminated public housing construction, as if real estate speculators had not gentrified thousands of formerly affordable single-room housing units.

The course of violent crime is complex, and inextricable from the fate of cities and the poor. Here is the real danger of the zero tolerance gospel: it severs crime from context, and instead of a clear vision of a safe society offers only an illusory obsession with order at all costs." (1997, p 6)

Shapiro underscores my argument; it is the social context, the structural problems of the system, which produce crime rates. It is obvious that the increased 'tolerance' levels of the criminal justice systems throughout the Western world were a product of the exceptional growth of pressure upon them rather than 'liberalism' and that the values of individualism and immediate gratification which contribute so greatly to our crime problem are not a product of a free-floating permissiveness but of the market society which flourished in the last part of the Twentieth Century (see Currie, 1997). Crime rates relate to the material conditions which occur within a society; the criminal justice system, whether scripted by liberal ideals or by a Draconian conservative morality, cannot make more than a marginal impact on the overall crime rates. It can contain a problem, but the problem, as Ramsey Clark so eloquently argued so long ago in *Crime in America* (1970), will simply recur unless the problem itself is addressed. It is necessary not merely to punish offenders for breaking windows, but to actually mend the windows. That is to engage in a thorough programme of social reconstruction in our cities. Zero tolerance of crime must mean zero tolerance of inequality if it is to mean anything.

Note

I turn my radio on as I write this (29th July, 1997), and hear the Home Secretary,

Jack Straw, solemnly inform the public that incivilities and crime: antisocial behaviour and 'real' crime, correlate highly. I can hardly believe my ears; for who could have believed otherwise? It is like pronouncing that there is a strong correlation between smoke and fire. Part of this is a result of the legacy of the modernist notion that 'crime' was a separate form of activity committed by 'criminals' and that this professional underworld, small in size, contrasted with a separate sphere of antisocial behaviour, much more widespread and 'amateurish'. Such an idea was given weight by numerous criminological studies which examined this correlation. Perfect correlation was never to be found. Wes Skogan (1988), for example, in his summary of North American Studies reports 0.45 to 0.60, whilst Hope and Hough in their analysis of British Crime Survey data found a higher 0.8, but noted that "rates of perceived incivilities are more strongly related to levels of fear of crime and neighbourhood satisfaction than the level of [criminal] victimisation itself" (1988, p 36)

Of course this disparity in evidence of incivilities and crime is bound to occur if one contrasts *actual* crime rates with *perceived* incivility rates, which is why perceptions of incivility and fear (i.e. perceptions) of crime correlates much higher. But it is out of such moonshine that criminological conundrums are made!

Bibliography

Beck, U (1992) *Risk Society.* London: Sage.

Bowling, B (1996) Zero Tolerance in *Criminal Justice Matters* (Autumn) No. 25 pp 11–12.

Clark, R (1970) *Crime in America.* London: Cassell.

Clarke, R and Hough, M (1984) *Crime and Police Effectiveness.* London: HMSO.

Cohen, S (1973) Protest, Unrest and Delinquency: Convergencies in Labels and Behaviour in *International Journal of Criminology and Penology* 1, pp 117–28.

Currie, E (1997) Zero Tolerance and its Alternatives. ESRC/University of Salford Colloquium. *The Quality of Life and the Policing of Incivility* (September)

Dennis, N (1997) (ed.) *Zero-Tolerance: Policing in a Free Society.* London: Institute of Economic Affairs.

Dennis, N and Erdos, G (1992) *Families Without Fatherhood.* London: Institute of Economic Affairs.

Foley, R (1993) Zero-Tolerance in *Trouble and Strife* (Winter) No. 27 pp 16–20.

Furedi, F (1997) *The Culture of Fear.* London: Cassell.

Garland, D (1996) The Limits of the Sovereign State in *British Journal of Criminology* 36(4) pp 445–471.

Giddens, A (1991) *Modernity and Self-identity.* Cambridge: Polity.

Gottfredson, M and Hirschi, T (1990) *A General Theory of Crime.* Stanford, Calif: Stanford University Press.

Gottfredson, M and Hirschi, T (1995) National Crime Control Policies in *Society* (Jan/Feb) pp 30–36.

Gusfield, J (1989) Constructing the Ownership of Social Problems in *Social Problems* 36, pp 432–41.

Home Office (1996) *Criminal Statistics, England and Wales 1995.* London: The Stationery Office.

Hope, T (1996) Inequality and the Future of Crime Prevention in S Lab (ed.) *Crime Prevention at a Crossroads.* Cincinnati: Anderson Publishing.

Hope, T and Hough, M (1988) Area, Crime and Incivility in T Hope and M Shaw (eds.) *Communities and Crime Reduction.* London: HMSO.

Jacobson, M (1997) New York City: An Overview of Corrections, Probation and Other Criminal Justice Trends. *Symposium on Crime and Prisons in the City* (19 September). Centre for Criminology Middlesex University.

Kelling, G and Cole, C (1997) *Fixing Broken Windows* New York: Free Press.

Kelly, L (1987) The Continuum of Sexual Violence in J Hanmer and M Maynard (eds.) *Women, Violence and Social Control.* London: MacMillan.

Kelly, L and Radford, J (1987) The Problem of Men: Feminist Perspectives on Sexual Violence in P Scraton (ed.) *Law, Order and The Authoritarian State.* Milton Keynes: Open University Press.

Kinsey, R; Lea, J; Young, J (1986) *Losing the Fight Against Crime.* Oxford: Blackwells.

Kutzinger, J and Hunt, K (1993) *Evaluation of Edinburgh District Council's Zero Tolerance Campaign.* Edinburgh: District Council Women's Committee.

Lardner, J (1997) Can You Believe the New York Miracle?. *New York Review of Books*, Vol.44 (13) (August 14th) pp 54–58.

Lea, J and Young, J (1984) *What is to be Done About Law and Order?* Harmondsworth: Penguin.

Matthews, R (1992) Replacing Broken Windows: Crime, Incivilities and Urban Change in R Matthews and J Young (eds.) *Issues in Realist Criminology* London: Sage.

Medea, A and Thompson, K (1972) *Against Rape* New York: Farrar, Straus & Giroux.

Metropolitan Police (1986) *Strategy Plan.* London: Metropolitan Police.

Mooney, J (1998) *Gender, Violence and the Social Order.* London: Macmillan.

Morris, P and Heal, K (1981) *Crime Control and the Police.* London: HMSO.

Moynihan, D P (1993) Defining Deviancy Down in *American Scholar.*

Murray, C (1984) *Losing Ground* New York: Basic Books.

Murray, C (1997) *Does Prison Work?* London: Institute for Economic Affairs.

Newman, K (1985) *Report of The Commissioner of Police of the Metropolis.* London: HMSO.

Pearson, G, Gilman, M and McIver, S (1985) *Young People and Heroin Use in the North of England.*

Pollard, C (1997) Zero-Tolerance: Short Term Fix, Long Term Liability? in Dennis, N *OpCit.*

Potter, K (1997) Zero-Tolerance Time Bomb in *Police Review* (18 April) pp 24–6.

Shapiro, B (1997) Zero-Tolerance Gospel. http:www.oneworld.org index oc/issue 497/shapiro.html.

Skogan, W (1988) Disorder Crime and Community Decline in T Home and M Shaw *Communities and Crime Reduction.* London: HMSO.

Walsh, B (1997) Can Fixing Windows Help Mend Cities? in *Urban Environment Today* 23 pp 8–9.

Wilson, J Q (1985) *Thinking About Crime* 2nd Edition. New York: Vintage Books.

Wilson, J Q (1992) Against the Legalization of Drugs in *Drug Legalization: For and Against* (eds) R Evans and I Berent. LaSalle, Illinois: Open Court.

Wilson, J Q and Kelling, G (1982) Broken Windows in *The Atlantic Monthly* (March) pp 29–38.

CHAPTER 8

Young People, Crime and Citizenship

John Pitts

In this chapter I shall present some of the results of a research programme which aims to throw light on changes in the volume and nature of youth crime in the 1980s and 1990s. As a result of this work, initiated in the early 1990s, my colleagues and I are coming to a clearer understanding of the political and economic forces which have led not only to an increase in youth crime, but parallel increases in child abuse, youth homelessness, youth suicide, drug abuse, running away and youth prostitution over the period. While it is clear that these problems are not a simple a product of the social and economic policies of the 1980s and 1990s these policies have, nonetheless, played a key role in their intensification.

I shall explore a strand of this research which grew out of an ESRC-funded comparative study of the responses of public professionals and local politicians to youth crime and victimisation in two neighbourhoods, one in East London and one in Paris. In Paris, we were introduced to the idea that youth crime could be usefully understood as a crisis of citizenship. This crisis, the explanation ran, was precipitated by rapid, social and economic change which segregated the residents of the banlieu, the poor suburbs, from the local economy and eroded established political and cultural ties. It followed from this that if youth crime was to be reduced, measures which strove to develop new forms of social solidarity, political connectedness and economic involvement must be introduced (Bonnemaison 1983). *(For a fuller account of the French Social Prevention Initiative see Chapter 19).*

Now it will be immediately obvious that this account of the problem and the prescriptions for action which flow from it are at odds with the beliefs about, and attitudes towards, youth crime espoused by most senior politicians, not a few representatives of local government and the police and many of Britain's most eminent criminologists. These beliefs and attitudes are stated succinctly by Messrs. Mandelson and Liddle in their book *The Blair Revolution* in which they write:

> "Schools require a new, much tougher, set of disciplinary sanctions to deal with the unruly and uncooperative pupils - such as compulsory homework on school premises, weekend and Saturday night detention, and the banning of favourite leisure pursuits such as football matches.
>
> This greater emphasis on discipline should be matched in the local community. The police, schools and local authority services must work together closely to crack down on vandalism and other anti-social behaviour. Excessive tolerance of low-level sub-criminal behaviour by unruly young people undermines general respect for the rule of law, ruins the environment and makes a misery of the lives of many innocent people – and provides a breeding ground for more serious crime." *(The Blair Revolution*, London, Faber 1996)

We are therefore faced with one account of events, couched in a moral/ scientific language, which ascribes the problem of youth crime to the characteristics of individuals, families and classroom regimes, and another which ascribes it to a loss of social cohesion and the erosion of citizenship. Thus in one, the object of intervention is the child, the family or the classroom, while in the other it is the quality of citizenship within 'socially excluded' neighbourhoods. But what is citizenship?

The nature of citizenship

The following working definition of citizenship, derives from a reading of the literature on citizenship, relevant French policy documents and our observations of professionals, local politicians and groups of young people on a large housing estate to the west of Paris, as they have tried to effect change.

1. Citizenship is **active,** it connotes a form of participation in public life which is not limited to the periodic re-election of governments, but encompasses an active engagement with, and a concern for, the well-being of one's community and one's society.

2. Citizens have **a political voice and a political stake.** They are governed, but through their involvement in political life they also have a hand in government thus, as van Gunterstein (1994) suggests, to be a citizen is to assume an 'office'.

3. Because of these responsibilities citizens must be prepared, if necessary, to **subordinate their interests** to the general interest.

4. Because a capacity for **autonomy, judgement and loyalty** will therefore be demanded of them, it is the job of the educational system to equip them for this office, and the job of the political system to facilitate their involvement in the political process.

5. Citizens are not the passive objects of historical and cultural processes, they are **actively engaged in shaping and re-shaping their history and their culture** and it is the job of those with responsibility for cultural affairs and the educational system to equip them with the knowledge and discernment to enable this process to occur.

6. Citizens are **productive,** they contribute to the common wealth through their participation in economic life and it is a central task of government to ensure that their skills and abilities are used to the full for the common good.

7. Citizens are engaged in a relationship of **mutuality**, one with another, and it is upon this intricate and infinitely complex network of mutual obligation that social cohesion or social solidarity is founded. As such, the citizenship of the majority is diminished if the rights and obligations of citizenship are denied to a minority.

8. While the citizen has an obligation to uphold the law, **the state has a reciprocal obligation to protect the property and person of citizens**. Indeed for the radical right, this is the sole justification for the existence of the state.

By these criteria, it is evident that the citizenship of those young people most likely to be involved in youth crime in the UK, whether as perpetrators or victims, has been progressively eroded in the period since the late 1970s.

Economic change

The political and economic changes which have occurred in the past two decades, and the redistribution of wealth, opportunity and political power which have accompanied them have transformed social life in the UK. Between 1981 and 1991 the number of workers earning half the national average wage or less, the Council of Europe poverty line, rose from 900,000 to 2,400,000. In the same period those earning over twice the national average rose from 1,800,000 to 3,100,000. It is poor young families which have borne the brunt of these changes. These economic changes have both precipitated and paralleled profound demographic changes.

Housing the 'Have Nots'

As the 1980s progressed a combination of the government's 'right to buy' policy, the curtailment of the right of local authorities to spend housing revenue on housebuilding, and progressive reductions in central government's financial contribution to local government ensured that less and less public housing stock was available for rent. These developments presaged significant demographic changes in which relatively prosperous elderly and higher income families left housing estates in the inner city or on its periphery, to be replaced by poorer, younger families (Page 1993). As a result, whereas at the beginning of the 1980s the average council house tenant's income was 73 per cent of the national average, by the beginning of the 1990s it had fallen to 48 per cent. By 1995, over 50 per cent of council households had no breadwinner (Rowntree 1995). The estates which experienced the greatest changes saw increasing concentrations of children, teenagers, young single adults and young single parent families. These neighbourhoods also became a last resort for residents who had previously been homeless, hospitalised or imprisoned, and for refugees from political persecution. By 1997 20 per cent of the children and young people in the UK lived in these neighbourhoods (Dean 1997).

Neighbourhood destabilisation

These rapid demographic changes quickly eroded relationships of kinship and friendship, transforming these neighbourhoods into aggregates of strangers, who were often deeply suspicious of one another. This had a number of consequences.

1. These changes meant that those people most vulnerable to criminal victimisation, young single parents, black and Asian families and the single elderly . . . and those most likely to victimise them, adolescent boys and young men, were progressively thrown together on the poorest housing

estates. In their study of one such neighbourhood in the early 1990s, Tim Hope and Janet Foster (1992) found that a 40 per cent turnover in population over three years was paralleled by a 50 per cent rise in burglaries. However, rapid population change meant that traditional forms of informal social control also disappeared.

2. Alongside the disappearance of informal systems of social control we saw the erosion of traditional systems of informal social support for parents, young people and children which often made the difference between whether a child or young person could be sustained in a fragile or volatile home or not. The American criminologist Elliott Currie (1991) writes:

> "Communities suffering from these compounded stresses begin to exhibit the phenomenon some researchers call 'drain': as the ability of families to support themselves and care for their children drops below a certain critical point, they can no longer sustain those informal networks of social support and help that can otherwise be a buffer against the impact of the economic grinding of the market.
>
> (p 346)

3. Because people were disconnected from one another, participation in local political and social life was minimal and so people had no basis upon which to join together to exert political pressure, bid for resources and make demands on the local and central government agencies with responsibility for the problems they confronted.

4. High crime neighbourhoods tend to be highly concentrated and have a distinctive economic structure. In Britain in the 1980s, neighbourhood destabilisation, by eroding economic links between poor neighbourhoods and their local economies reproduced this structure in growing numbers of poor neighbourhoods. In the process inner city retail, industrial and commercial concerns, which had once been central to the social and demographic stability of working class neighbourhoods, either went out of business or relocated in the industrial and retail parks on the periphery of the city. The impact of this mass evacuation was compounded by a policy shift in the mid-1980s which meant that training resources followed employers rather than 'job-seekers'.

Harrison (1972) identifies a 'dual economy' in urban centres in which the labour market is divided into primary and secondary sectors. The primary sector labour market is characterised by steady jobs with reasonable wages and prospects for advancement. Workers in this sector tend to be older, better qualified, more reliable and better motivated, but these are qualities which are strengthened and reinforced by the higher quality and the greater stability of their jobs. The secondary sector labour market, by contrast, is characterised by low wages, sporadic, dead-end jobs which attract younger, less skilled, less well educated and less reliable employees. Like primary sector employment, the characteristics of the work force are shaped by, and mirror, their conditions of employment. Residents in poor, high crime, neighbourhoods tend to derive their livelihood from a variety of sources; government transfers, employment and training programmes, crime and illegal hustles which, as McGahey (1986) has suggested, 'constitute important additional sources of income, social organisation and identity for the urban poor'. In low crime neighbourhoods, residents tend to derive their income, identity and sense of self-esteem from one, primary sector, employment source. The economic, demographic and policy changes of the 1980s were instrumental in eroding primary sector employment in the poorest neighbourhoods and, by default, promoting the development of secondary sector employment with its inevitable concomitant; the proliferation of illegitimate economic enterprise.

The Vera study, undertaken in New York in the 1980s, showed that the key factor determining the level and nature of crime in working class neighbourhoods was adult involvement in primary sector employment (Sullivan 1989). The study found that the quality and quantity of jobs in a neighbourhood determined the ways people formed households, regulated their own, and the public behaviour of others and used public services. The resulting neighbourhood atmosphere then helped to shape the incentives for residents to engage in legitimate employment or income oriented crime. A high level of adult involvement in primary sector employment spawned stable households, stable families, stable social relationships and enhanced vocational opportunities for the next generation. A low level of involvement had the opposite effect. This study also revealed that, in the first instance, the factors determining a neighbourhood's crime rate and its capacity to contain crime, were almost all visited upon it from the outside in the form of social and economic policies, economic fluctuations, the drugs trade, demographic destabilisation and benefit levels.

A youth crime implosion

The bulk of the crime and violence in these neighbourhoods is committed by local children and young people and is often directed against other local children and young people, in and out of school. These are the neighbourhoods where racially-motivated violence and gang fighting is most prevalent. In a period of economic boom, the young people in these neighbourhoods would have cut their ties with the school and the neighbourhood and got on with adult life. Now, people of eighteen and older are condemned to seek such status as they can from a peer group whose members may be as young as twelve. Thus, they are only semi-detached from the neighbourhood and the school, its social networks and its tensions. As a result, conflicts which begin in the school can spill over into the neighbourhood where they attract older unemployed teenagers and young adults. Similarly, conflicts which begin in the neighbourhood are often fought out in the school. We are therefore confronted once again with the paradox of economic globalisation, paralleled by the development local tribalism. Condemned to a ghettoised form of life, these young people are progressively cut off from active participation in the socio-cultural and economic mainstream with only the school to offer them a way out.

The destabilised school

The capacity of the school to resist these tendencies towards lawlessness and offer young people the means to transcend their social predicament is undermined by the knock-on effects of neighbourhood destabilisation. In the north London school where our current research is based, the transience of the neighbouring estate is reflected in a 50 per cent turnover in the school roll between years 7 and 11. Because the nature of the changes in the neighbourhood has been to replace more prosperous residents with less prosperous ones, by 1997 over 50 per cent of school students qualified for free school meals.

Because poverty and transience generate educational disadvantage in children, and erode the capacity of adults to offer consistent parenting, schools in these neighbourhoods must absorb a higher proportion of children with special educational and behavioural needs. Thus, the school currently has twice the borough average of 'statemented' students on its roll. As a result, behaviour in the playground and the corridors has deteriorated. The impact of the resultant atmosphere can be measured in increased truancy and lateness amongst students who were previously seen to pose no particular problems and are now avoiding this increasingly hazardous environment.

A recent study of 15 schools identified by OFSTED as 'failing' revealed that they were all serving communities with high levels of social deprivation and unemployment, a high proportion of single parent families and a high uptake of free school meals (Centre for Educational Management 1997). The report notes that these schools tended to have poor premises and that their intake represented the residuum of children that grant maintained or grammar schools had not selected. Many of the schools in the sample had recently amalgamated or reorganised in the face of demographic change and local competition. Whereas most of the failing schools were serving pupils from areas with a high level of deprivation, better off pupils were increasingly congregating in other, better-resourced, schools. Nonetheless, between 1988 and 1996 the proportion of pupils in poorer neighbourhoods gaining 5 or more A-C grades at GCSE rose from 20–32 per cent. However, in the most affluent local authorities, there was an increase from 30–48 per cent. Ironically, the 'additional needs' formula devised by the Conservative government to help the least prosperous local authorities, benefits Harrow more than Barnsley and Westminster more than Birmingham or Liverpool.

Absorbing trouble
A further consequence of rapid student turnover is that schools have a large number of vacancies. In the current economic climate, in which local education authorities are striving to reduce surplus capacity, these schools are under constant pressure to absorb students who wish to transfer from other schools. In the school in our study, 30 per cent of year 10 and 64 per cent of year 11 students have previously attended another secondary school. Beyond the destabilising effect of this steady influx of new students, is the fact that many of them bring additional academic and behavioural problems with them.

Student victimisation
At this school, between September 1996 and April 1997, 41 per cent of year 11 students were assaulted, with 30 per cent of these assaults occurring in the vicinity of the school or on the way home from school, in the hour or so following the end of the school day. 80 per cent of the perpetrators were male, and 48 per cent were described as being either strangers or students from another school. 24 per cent of respondents reported being threatened or assaulted with a weapon. In a similar study undertaken in a similar neighbourhood in east London, over 30 per cent of victimised students identified their assailant as being older than them and, in some cases, as an adult (Pitts 1993, Pitts and Smith 1995). It is, of course, ironic that schools in 'destabilised neighbourhoods', confronting formidable social problems, are nonetheless required to import further problems of disruption, crime and violence from other neighbourhoods. But it doesn't stop there.

Taking flight
As the *Centre for Educational Management* study cited above indicates, seeing the writing on the wall, some parents seek to transfer their children to other schools, further destabilising the school. This has the effect of reducing the proportion of parents who have effected a positive choice in

favour of the school and increasing the proportion who are unwilling, or unable, to effect a choice about their child's education. These are not simply neglectful parents. Some of them, like the refugees from Eritrea, Ethiopia or Bosnia, speak little English and have been traumatised by the experience of violence, change and loss. The parents who seek a transfer tend to be more prosperous and articulate and are often active in fund raising efforts and the PTA. They are also the parents who are most likely to reinforce the school's espoused ethos at home. Their departure is a double blow for the school, diminishing both the material and moral resources crucial to the development of 'social capital'.

Staff morale
Not surprisingly, these changes undermine staff morale, and so, as OFSTED has observed, the problems in the student group are mirrored in staff absenteeism and a rapid turnover of teachers. Last year at the school in our study, one third of the teachers left. Increasingly, 'destabilised schools' are staffed by probationary teachers, supply teachers and, as a result of the transfer of teacher education to the schools, student teachers. This is particularly ironic since all the teachers we speak to are agreed that their students do not like 'new faces', take time to trust people, and need to gain experience in forming positive relationships with adults.

The changes afflicting these schools have, of course, been paralleled by the introduction of the national curriculum, league tables, the local management of schools, real cuts in funding, serious reductions in the education social work service, school counselling, pastoral care, home-school liaison, home tuition, off-site units, Child and Family Guidance Clinics, the Youth Service and those parts of the voluntary sector not undertaking statutory youth justice and child protection work. These changes have steadily eroded the ability of these schools to deal with the problems presented by its students. In consequence, the additional work generated for teachers by problematic students; meetings with students, their parents, social welfare and criminal justice agencies, the production of reports for, and attendance at, case conferences, court hearings etc., has burgeoned. The school's predicament has been compounded by the disappearance of the Inner London Education Authority whose banding policies once distributed children with special needs more equally between schools and contributed to their social mix.

A combination of regressive taxation, council house sales, the demolition of the large metropolitan education authorities, under-funding and 'parental choice' are pushing many schools in socially deprived neighbourhoods into a downward spiral which, despite their best efforts, they are powerless to reverse. This does not mean, of course, that the situation is irreversible. It is an unintended consequence of government policy and, as such, it is amenable to an intervention which eschews the tired rhetoric of 'standards' and 'discipline' and instead pays studious regard to the political and economic forces which have progressively undermined the ability of some of our best state secondary schools and most committed teachers to act as a bulwark against the crime and violence emanating from the impoverished neighbourhoods they serve.

A concentration of disadvantage

These are the neighbourhoods in which racist attacks, small-scale riots and drug-related crime and violence proliferated in the 1980s. (Pearson 1987, Lea and Young 1988, Campbell 1993, Sampson and Phillips 1995). Geoffrey Pearson observes that:

"... even within a town or a city with a major problem it will tend to be concentrated in certain neighbourhoods and virtually unknown in others. Moreover, where the problem has tended to gather together in dense pockets within our towns and cities, this will usually be in neighbourhoods which are worst affected by unemployment and wretched housing" (pp 190–191)

Not surprisingly, perhaps, these are also the neighbourhoods from which the bulk of the children in care, or being 'looked after' by the local authority are drawn and where the preponderance of young people who run away, and stay away, from home originate (Currie 1991, Pitts M. 1992, Shriane 1995, Pitts J. 1996). An analysis of data supplied by the homelessness charity *Centrepoint* reveals that, overwhelmingly, young people who run away from, or are thrown out of, home come from regions with the highest levels of unemployment in general, and youth unemployment in particular. Many of them have spent some time in care. Many report that they leave home as a result of conflict with parents, and this conflict often concerns money, or its absence. An analysis of the data for London reveals that over 70 per cent of the runaways who reached *Centrepoint* came from the poorest Inner London boroughs. A study undertaken by Hugh Shriane in Luton showed that 46 per cent of the young people who ran away from home came from the poorest public housing estate with the highest crime rate and lowest levels of youth employment and political participation in the borough.

Domestic violence and child abuse

While it is possible to produce evidence to support a link between economic and political change, neighbourhood destabilisation and running away, surely abuse is of a different order altogether? Well yes and no! Most people today would accept that child abuse, in the forms of sexual violation and violence is, for the most part, perpetrated by men and that it occurs throughout the social structure. However, recent scholarship (Messerschmidt 1993, Segal 1990, Campbell 1993) suggests that rather than being randomly distributed, crimes against women and children tend to be concentrated in the poorest neighbourhoods. If as many commentators argue, the violent sexual abuse of women and children is essentially about power rather than sex, it should not surprise us, that this violence is most prevalent amongst men who experience the greatest discrepancy between what they have become and what they believe, as men, they are supposed to be (Segal 1990). This begins to explain the prevalence of child abuse and domestic violence in destabilised neighbourhoods. In response to these developments Currie has advocated 'a wide range of supports for parents in coping with real world stresses in their communities', however, the political changes of the 80s and 90s have served only to erode these services.

The decline of public services
The plight of the families in these neighbourhoods has been compounded by cutbacks in local government expenditure which have resulted in the withdrawal of many of the educational, youth service, community development and social welfare services which had previously contributed to the quality of communal life and social cohesion in their neighbourhoods. However, it is not simply that there was greater need and fewer organisations and individuals available to respond to that need. In the 1980s, the nature of both public services and 'publics' themselves has changed. The 1980s witnessed swingeing cuts in local authority budgets, a substantial redistribution of political power from local to central government and the parallel introduction of 'market forces' into public services (Hutton 1995). In this period, decisions about the goals to which public services should strive, their spending priorities, and the day to day conduct of their staff were increasingly taken by central government or the government's appointees in the burgeoning, and largely unaccountable, QUANGOcracy which progressively annexed public services in the 1980s. Together, these forces have seriously restricted the capacity of local agencies to make a concerted collaborative response to the profound problems experienced by the residents of destabilised neighbourhoods.

Conclusion

We live in a time in which social solutions to social problems are deeply unpopular. It is much easier to talk of the need to inject a new sense of responsibility into lax parents and a new discipline into the education of the young, than to confront what is really happening in our cities and the run-down housing estates on their periphery. This tedious rhetoric belies a stark reality in which growing numbers of young people are being driven to desperate, often self destructive, lengths in order to salvage a livelihood and a plausible identity from an increasingly barren social and economic landscape.

However, the foregoing analysis suggests that if they are to be effective, local authorities, which will not only play the lead role in the development of community safety, but also provide access to the political process at a local level should, as a number of them already are, consider how they might help to construct new forms of social solidarity and new forms of citizenship which will reassert our connectedness with those young people who have shouldered more than their fair share of the costs of the free market experiment. They will, to paraphrase C. Wright Mills (1959), need to consider how we might transform these 'private troubles' into 'public issues'.

But this is not simply another task for which local authorities must devise new performance indicators and novel 'inputs', 'outputs' and 'upshots'. There is a broader question which each of us must answer if we are to claim to be taking the problem of youth crime seriously. It is a philosophical and political question but the way we answer it will have profound practical consequences for young people. And the question is, are the young people I have been discussing an unruly 'underclass' whose behaviour and attitudes must be modified in order to bring them back into line, or are they socially excluded citizens who have been denied both the rights and duties of citizenship. We need to be clear in our interventions whether we are aiming merely to remedy some behavioural or developmental deficit or striving to open up genuine opportunities for significant participation in economic, social and cultural life.

'But', you may say, 'this is all very well, but does the way we define the problem make any real difference, surely its all the same in the end, aren't you just talking about two sides of the same coin'?

In 1981 in both Britain and France, approximately 3,500,000 offences were recorded by the police. Both countries had witnessed steady increases in recorded crime in general, and recorded youth crime in particular, and both confronted youth riots on the streets of their major cities. However, by the end of the 1980s the number of offences recorded in Britain was approaching 6,000,000 while in France, between 1983 and 1986 there was a decline in recorded offences to around 3,000,000 where it remained for the rest of the decade (Parti Socialiste Francais 1985, De Liege 1991). In Britain crime appears to have risen fastest in the poorest neighbourhoods

(Hope 1994). In France, by contrast, it was in the poorest neighbourhoods that the fall in the crime rate was most marked (King 1989, De Liege 1991).

We appear to be faced with a choice between the pursuit of 'discipline' and the pursuit of 'solidarity'. The choice is yours.

Bibliography

Bonnemaison (1983) *Face à la Delinquence: Prevention, Repression, Solidarité: Rapport a le Prime Ministre de la Commission Des Maires sur la Securité*, Paris, La Documentation Francaise

Campbell B. (1993) *Goliath, Britain's Dangerous Places*, London, Methuen

Centre for Educational Management (1997) *Learning From Failure*, London, The Roehampton Institute

Currie E. (1991) *International Developments in Crime and Social Policy* in NACRO, Crime and Public Policy, London, NACRO

Dean M. (1997) *Tipping the Balance*, Search, York, Joseph Rowntree Foundation

De Liege M-P. (1991) *Social Development and the Prevention of Crime in France: a Challenge for Local Parties and Central Government* in Farrell M. and Heidensohn F. *Crime in Europe*, London, Routledge

Harrison B. (1972) *Education, Training and the Urban Ghetto*, Baltimore, Johns Hopkins University Press

Hope T. and Foster J. (1992) Conflicting Forces: Changing the Dynamics of Crime and Community on a Problem Estate in *British Journal of Criminology* 32/92

Hope T. (1994) *Communities Crime and Inequality in England and Wales*. Paper presented to the 1994 Cropwood Round Table Conference *Preventing Crime and Disorder* Sept. 14–15, Cambridge

Hutton W. (1995) *The State We're In*, London, Jonathan Cape

King M. (1989) Social Crime Prevention ala Thatcher in *The Howard Journal* 28, pp 291–312

Lea J. and Young J. (1988) *What Is To Be Done About Law & Order?*, Harmondsworth, Penguin

Mandelson P. and Liddle P. (1996), *The Blair Revolution*, London, Faber

McGahey R. (1986) *Economic Conditions, Neighbourhood Organisation and Urban Crime* in Reiss J. A. and Tonry M. Communities and Crime, Chicago, Chicago University Press

Messerschmidt J. W. (1993) *Masculinities and Crime: Critique and Reconceptualisation of Theory*, Maryland, Rowman & Littlefield

Mills C. W. *The Sociological Imagination*, Harmondsworth, Penguin

Page D. (1993) *Building for Communities: a Study of New Housing Association Estates*, York, Joseph Rowntree Foundation

Parti Socialiste Francais (1986) *Les murs d'argent. Manifeste contre la privatisation des prisons*, Paris, Parti Socialiste

Pearson, G. (1983) *The New Heroin Users*, Oxford, Blackwell

Pitts J. (1993) *Developing School and Community Links to Reduce Bullying*, Tattum D (ed.) Understanding and Managing Bullying, London, Heinemann

Pitts J. (1996) *The Politics and Practice of Youth Justice*, Mclaughlin E. and Muncie J. (eds.), Controlling Crime, Sage Publications/Open University Press

Pitts J. and Smith P. (1995) *Preventing School Bullying*, Home Office Crime and Prevention Series, Paper 63, London, Home Office

Pitts M. (1992) *Somewhere to Run*, Unpublished BA Dissertation, Exeter University

Rowntree Foundation (1996) *The Future of Work: Contributions to the Debate*, York, Joseph Rowntree Foundation

Sampson A. and Phillips C. (1995) *Reducing Repeat Racial Victimisation on an East London Estate*, London, Home Office

Segal L (1990) *Slow Motion: Changing Masculinities*, Changing Men, London, Virago

Shriane H. (1995) *Luton Runaways Profile*, Luton, Community Links Project

Sullivan M. (1989) *Getting Paid, Youth Crime and Work in the Inner City*, London, Cornell University Press

Van Gunsteren H. (1994) *Four Conceptions of Citizenship*, Van Steenbergen B. (ed.) The Condition of Citizenship, London, Sage

CHAPTER 9

Preventive Work with Children and Young People at Risk of Offending

John Graham

Introduction

During the last thirty years there has been a considerable expansion of activity aimed towards preventing crime, both in Europe and North America. This has been largely generated by the relentless rise in crime, the pervasive spread of fear and insecurity and by a certain loss of faith in the ability and capacity of the criminal justice system to control the crime problem (Graham and Bennett, 1995; Audit Commission, 1996; Bright, 1997). Much of this crime prevention activity has focused on the manipulation of environments and situations to reduce opportunities for committing offences. The essence of this situational approach to crime prevention is that offenders weigh up the costs and benefits of committing a crime and only proceed if the latter outweigh the former. It presents an attractive option to those seeking practical, short term solutions at relatively little cost. But while it lends itself well to situations where individuals are already predisposed to exploiting opportunities for illegal gain, it is unlikely to influence the development of such individual predispositions in the first instance. It also contains inherent weaknesses which may even exacerbate certain aspects of the crime problem.

One of the by-products of efforts to persuade citizens of the need to protect their property and lock up their possessions is that it can lead to a kind of 'fortress' mentality, which feeds on fear and insecurity and leads in turn to renewed efforts by citizens to protect themselves from potential predators. This in turn feeds a climate in which the segregation of the 'haves' from the 'have nots' can flourish and the least well-off are separated, both physically and socially, from the rest of society. Given the links between social isolation and crime, it is feasible that the situational approach may inadvertently aggravate some of the very conditions which feed crime – fear, insecurity and exclusion.

In the USA, where both the fear and the reality of crime is so pervasive, the reaction has been to resort increasingly (and perhaps desperately) to the principle of incapacitation to 'win the war' against crime. With other justifications for imprisonment, such as rehabilitation, deterrence and 'just deserts', losing favour, incapacitation is left as the prime policy for tackling serious and violent crime in the USA (Zimring and Hawkins, 1995). The main justification for incapacitation is that it stops offenders committing crimes which they might commit if at large. It has a popular appeal. But preventing crime through incapacitation is extremely expensive, both in terms of human and financial costs. In the last two decades, the American prison population has increased from less than 300,000 to over 1.5 million and in the State of California public expenditure on imprisonment exceeds expenditure on education.

Fortunately, there are alternatives to imprisonment which are not only less expensive, but also more cost-effective. Last year RAND, a non-profit making institution which advises on various aspects of public policy in the US, published the findings of a study which measured the cost-effectiveness of a number of crime prevention strategies, including early interventions with children and families at risk and the Californian 'three strikes and you're out' incarceration programme (Greenwood et al., 1996). The results are highly encouraging; parent training, graduation incentives and delinquent supervision were all found to be more cost-effective than incarceration. Whilst the authors caution against taking these findings at face value, they suggest that shifting resources from the criminal justice and penal system to a more proactive approach may be financially and conceptually sensible.

This mirrors precisely the conclusion reached by the Audit Commission in its detailed appraisal of arrangements for dealing with youth crime in England and Wales (Audit Commission, 1996). Their study concluded that the youth justice system was expensive and ineffective in terms of reducing reoffending and recommended shifting resources from processing young offenders through the courts to interventions to prevent offending. In practice, the amount of money spent on preventing crime is still only a tiny fraction of the amount spent by the criminal justice system on the processing of offenders. But with increasing constraints on public expenditure budgets and burgeoning prison populations, governments need to consider alternative ways of tackling the growing crime problem. A serious option must now be to invest in resources for preventing children and young people from becoming offenders in the first place.

The purpose of this chapter is to set out the case for developing an evidence based approach to preventing criminality, drawing on what is known from research on what predisposes children and young people to engage in criminal behaviour and what prevents them from so doing. It is divided into three main sections. The first section briefly describes the current situation which children and young people face and how this is related to their propensity to engage in criminal activity. The second section summarises what is known from research about the main risk factors which underpin a propensity to engage in criminal behaviour and what is likely to be effective in reducing such a propensity. The third and final section sets out the government's new proposals for reforming youth justice, community safety and crime prevention and discusses some of the issues which will need to be addressed in developing and implementing an effective, multi-agency approach to preventing criminality at the local level.

The changing lives of young people

The lives of children and young people today are very different from what they were 50 or even 20 years ago. In some respects their outlook has improved – they are physically healthier, their life expectancy is longer, they are better educated and they have considerably more spending power. But compared with 20 years ago, today's children and young people are also more likely to experience long spells of unemployment, experiment with psychoactive drugs, suffer from psychosocial disorders (especially depression, suicide amongst young men and eating disorders among young women), cohabit rather than marry, experience the separation or divorce of their parents, be brought up in single or step parent families and, last but not least, engage in criminal behaviour. The reasons for these trends are not fully understood, but at least two major changes which have fundamentally affected the lives of young people deserve closer scrutiny – changes in the structure and functioning of families and changes in the transition from childhood to adulthood.

One of the key influences on the changing lives of young people is the decline of the traditional nuclear family. Over the last thirty years, marriage rates have fallen, divorce rates have increased sixfold and the proportion of children born outside wedlock has increased by more than threefold (although most births outside marriage are still jointly registered by two adults living at the same address). Compared with twenty years ago, children are twice as likely to experience the divorce of their parents and nearly three times as likely to live in single parent families (Utting, 1995). Today, approximately 1 in 5 children live in single parent families and 1 in 12 live in step parent families. Concurrently, there has been a shift in employment patterns within families. Mothers, particularly those with children under five, are more likely to be working, whilst fathers are more likely to be absent altogether. The proportion of households in which either both parents or no parent is working has increased, resulting in a bifurcation between work-rich (i.e. time-poor) and work-poor households. These structural changes are likely to have impacted upon the capacity of families to exert effective supervision and control over their children as well as ensure they receive the emotional care and support they need whilst growing up.

Findings from a national self-report offending study of young people aged 14 to 25 show that young people brought up predominantly in single parent or step families are more likely to offend than those brought up in two parent families (Graham and Bowling, 1995). This was found to be related to poor family functioning (particularly poor relations with one or both parents and low levels of parental supervision) and, for children living in single parent families, poverty. Thus although poverty has not been found to be directly related to the overall rise in crime since the second world war (Rutter and Smith, 1995), it is known that poverty increases the risk of psychosocial disorder and crime at the individual level and it would appear that the effects of poverty on crime are mediated through their impact on family functioning.

In the UK, the proportion of children living in households below half the national average disposable income rose from 1 in 10 to 1 in 3 over the last fifteen years (i.e. from about 1.25 million to about 4.3 million children) (Utting, 1995). Since the proportion of the whole population living in households below average income increased by less than this (from about 1 in 11 to 1 in 4), it can be concluded that children are increasingly being concentrated in less prosperous households. Households with below half the national average income are also approximately 10 per cent worse off in absolute terms than they were fifteen years ago. Therefore children living in the poorest households are both absolutely and relatively more deprived than they were fifteen years ago.

Research has also shown that, over the last ten to fifteen years, low-income families have become increasingly concentrated in socially disadvantaged council estates. The life chances of young people are critically affected by where they live and in neighbourhoods which contain high proportions of low-income, single parent and multi-problem families, crime and victimisation rates are particularly high. Research indicates that young people living in such neighbourhoods are approximately five times more likely to have a criminal record by their early thirties than those living in more stable communities. For males, the risks are twice as high (Kolvin et al., 1990).

Structural changes in the employment market have increased the vulnerability of young people, especially those leaving school at 16, to long term unemployment and all its negative implications. Over the last twenty years there has been a sharp decline in the availability of full time jobs for school leavers, a large increase in the proportion of children staying on in full time education after the age of 16 and a shift in the burden of responsibility for looking after young people from the state to the family. In areas where rates of long term unemployment are high and young men have no role models to emulate, the risks of drifting into criminal behaviour are further compounded. Rutter and Smith (1995) concluded that crime rises rapidly in areas where there are concentrations of people who have no attachment to the labour market.

Twenty years ago, criminal policy makers were comforted by the knowledge that the vast majority of young people grow out of crime. On reaching their late teens, they got a permanent job, found a place to live in of their own and began to think about settling down and starting a family of their own. But data from the Home Office national survey of self-reported offending by 14 to 25 year olds throws some doubt on the notion that young people, at least young men, begin to 'grow out of crime' in their late teens. The findings from this survey suggest that rather than growing out of crime, many young male offenders merely switch to offences with lower detection rates as they get older (Graham and Bowling, 1998). Their transitory status prolonged, they are effectively excluded from acquiring an independent livelihood through legitimate means.

The lengthening transition from childhood to adulthood is also characterised by increasing diversity. The paths to adulthood are rarely linear and very few young people today simply leave school, get a job, find a partner and form a new family. As a consequence, young people are more likely to lose their way and drift into a range of high risk lifestyles for relatively longer periods of time (Furlong and Cartmel, 1997). One particularly risky aspect of young people's lives, which has changed considerably for the worse, is the heavy misuse of drugs. Since the late 1960s, there has been a sixfold increase in drug-related deaths among young males aged 15–24 and research suggests that drug and alcohol misuse are important influences on the persistence of offending behaviour (Graham and Bowling, 1995). So the increasingly complex and lengthy transition to adulthood is characterised by exposure to greater risks for longer periods of time and as a consequence, some young people will become separated or excluded from the principal institutions which enable them to feel part of, and contribute to society. Some of these, in turn, will drift into serious and persistent criminal careers.

Risk and protective factors

Although it is not possible to predict with any degree of certainly who will become an offender on the basis of the level of risk to which they are exposed, it is known that children exposed to multiple risks are disproportionately likely to end up as serious or persistent offenders (Graham and Bowling, 1995). A considerable body of research-generated knowledge now exists about the main risk factors which characterise a propensity to engage in criminal behaviour and there is now considerable agreement as to what the main influences on criminality are.

Risk factors are generally part of a pattern of childhood anti-social behaviour (Capaldi and Patterson, 1996) and differ little from risk factors associated with other youthful deviant behaviour (Dryfoos, 1990; Hawkins and Catalano, 1992). Those who engage in anti-social or criminal behaviour an early age are more likely than others to become serious and persistent offenders (Home Office, 1987) and it is now accepted that the earlier one intervenes in the lives of young people, the greater the potential for preventing a range of adverse outcomes in later life.

The main risk factors for criminal behaviour, most of which tend to coincide and interact, can be broadly classified under three headings:

- The family
- The school
- The peer group

The family
Children who show signs of aggressive and anti-social behaviour at an early age are more likely to become offenders as adults. Such children tend to be impulsive, hyperactive and egocentric and have difficulty perceiving events from the perspective of others, negotiating reasonable agreements with others and thinking through the consequences of their actions. They often come from families characterised by multiple social and personal problems, discord and interpersonal conflict. Their parents are likely to:

- suffer from socio-economic deprivation and stress;

- have a history of involvement in crime, violence, alcohol and drug abuse;

- exercise harsh and erratic discipline (including corporal punishment);

- neglect and/or abuse their children;

- exercise low levels of supervision; and

- come themselves from similar families.

Where children have only one parent, they are more vulnerable to social maladjustment, especially if the parent is young, socially isolated and dependent on welfare. Such a situation is often accompanied by poverty, low educational attainment, and lower levels of supervision, all of which are associated with offending. However living in a one parent household does not necessarily predispose children to anti-social behaviour; it is the discord prior to, during and after separation which appears to be damaging, rather than separation itself (McCord, 1982).

The school
Some school pupils are more likely to engage in violent behaviour than others. They tend to be those who:

- are low achievers;

- behave disruptively or are involved in bullying;

- persistently truant; and

- are excluded from school.

The main predictors of academic failure, disruptive behaviour, persistent truancy and school exclusion are not entirely clear, but research suggests that aspects of schools themselves – antagonistic relations between staff and pupils, poor classroom management, lack of leadership and low morale – have a significant influence on these outcomes irrespective of the types of pupils who attend the school (Graham, 1988).

The peer group
During the transition from childhood to adulthood, the influence of parents decreases as the influence of peers increases. Research shows that those who spend considerable periods of time away from their home in unstructured and unsupervised activity 'on the streets' are more at risk of engaging in criminal activities. Association with violent older siblings or a peer group characterised by aggressive, 'macho' norms are powerful predictors of violent behaviour and where such peer groups feel isolated and excluded from mainstream lifestyles, the danger of forming a sub-culture based on oppositional and sometimes violent norms is high. A perceived lack of respect, feelings of powerlessness and low self-esteem are commonly associated with such sub-cultures.

Of course, not all children exposed to high levels of risk end up as criminals. Some are resilient and cope with disruption and upheaval more readily; others are particularly intelligent, or learn to adapt to risks in a constructive way. An anchor in the life of all children is important. They may be helped by a particularly committed adult (for example, a member of their family, a teacher with whom they have an especially good relationship or a close friend). They may come from families with strong religious or moral beliefs. They may find some way to succeed at school, against the odds, or excel at some form of sporting activity. Above all, they may enjoy strong, warm and consistent relationships with one or both of the parents. Preventing children from becoming offenders is therefore also about finding ways to increase these protective factors as well as decreasing the risks.

What works in preventing criminality?

On the basis of increasing knowledge about the risk factors which can lead to criminal behaviour, a number of programmes have been set up and evaluated in terms of their impact on criminality and associated outcomes. Based on this body of knowledge, it is now possible to state with some degree of certainty not only what kinds of interventions work and why, but also how cost effective they are (see, in particular, Greenwood et al., 1996 and Welsh, 1997). A number of reviews summarise this evidence (see, for example, Farrington, 1996; Utting, 1996).

Most recently Sherman (1997) has presented a comprehensive review of family, school and community based programmes for preventing crime and criminality to the US National Institute of Justice. He states that the most promising results in all areas of crime prevention are programmes which provide high risk children and families with home visits, pre-school education and high quality day care. Evaluations of such programmes have consistently shown positive effects on crime or crime risk factors and Sherman reviews 18 such programmes in all. Two of the most important the Syracuse Family Development Programme and the High/Scope Perry Pre-School Programme – both measured the long term impact on delinquency.

The **Syracuse Family Development Programme** which provided pre and post natal advice and support to low income, predominantly African-American women, provides outcome data on the children at age 15. Whereas 22 per cent of the control group had been convicted for criminal offences by age 15, only 6 per cent of the experimental group had convictions and these tended to be for less serious offences (Lally et al., 1988).

The **High/Scope Perry Pre-School Programme** combined high quality pre-school education with home visits to disadvantaged black children and their mothers. By age 19, arrest rates were 40 per cent lower for the experimental group and teenage pregnancies 50 per cent lower. By age 27, the children who had attended pre-school were significantly more likely to have completed their education, to own their homes and to be earning more than $2,000 a month. In the control group 35 per cent had been arrested five or more times, compared with 7 per cent of those in the experimental group (Schweinhart and Veikart, 1993). A cost-benefit analysis based on these figures concluded that for every $1 invested, the programme would produce a return of $7. The multiple benefit of the Perry pre-school project have led to insurance companies funding similar programmes on the grounds that the recipients do well as school, find long term stable employment and are therefore more likely to purchase a house or a car.

Other evaluations reviewed by Sherman (1997) focus on crime risk factors and measured outcomes in terms of later reductions in anti-social behaviour and improvements in children's cognitive skills, parental attachment and parenting skills or their impact on child abuse. All show positive outcomes. Furthermore, such programmes often have large effects. The Rochester University study, for example achieved a 79 per cent relative reduction in child abuse (which is a strong predictor of delinquency) (Olds et al., 1986). Whilst such an effect size is unlikely to persist, positive effects do ensure, albeit at a lower level. In a 15 year follow up, Olds et al. (1997) report 69 per cent fewer arrests, 44 per cent fewer substance abuse related behavioural problems experienced by the mothers and 46 per cent fewer reports of child abuse in the experimental group. Sherman (1997) estimates that, on the basis of the evidence on reductions in child abuse alone, the delivery of a universal home visitation programme in the US would prevent over half a million serious crimes.

Sherman (1997) also reviews family therapy and parent training programmes, of which three measured their impact on delinquency and showed moderately positive effects. Overall, parent training courses do seem to be able to help parents respond more constructively, use discipline less harshly and more consistently and avoid situations which precipitate conflict. Unfortunately, there are few examples of such programmes in the UK, although work is being undertaken at Maudsley Hospital in London with severely aggressive children and their families. Based on clinical and therapeutic methods developed in the USA (see Webster-Stratton et al., 1988), the work uses video-tapes and one-way mirrors to show parents how to control the behaviour of their children without resorting to physical punishments or threats. Unpublished findings from a pilot study suggest that improvements in children's behaviour are sustained for two years beyond the 10 to 12 week course (Utting, 1996).

Whilst early interventions show much promise and are necessary for effective prevention in the early years, they need to be supplemented with other strategies as the child begins to explore the outside world. As the child grows older, the importance of family life and parenting tend to be superseded by school and peer group influences.

Research on school effectiveness shows that schools which are characterised by high quality classroom management, good leadership and organisation and where children feel emotionally as well as educationally supported, are those which are best placed to protect their pupils from engaging in criminal behaviour (Graham, 1988). High quality evaluations of school based programmes are few and tend to be less promising than family based initiatives, but there have been some notable successes, particularly where schools are adopted a 'whole school' approach to reducing problems of disaffection and delinquency.

One good example which has been carefully evaluated is the *PATHE project,* which included the additional benefit of comparing the effects of institutional change with individually-based interventions (Gottfredson and Gottredson, 1986). The results show that the *institutional change elements* had a small but measurable effect on delinquency and school conduct one year after the programme was implemented. The most dramatic improvement occurred in the rate of suspensions in the three experimental high schools, which dropped by 14 per cent on average. In the control high school, the suspension rate increased by 10 per cent. In contrast, the *individual measures* had no effect on delinquency, but did improve the commitment of at risk pupils to education as indicated by small improvements in attendance and academic performance. A similar initiative – the Effective Schools Project – reported considerably larger reductions in delinquency, two years after the programme was implemented (Gottredson, 1987).

In England, a similar 'whole school' approach has been implemented in 23 schools in Sheffield to tackle bullying and associated problems. The initiative was based on similar work undertaken in Bergen in Norway, which produced marked reductions in bullying and anti-social behaviour inside and outside school (see Olweus, 1990 and 1991). It involved the introduction of a wide range of measures, including precise procedures for preventing and responding to bullying, improvements in playground supervision and courses for improving problem-solving skills and assertiveness. The programme was successful in reducing bullying in primary schools, but had relatively small effects in secondary schools (Smith and Sharp, 1994). A similar initiative implemented in East London and Merseyside resulted in reductions in bullying in three out of four schools (Pitts and Smith, 1995).

To be effective, early intervention needs to improve both the parenting and the education of children at risk, preferably sustained throughout childhood. The best way to accomplish this is to forge partnerships between the two principal sources of socialisation and informal social control – families and schools (Graham and Utting, 1996). A few projects in the USA have begun to adopt this approach. LIFT (Linking Interests of Families and Teachers), for example, focuses on encouraging pro-social and discouraging anti-social behaviour at home and at school through parent training, social skills classes for the children, playground behaviour strategies and the installation of a school-to-home telephone line. Initial findings suggest an immediate impact in terms of reducing aggressive and anti-social behaviour (Reid et al., 1994).

Influencing peer groups, especially criminal peer groups, is very difficult and there are very few examples of successful programmes. One exception is the South Baltimore Youth Centre project, which has built on the work of the Milton S. Eisenhower Foundation for the Prevention of Violence. The project incorporates the best elements of two other projects, El Centre and Argus, both of which are community based projects set up to tackle drug misuse and serious crime (see Graham and Bennett, 1995). The project provides a safe environment for young people at risk who are encouraged to form an extended family, with youth workers acting as their mentors and advocates. Contracts are signed and peer pressure is used to exercise discipline and control. Members are taught to control their anger and confront their fears and where possible are offered job training linked to real jobs. Serious delinquent behaviour decreased by a third among those on the programme, compared to a small increase in the control group over a period of 19 months (Baker et al., 1995).

Are criminality prevention programmes cost-effect?

Welsh (1997) has reviewed the literature on the cost-effectiveness of initiatives to prevent criminality. In all, Welsh found nine studies which provided cost data, of which seven provided sufficient detail to allow some form of economic analysis. All the studies are from North America. At the point of intervention, subjects ranged in age from pre-birth to 18. Most projects targeted children in their early years and most were implemented in the home. All but two of the studies had follow-up periods of 16 months or more and all were exposed to high quality evaluations (experimental or quasi-experimental designs).

Of the seven studies, six show a positive cost-benefit outcome. The economic return on one unit of investment ranged from 1.06 units to 7.16 units. The most promising were found to be those which targeted babies, infants and pre-school children. Savings from reduced crime and delinquency (measured through less involvement with the criminal justice system and fewer victims of crime) accounted for a substantial proportion of the measured benefits. Other monetary benefits included less reliance on welfare payments, more subjects employed (and therefore increased tax revenues), less use of remedial education and less use of security and emergency services.

Welsh concludes his review by drawing attention to three important requirements for the development of more economically efficient strategies for reducing crime. Firstly, all programme evaluations need to include a prospective cost-benefit or economic dimension; secondly, evaluation designs need to be of the highest scientific quality and thirdly, funding bodies must be prepared to finance such economic evaluations. Further research, he suggests, needs to identify which interventions work best with which populations, how long the benefits last and at which point in time is it more appropriate and effective to intervene. Although similar prevention programmes exist in the UK, they have either not been evaluated, or not been evaluated to the same high scientific standard as in the USA. None provide cost data in a form which allows any kind of economic assessment. It is therefore also important to discover whether the projects described above could be successfully replicated in the UK.

The Government's new proposals

In November 1997, the government published a white paper outlining their new strategy for tackling youth crime (Home Office, 1997). It incorporates a comprehensive overhaul of the youth justice system and proposes that the statutory aim of the youth justice service is the prevention of offending.[1] The preventive focus of the government's new strategy is encompassed in a number of measures, some of which impinge directly on the workings of the youth justice system, some of which are directed at agencies working outside the youth justice system. The former largely comprise new sentencing options,[2] whilst the latter are concerned primarily with identifying children and young people at risk of becoming involved in criminal activity and changing their behaviour before bad habits take root. To this end, the new Crime and Disorder Bill proposes two new orders, the child safety order and local child curfews.

The child safety order is designed to protect children under the age of ten who are at risk of becoming involved in crime or who have started to display anti-social or criminal tendencies. It will only be used where the local authority can show that:

---

[1]The preventive focus of the Government's new strategy actually goes much wider than this, including the provision of a statutory responsibility to local authorities and the police to develop a community safety and crime reduction strategy.   (Home Office, 1997b)
[2]In addition to the new sentencing options, the Crime and Disorder Bill also introduces the Final Warning. This replaces the current system of cautioning for young offenders and insofar as it will usually be accompanied by a community intervention programme, involving the offender and his or her family to address the causes of the offending, it will also have the aim of reducing the risk of further offending.

- a child under the age of 10 has done something that would constitute an offence if he or she were over 10;
- a child's behaviour suggested he or she was at risk of offending;
- a child's behaviour was disruptive or harassing to local residents; or
- a child had breached a local curfew order.

The order would specify that certain requirements be undertaken to support the child, protect him or her from the risk of being drawn into crime and ensure proper care and control. To secure this, the Family Proceedings Court will be able to require a child, for example, to attend school, be at home at certain times or stay away from certain people or places.

The local child curfew is designed to protect young children and their local communities through the application of an area curfew, which would prohibit children under ten from being in specified public places, unless supervised by a responsible adult, between certain times (e.g. 9.00 p.m.to 6.00 a.m.). Such curfew schemes will be integrated into the area's wider community safety strategy, as will other measures aimed at tackling youth crime.

In addition to targeting children under ten who are identified as at risk of offending, the new Bill also includes a new order, the Parenting Order, which reflects a shift towards placing greater emphasis on the responsibility of parents for the offending or irresponsible of their children. A court could require the parent to attend regular counselling or guidance sessions for a period not exceeding three months. The order will be available for parents of convicted young offenders, parents who have been convicted of failing to send their child to school or those subject to other orders, such as the child safety order or the anti-social behaviour order. In some cases courts may impose additional requirements, such as requiring parents to ensure their children attend school or that they are at home during certain hours of the day or night. Such additional requirements may apply for up to one year.

Much of government's current efforts to tackle youth crime are firmly grounded in research-based evidence on the causes of crime. The child safety order, for example, has evolved from research which has shown that the earlier children start to offend, the greater the chances that they will go on to become serious and persistent offenders (Home Office, 1987). Equally, the parenting order reflects the considerable body of evidence which suggests that family functioning is an important factor in the aetiology of crime.

Alongside the new measures outlined in the Crime and Disorder Bill, the government is developing a range of social policies to reduce juvenile crime. These include the development and coordination of family policy, including measures to reduce the incidence and fall-out associated with family breakdown and getting single parents off welfare and into work; measures to reduce social exclusion; policies for improving educational achievement and reducing truancy and associated exclusion from school; and measures for improving employment and training opportunities, including the New Deal programme for unemployed 18 to 24 year olds.

The new bill also places a statutory duty on local authorities to draw up a strategic plan for youth justice work, including the setting up of multi-agency Youth Offending Teams (YOTs) to deliver community-based intervention with, and supervision of, young offenders. Although the work of the new YOTs will be predominantly with young offenders, the white paper suggests they should also have a role in the prevention of youth offending and recognises the importance of making connections at the strategic level with other related multi-agency partnerships.

Inter-agency arrangements for preventing criminality

What are the key partnerships with which YOTs will need to develop close working relationships and what problems might they face? Currently, there is a plethora of multi-agency partnerships at the local level. Some specifically target the problem of criminal behaviour (or substance misuse), others focus more widely on the needs and problems of children (and their families) in general. Some involve collaboration between just two or three agencies, others are wide-ranging partnerships involving local authority departments, police and health authorities, the voluntary and private sectors and local communities.

The starting point, however, will be to develop a strategic framework for the work of YOTs which fits with the new statutory community safety partnerships. It may be possible, for example, for one multi-agency steering group to oversee both the work of YOTs and the development of work on comunity safety. But it remains to be seen how work to prevent criminality can best be fitted within this framework.

One advantage of developing close links at the strategic level with community safety partnerships is that they have a statutory mandate to tackle the problem of crime, they involve all the key agencies and they have at their disposal a detailed information base on the nature and extent of the problem of juvenile crime. Furthermore, much of their work will be in the form of individual projects which are time limited and problem oriented, both of which are likely to be features of criminality prevention initiatives. On the other hand, it could be argued that the most effective approach to preventing criminality requires the routine delivery of services to children and families at risk throughout childhood. Research evidence suggests that preventive interventions need to be developmentally appropriate and continuous. This is not compatible with the short term funding arrangements which currently characterise the work of crime prevention/ community safety partnerships. Furthermore, measures to prevent criminality are unlikely to yield results in the short term and some way needs to be found to protect investments in children and young people from the pressure to demonstrate short term gains.

Children's services plans, which provide a statutory framework for the delivery of services to children and families, may be a more appropriate vehicle for delivering criminality prevention. Section 19 of the Children Act 1989 requires local authorities to conduct joint reviews (involving education, social services and health) of early years service, including early intervention measures with children and families at risk. Paragraph 7 of Schedule 2 to the 1989 Act requires local authorities to take steps to encourage children and young people not to commit offences. It will be a matter for local authorities to determine the extent to which they wish to discharge this responsibility for preventive work through the new YOTs. There will therefore be an important linkage between children's services plans and youth justice plans.

The work of children's service plans and YOTs is also likely to be relevant to the work of child protection committees. Some of the principles which characterise the policies and procedures of such committees are clearly relevant to preventive work with young children at risk. They include the requirement for agencies to work closely with parents and maintain the child within the family wherever possible; the requirement to consider the possible negative effects of any intervention; the need to take account of the right to confidentiality, with information only being shared if it is in the interests of the child; and the importance of developing effective working relationships between the police and social services. Certainly much of the experience child protection committees have of working with children and families with multiple problems, of undertaking risk assessment and of working with both the civil and the criminal courts may provide valuable lessons for the new YOTs.

Conclusion

The government's new approach to tackling youth crime is timely. Most young people today face a riskier and more protracted transition to adulthood and many have to cope with unstable family lives and insecure employment prospects. They are more likely to suffer from psycho-social disorders and young men who offend are not growing out of crime during their teens or early twenties. Against this backcloth, it is now accepted that the criminal justice system alone cannot cope with the problem of crime and that reducing opportunities for committing offences does little to prevent individuals from developing a propensity to engage in criminal behaviour in the first place, and may even act counter-productively.

Fortunately, there is now sufficient evidence to support a policy of investing in children and families, preferably when children are still very young. Programmes which prevent criminality by intervening early in the lives of children at risk have been shown to be cost-effective. The Audit Commission's report Misspent Youth recommends shifting resources to preventive work, but there is also a need to shift the climate towards perceiving the problem of criminality (and hence its prevention) as one which germinates at a very early age, even though it only manifests itself much later. Only with such a shift in climate will it be possible to justify the development of a long term preventive programme of investment in children and families at risk and hence tackle the roots of crime.

At least three provisos need to accompany such a shift. Firstly, it is still necessary to learn more about what works in preventing criminality, with what populations under what conditions and at what cost. So far most of the high quality evidence of effectiveness comes from North America and similar programmes need to be set up and tested here in the UK. Evaluations need to measure effectiveness in terms of multiple outcomes in the long as well as the short term. This requires a degree of faith and a modicum of political will.

Secondly, schools (as well as families) need to be persuaded that they are an essential part of the solution. They offer a natural focus and location for a community based, inter-agency managed initiative to prevent criminality. Together with families, they can form a potent force for exerting informal social control and exercising authority in the lives of young people and just as the boundaries of parental responsibility are being widened, perhaps so too should the boundaries of teachers' responsibilities. Ironically, it is those young people who are most in need of such care and discipline – the disaffected, the disruptive, the excluded – which schools increasingly relinquish responsibility for.

Thirdly, an important limitation of the proposed legislation is that the new orders are unlikely to be placed on very young children, for whom the potential gains of preventive interventions are likely to be the greatest. To develop an evidence-based approach to prevention, this gap will need to be addressed. Perhaps the year 2000 will witness the beginnings of a real change in climate as the foundations of a long term investment strategy for a future generation better prepared for avoiding a life of crime are laid.

References

Audit Commission (1996) *Misspent Youth*. Audit Commission Publications: Abingdon

Baker, K. et al. (1995) Violence Prevention Through Informal Socialisation: An Evaluation of the South Baltimore Youth Centre in *Studies on Crime and Crime Prevention*, vol. 4, no. 1. National Council for Crime Prevention: Stockholm, Sweden

Bright, J. (1997) *Turning the Tide: Crime, Community and Prevention*. Demos: London

Capaldi, D.M. and Patterson, G.R. (1996) Can Violent Offenders be Distinguished from Frequent Offenders: Prediction from Childhood to Adolescence in *Journal of Research in Crime and Delinquency*, 33, pp 206–231

Dryfoos, J.G. (1990) *Adolescents at Risk*. New York: Oxford University Press.

Farrington, D.P. (1996) *Understanding and Preventing Youth Crime*. Joseph Rowntree Foundation: York

Furlong, A. and Cartmel, F. (1997) *Young People and Social Change: Individualization and Risk in Late Modernity*. Buckingham: Open University Press

Gottfredson, D.C. (1987) An Evaluation of an Organisation Development Approach to Reducing School Disorder in *Evaluation Review*, 11, pp 739–763

Gottfredson, D.C. and Gottfredson, G.D. (1986) *The School Action Effectiveness Study: Final Report*. Baltimore: Johns Hopkins University

Graham, J. (1988) *Schools, Disruptive Behaviour and Delinquency*. Home Office Research Study No. 96. London: HMSO

Graham, J. and Bennett, T. (1995) *Crime Prevention Strategies in Europe and North America*. HEUNI: Helsinki

Graham, J. and Bowling, B. (1995) *Young People and Crime*. Home Office Research Study No. 146. London: HMSO

Graham, J. and Utting, D. (1996) Families, Schools and Criminality Prevention in Bennett, T. (ed.) *Preventing Crime and Disorder: Targeting Strategies and Responsibilities*. Institute of Criminology, University of Cambridge: Cambridge

Greenwood, X. et al. (1996) *Diverting Children from a Life of Crime: Measuring Costs and Benefits*. Rand Corporation: Santa Monica, California

Hawkins, J.D. and Catalano, R.F. (1992) *Communities That Care*. Jossey Bass: San Francisco

Home Office (1987) *Criminal Careers of Those Born in 1953: Persistent Offenders and Desistance*. Home Office Statistical Bulletin. London: HMSO

Home Office (1997a) *No More Excuses – A New Approach to Tackling Youth Crime in England and Wales*. Home Office: London

Home Office (1997b) *Getting to Grips with Crime: A New Framework for Local Action*. Home Office: London

Kazdin, A.E. (1985) *Treatment of Anti-Social Behaviour in Children and Adolescents*. Homewood, IL: Dorsey

Kolvin, I., Miller, F.J.W., Scott, D.M., Gatzanis, S.R.M. and Fleeting, M. (1990) *Continuities of Deprivation? The Newcastle 1000 Family Study*. Aldershot: Avebury

Lally, J.R. et al. (1988) More Pride, Less Delinquency: Findings from the Ten Year Follow-up Study of the Syracuse University Family Development Research Program in *Zero-to-three*, vol. 8, no. 4, pp 13–18

McCord, J. (1982) A Longitudinal View of the Relationship Between Paternal Absence and Crime in Gunn, J. and Farrington, D.P. (eds.) *Abnormal Offenders, Delinquency and the Criminal Justice System*, pp 113–128. Chichester: Wiley

Olds, D.L. et al. (1986) Preventing Child Abuse and Neglect: A Randomized Trial of Nurse Home Visitation in *Pediatrics*, No. 78, pp 65–78

Olds, D. et al. (1997) Long Term Effects of Home Visitation on Maternal Life Course and Child Abuse and Neglect: Fifteen Year Follow-up of a Randomized Trial in *The Journal of the American Medical Association*, August 27, vol. 278, pp 637–643

Olweus, D. (1990) Bullying Among Schoolchildren in Hurrelmann, K. and Losel, F. (eds.) *Health Hazards in Adolescence*. Berlin: De Gruyter

Olweus, D. (1991) Bully/Victim Problems Among Schoolchildren: Basic Facts and Effects of a School Based Intervention Programme in Pepler, D.J. and Rubin, K.H. (eds.) *The Development and Treatment of Childhood Aggression*. Hillsdale, NJ: Erlbaum

Pitts, J. and Smith, P. (1995) *Prevention School Bullying*. Crime Prevention and Detection Series, no. 63, Police Research Group. London: Home Office

Reid, J.B. et al. (1994) *A Universal Prevention Strategy for Conduct Disorder: Some Preliminary Findings*. Paper presented to SRCAP Conference, June 1994, London

Rutter, M. and Smith, D. (1995) *Psychosocial Disorders in Young People: Time Trends and Their Causes*. Wiley: Chichester

Schweinhart, L.J. and Weikart, D.P. (1993) *A Summary of Significant Benefits: the High/Scope Perry Pre-school Study Through Age 27*. High/Scope Press: Ypsilanti/Michigan

Sherman, L.W. (1997) Family-Based Crime Prevention in Sherman, L.W. et al. *Preventing Crime: What Works, What Doesn't, What's Promising*. US Department of Justice: Washington

Smith, P.K. and Sharp, S. (1994) *School Bullying*. London: Routledge

Utting, D. (1995) *Family and Parenthood: Supporting Families, Preventing Breakdown*. York: Joseph Rowntree Foundation

Utting, D. (1996) *Reducing Criminality Among Young People: A Sample of Relevant Programmes in the United Kingdom*. Home Office Research Study, No. 161. London: HMSO

Utting, D., Bright, J. and Henricson, C. (1993) *Crime and the Family*. Family Policy Studies Centre. Occasional Paper 16. London.

Webster-Stratton, C., Kolpacoff, M. and Hollinsworth, T. (1988) Self-administered Video-tape Therapy for Families with Conduct Problem Children: Comparison with Two Cost-effective Treatments and a Control Group in *Journal of Consulting and Clinical Psychology*, no. 56, pp 558–66

Welsh, B. (1997) *Costs and Benefits of Primary Prevention: A Review of the Literature*. Paper presented to the Seminar on Primary Prevention of Adult Anti-social Behaviour, Department of Health, London

Zimring, F. and Hawkins, G. (1995) *Incapacitation: Penal Confinement and the Restraint of Crime*. New York: Oxford University Press

CHAPTER 10

Youth Justice Services and Community Safety Strategies

Mike Thomas and Peter Ashplant

The responsibilities of local authority youth justice teams in the development of community safety strategies has often been overlooked and misunderstood. Given the fractional development of youth justice services in recent years it is hardly surprising therefore to find the Morgan Report *Safer Communities* (1991) commenting on the lack of specific strategies within local authorities for preventing crimes being committed by young people. More recently a consultation document produced by the local authority associations *Crime the Local Solution* (1997) failed to include social services within a list of key agencies which should be involved in drawing up community safety plans.

In 1994 the Probation Inspectorate considered the structure of youth justice teams in their thematic inspection *Young Offenders and The Probation Service*. The inspection team found three approaches to the delivery of services for young offenders:

- integrated teams
- combined teams
- agency-based teams

However, while commenting that 'none of the approaches were without their problems' the inspectorate were unable to identify which approach was their preferred option.

The Home Affairs Select Committee into Juvenile Offenders (1993) were also unable to identify the most appropriate model for delivering youth justice services, proposing instead that a new national agency should be established which would manage the custody and supervision of young offenders.

It is clear therefore that the youth justice service has long held the mantle of a Cinderella service. Without a common national identity, without a common title for those working within it (social worker, probation officer, youth justice worker . . .), and without a clear definition of the age group it works with (10–15 years? 10–16 years? 10–17 years?) it is hardly surprising

116

that the youth justice service has found itself a soft target for those who wish to apportion blame for any perceived increase in juvenile crime both locally and nationally.

However in 1996 the Association of Directors of Social Services and the Association of Chief Officers of Probation, together with the Association of County Councils and the Association of Metropolitan Authorities jointly published their *National Protocol for Youth Justice Services.*

The protocol was intended to restate the principles on which youth justice services should be based and to emphasize the aims of work with young people involved with crime. The protocol also states unequivocally that "policies in respect of youth justice services should be placed in the context of local children's services plans and community safety strategies". Further it reinforced the view that community safety should be seen as the legitimate concern of all in the local community. The protocol has been fundamental in detailing for the first time the core services that should be available to young people in danger of involvement with crime, and for those already involved in the criminal justice system, as well as outlining the specific offence-related services which should be in place (Figure 1.). These include:

1. **Pre-court and diversion services**

   • 24 hour appropriate adult service
   • Diversion from prosecution and cautioning arrangements
   • Caution support services

2. **Remand services**

   • Remand management strategy
   • Bail information
   • Bail support
   • Range of safe local authority accommodation
   • Access to secure accommodation

3. **Court services**

   • Court liaison
   • Pre-sentence report preparation

4. **Management of community sentences**

   • Attendance centre orders
   • Supervision orders
   • Supervision orders and requirements (e.g. intermediate treatment)

Youth Justice Services

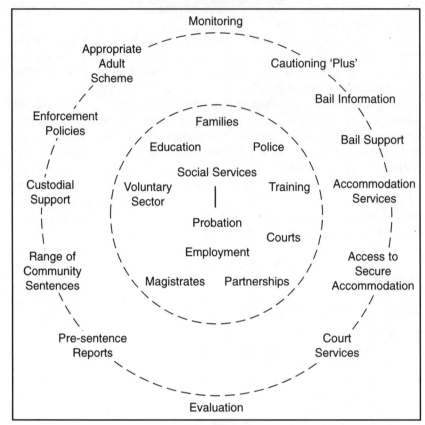

Figure 1

- Supervision orders and specified activities
- Probation orders
- Probation orders and requirements
- Combination orders
- Community service orders

5. **Enforcement of community sentences**

6. **Custodial support services**

   - Pre-custody service
   - Pre-release service
   - Post-release service

7. Monitoring and evaluation

Such services should be developed from a framework of the key principles which underpin the whole of the service. These include *Section 44* of *the Children & Young Persons Act 1933* which provides for all courts to have regard for the welfare of the child or young person who appears before them. *Section 1(1)* of the *Children Act 1989* which states that the child's welfare should be the court's paramount consideration in any proceedings under that Act and *Section 17(1)* which places a general duty on every local authority to safeguard and promote the welfare of children who are in need. Further, *schedule 2* Paragraph 7 states that every local authority shall take reasonable steps designed to encourage juveniles within its area not to commit offences and to reduce the need to bring criminal proceedings against juveniles, while the *UN Convention on the Rights of the Child* requires that in all actions concerning children (i.e. below 18 years) in courts of law, the best interests of the child should be the primary consideration. Fundamentally the Protocol has been written to assist authorities in the evaluation of their youth justice services by clearly specifying the aims, objectives, principles and types of services that should be provided in order to meet the agency's commitment to a community safety.

Community safety is a corporate strategy and as such it is imperative that youth justice services are developed within it and not away from it. During 1995 Solihull, in the West Midlands, agreed to carry out a community safety audit jointly between the council and the local police. The audit was the first stage in developing a community safety strategy that is understood, logical and can be used by communities as well as those delivering a service. Such an approach has three main components –

Victim   Offender   Opportunity

Figure 2. suggests the inter-relationship between the three components, where the removal of any one component also removes the grounds for a crime or incident to take place.

Solihull quickly realised that professionals were responding and working hard to provide services to the victim, the offender and reduce opportunity to but that they were doing so without planning policies and services together and often in total ignorance of the role of the other agencies. Gradually the corporate approach taken by a community safety strategy enabled the sharing of principles, aims and objectives, recognised the reactive and often negative impact on each other and began to facilitate a needs analysis where there could be a collective concentration of efforts.

The findings of the audit became the focus of a public, private and

Figure 2

voluntary sector steering group which agreed priorities at officer level and thereafter encouraged elected members to form a parallel but equally strategic Community Safety Advisory Group to recommend and advise on policy matters.

Like many areas Solihull already had a tried and tested multi-agency youth justice service which worked well for those who entered the criminal justice system. However the development of support for those outside the system was inconsistent with no coordinated approach to preventive strategies. Following the community safety audit a comprehensive youth strategy was developed which encouraged both statutory and voluntary services for young people.

The Audit Commission's report *Misspent Youth* (1996) highlighted the need for local authorities to establish local forums that bring together local government, youth courts, police, probation and health services which should be coordinated through the chief executive. However a local forum on its own is insufficient, and needs to ensure that it initiates action at the strategic level, the management level and the practitioner level.

There is however a word of warning that should be sounded. Community safety strategies need to be dynamic and to be regularly reviewed in order to take account of the changing aspects of the agencies involved. This is likely to be particularly important over the next 18 months as the new Labour government unveils its blueprint for law and order – and the likelihood of the competing demands for those agencies involved.

CHAPTER 11

School Exclusion, Risk and Community Safety

Isabelle Brodie

Introduction

Exclusion from school is an issue which has attracted increasing public and political attention in recent years. A small number of cases of exclusion have received high levels of media publicity and this, together with evidence of a significant rise in the number of exclusions overall, has led some commentators to suggest that the issue has attained the status of a 'moral panic' (Blyth and Milner, 1993). While political rhetoric may present the issue as one which is essentially related to the effectiveness of school discipline (Squire, 1996; OFSTED, 1996) exclusion from school clearly has wider implications. As Blyth and Milner (op. cit.) comment, the consequences of this phenomenon are sufficiently serious that school exclusion may be viewed as one of the constellation of factors which result in 'social exclusion'. Most obviously, the lack of educational qualifications is likely to damage employment prospects. It is also important to recognise that the effects of exclusion are not confined to the individual. The impact on families is considerable, notably in providing care for the child while out of school. Research also demonstrates that welfare and youth justice agencies are likely to have a substantial involvement in managing the consequences of exclusion. Inevitably, this has resource implications.

This chapter will begin by outlining some research findings regarding the scale of exclusion as a social problem and the groups of pupils most vulnerable to this sanction. It will go on to argue, however, that exclusion raises important issues for the community at large. These include the safety of young people excluded from school, the relationship between exclusion and criminal activity, and the impact of exclusion on other agencies.

The nature and scale of the exclusion problem

Exclusion from school is not new, though the term 'exclusion' has replaced the more familiar language of suspension and expulsion. Two forms of exclusion currently exist: fixed-term exclusion, which can take place for up to 45 days across the school year, and permanent exclusion. Exclusion is the most serious sanction available to head teachers and official guidance emphasises that it should be used only in response to extreme acts of misbehaviour (Department for Education, 1994). However, most recent research evidence indicates that an exclusion is usually the culmination of a long build-up of tension. The most common reasons stated for exclusions include verbal abuse to staff, violence to other pupils and disruption in the classroom (Galloway et al., 1992; OFSTED, 1996; Hayden, 1997).

Numbers of exclusions
Statistics regarding the numbers of exclusions have not, unfortunately, been collected on a systematic basis by any one agency. However, data from a range of sources has demonstrated that this is a problem of significant proportions. In 1990 the National Exclusions Reporting System (NERS) was set up with the purpose of monitoring the number of exclusions taking place. Findings from this were reported in 1993, and showed an increase in the number of exclusions from 2,910 in 1990–91 to 3,833 in 1991–92. In 1993–93 further government funded research demonstrated that the number of permanent exclusions had risen to over 11,000, a dramatic

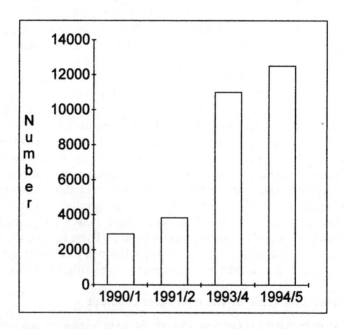

Figure 1.   Number of permanent school exclusions by year, England

threefold increase (Department for Education, 1995). A follow-up study carried out for the year 1994–95 showed a further increase to 12,500 (Parsons, 1996), though the collection of statistics on exclusions as part of the government's schools census suggested that numbers had stabilised. Research by market research groups and newspapers (for example, MORI, 1993; The Independent, 11 June 1995) has also emphasised the large numbers of exclusions taking place.

While these statistics are important in providing some indication of the scale of school exclusion as a problem, such data should not be accepted uncritically. The lack of national data prior to 1993 makes it impossible to assess the extent of the increase, thus heightening the sense of moral panic which surrounds the issue. More technical problems also exist, and three specific issues may be identified. Firstly, it has been pointed out that data does not always distinguish between the numbers of exclusions taking place and the number of children to which these refer (Hayden, Sheppard and Ward, 1996). Therefore, five fixed-term exclusions may be recorded without reference to the fact that these apply to only one child. Secondly, differences in the application of regulations regarding exclusion procedures means that information regarding the number and pattern of exclusions is more complete for local authority maintained schools than for independent, grant-maintained and voluntary aided schools. Thirdly, measurement of school exclusion on the basis of exclusions reported to the local education authority almost certainly underestimate the scale of the problem. Inevitably those exclusions which have been described as 'unofficial' or 'informal' are hidden. However, this problem may also extend to officially reported exclusions; Parsons (1996) claims that in the survey of permanent exclusions carried out by OFSTED (1996), for example, local education authorities under-reported the number of exclusions taking place.

Age, gender and ethnicity
Permanent exclusions take place mainly among pupils of secondary school age, and especially at Key Stages 3–4 (ages 14–16). In 1995–96, for example, more than 80 per cent of permanent exclusions involved young people at secondary school. However, the number of primary school pupils being excluded has also increased and in 1993–94 represented 12 per cent of the total number of exclusions (Parsons, 1996).

Gender and ethnicity are also important factors in understanding the nature of exclusion as a phenomenon. The majority of excluded pupils are boys, who outnumber girls at a rate of at least four to one, and by as many as 21 to one at primary school level (Galloway et al., 1982; Department of Education, 1995; Hayden, Sheppard and Ward, 1996; OFSTED, 1996). In research using smaller numbers of case studies, we also find few examples of excluded girls (see, for example, Parsons et al., 1994).

Understanding of the relationship between ethnicity and exclusion is hampered by the fact that local authorities frequently fail to distinguish between different ethnic groups when collecting data on exclusions (Hayden, Sheppard and Ward, op. cit.). Generally, however, existing evidence indicates that a disproportionate number of African-Caribbean males are excluded from school. Data collected during OFSTED inspections in 1993–94 show that black African-Caribbean pupils were excluded at almost six times the rate of white pupils (Gillborn and Gipps, 1996). In some cases the decision to exclude has been identified as overtly discriminatory, including religious or cultural 'non-conformity', the failure to recognise racist elements in incidents which occur within the school and the misdiagnosis or disregard for medical or educational problems within an ethnic group (Bourne, Bridges and Searle, 1994). However, it has been argued that it is important to consider that importance of pupil/teacher interaction in explaining the high level of exclusions among black pupils. Ethnographic studies have shown that black pupils experience proportionately more punishments of all types (for example, detentions and report cards) and are criticised more often than white pupils (Gillborn, 1990). This has been linked to cultural styles among black pupils, and a perception by teachers that black males in particular are threatening and aggressive.

Exclusion and social disadvantage

However, the most striking aspect of the backgrounds of children excluded from school is the high level of disadvantage that many have experienced, including poverty, homelessness and parental illness and bereavement. This appears to be true for young people of both primary and secondary school age. Research involving case studies of 65 primary school pupils excluded from school found evidence of child protection concerns, family disruption and contact with a range of external agencies including social services, the police and educational welfare (Hayden, Sheppard and Ward, op. cit.). Given these levels of disadvantage, it is unsurprising to find that many children who are excluded from school have been looked after 'in care' by the local authority (Stirling, 1992; SSI/OFSTED, 1995; Firth, 1996; Brodie and Berridge, 1996). Indeed, children excluded from school become 'children in need' according to the Children Act 1989 as a result of their lack of education. In view of the multiple disadvantage experienced by a high proportion of excluded pupils, many will already have fallen into this category.

In many respects, then, it seems that exclusion is a phenomenon rooted in existing disadvantage. Consequently the increase in the problem cannot be attributed simplistically to a sudden increase in challenging behaviour amongst young people. However, it seems likely that when exclusion occurs, further problems will be triggered. Exclusion is likely to place further stress on families already experiencing difficulties (Cohen et al., 1994). It may even precipitate entry to foster or residential care (see, for example, Parsons et al., *op. cit.*). In some highly publicised cases of exclusion, notably those where the appeal process has been used, the young person's behaviour and exclusion has stigmatised families and damaged relationships within communities.

For the young person, exclusion has immediate and serious consequences. Although, as shown earlier, exclusions tend to be preceded by a long build-up of tension, children may still be surprised and shocked by what has occurred (Gersch and Nolan, 1994; Hayden, op. cit.). Nor is the situation likely to be quickly remedied. Research findings suggest that many excluded pupils spend a considerable amount of time without education (Parsons et al., *op. cit.*). Only 27 per cent of primary age pupils and a mere 14 per cent of secondary school pupils are reintegrated into mainstream schooling (Department for Education, 1995). Even where alternative educational provision is found, this is likely to be part-time. The Department for Education survey showed that home tuition caters for about a quarter of pupils permanently excluded from secondary school and for just over two-thirds of primary school aged pupils. However, on average this consists of some three to five hours teaching each week. Provision at pupil referral units (PRUs) is also likely to be part-time. It is widely accepted that this level of provision is inadequate, opening the way to further stress and difficulty for children's families as well as creating difficulties for individual young people. It is especially alarming in view of the high proportion of young people who are excluded and who also have statements of special educational need (Association of Metropolitan Authorities, 1995; Hayden, op. cit.).

The lack of alternative educational provision leaves substantial amounts of time during which these young people have no form of education. The irony of this is considerable in the sense that, for most children, school is essential in organising their daily and weekly routines. Yet for pupils permanently excluded from school, who are perhaps in greatest need of such structure, only very limited provision exists. The lack of any gainful occupation for the majority of weekdays clearly leaves these young people at considerable risk. While no research study has focussed specifically on the way in which excluded pupils manage their time, the evidence which exists suggests that much of the day is spent 'hanging around'. Participant observation in children's homes, for example, has shown that adolescents who are excluded often receive little supervision from residential staff and may spend substantial amounts of time outside the building (Berridge et al., 1996; Berridge and Brodie, op. cit.). This raises some potentially serious child protection issues. Although little research has been carried out in Britain, there is some evidence from the United States that children are at greater risk of abuse during periods when time is unstructured (see, for example, Blatt, 1992).

Exclusion and offending

The way in which young people spend their time while excluded from school is also important when considering the relationship between exclusion and offending behaviour. While there is likely to be some diversity in the type of care arrangements available for young people, research has shown that adolescents who receive little parental supervision are more likely to offend (Steinberg, 1986; Home Office, 1995). Aside from this, the relationship between school factors and offending is well-established, and it is important that exclusion is not isolated from issues such as truancy and disaffection.

However, evidence has mounted regarding the link between exclusion and offending. An Audit Commission survey found that 42 per cent of offenders of school age who are sentenced in the youth court have been excluded from school (Audit Commission, 1997). The Home Office survey of young people aged between 14 and 25 found a strong relationship to exist between both temporary and permanent exclusion and offending. Eleven per cent of males in the sample had been excluded on a fixed-term basis and three-quarters of these had offended. Of those females who had been temporarily excluded – four per cent of the sample – nearly half were offenders. Though numbers were small, this relationship was even stronger in regard to young people permanently excluded from school (Home Office, op. cit.). Younger children are also affected (Hayden, 1994).

There are clearly dangers in assuming links between all forms of non-attendance and involvement in offending; as Carlen, Gleeson and Wardhaugh (1992) point out, to equate non-attendance at school with delinquency may serve to further pathologise not only the young people involved but also their families. Given that exclusion may result from a young person's offending behaviour, there are also difficulties in understanding the nature of the causal link between the two. It is therefore 'sensible to consider exclusion from school to be both a cause and a consequence' of offending (Home Office, op. cit.), p 42).

There is, however, some evidence that the exclusion itself can lead to further offending. In one local authority, 58 per cent of those children aged 11 or more who were permanently excluded offended either in the year before or the year after exclusion. However, this group was known to commit 50 per cent more offences in the year after the exclusion had taken place (Audit Commission, op. cit.). The Audit Commission argues that the excluded group, while relatively small, contains some of the most persistent offenders. A study of the costs of exclusion also found that the cases of approximately a quarter of excluded pupils generate costs for the police, and indeed that costs to the police and criminal justice services form over 70 per cent of the total costs of agencies other than education (Commission for Racial Equality, 1997).

In addition, account should be taken of other trends in offending patterns which may place children excluded from school at heightened risk of offending. Research has shown that young people involved in crime are now less likely to outgrow this, with the result that delinquent peer groups are likely to be older (Home Office, op. cit.). Consequently, 'links may be forged between criminal neophytes of 14 and old stagers of 25' (Pitts, 1997, p 4). Such peer groups are a key source of social status for young people who may have few other social networks. In turn this may lead to involvement in more serious types of offending.

Conclusion

It is important that the problem of exclusion from school is placed in perspective. Even with rising numbers, the 1995–96 statistics show that one secondary school pupil in every 240 is excluded, and only one in every 2,300 primary school pupils (Parsons, 1996). This might be compared with truancy statistics – one recent survey of pupils in Years 10 and 11 found that one in 10 young people missed school at least once a week, and it is probable that this is an underestimate (Audit Commission, op. cit.). It is also important to emphasise that while exclusion rates vary considerably between schools and local authorities, research has not generally shown schools to exclude carelessly.

Nevertheless, as the evidence above demonstrates, the problems of young people excluded from school are usually extreme in nature and are likely to require intervention from a variety of agencies. It seems that exclusion can only exacerbate these difficulties by placing young people at risk of involvement in offending and reducing their chances of employment. Families are also placed under greater stress.

In these circumstances the importance of preventive work cannot be underestimated. This may involve more than one agency. Initiatives aimed at young people at risk of exclusion, or working with pupils already excluded, appear to be most effective when some form of inter-agency work is involved. However, the range and complexity of the problems presented by excluded pupils also makes it essential that the lines of responsibility are drawn clearly. Where this does not happen, there is a danger that these young people may fall through the net of existing provision (Roaf and Lloyd, 1995). This can only lead to the further marginalisation of a highly vulnerable group.

Bibliography

Audit Commission (1997) *Misspent Youth – Young People and Crime*. London: Audit Commission.

Association of Metropolitan Authorities (1995) *Reviewing Special Educational Needs* London: Association of Metropolitan Authorities.

Berridge D. and Brodie I. (1997) *Children's Homes Revisited*. London: Jessica Kingsley.

Blatt E. (1992) Factors associated with child abuse and neglect in residential care settings, *Children and Youth Services Review*, 14, 493–517.

Blyth E. and Milner J. (1993) Exclusion from school: a first step in exclusion from society?, *Children and Society*, 7, 3, 255–268.

Bourne J., Bridges L. and Searle C. (1994) *Outcast England: How Schools Exclude Black Children*. London: Institute of Race Relations.

Brodie I. and Berridge D. (1996) *School Exclusion: Research Themes and Issues*. Luton: University of Luton Press.

Carlen P., Gleeson D. and Wardhaugh J. (1992) *Truancy: The politics of compulsory schooling*. Buckingham: Open University Press.

Cohen R., Hughes M., Ashworth L. and Blair M. (1994) *School's Out: The Family Perspective on School Exclusion*. Ilford: Barnardo's.

Commission for Racial Equality (1997) *Exclusion From School: The Public Cost*. London: Commission for Racial Equality.

Department for Education (1994) *Exclusions from School. Circular 10/94*. London: Department for Education.

Department for Education (1995) *National Survey of Local Education Authorities' Policies and Procedures for the Identification of, and Provision for, Children Who Are Out of School by Reason of Exclusion or Otherwise*. London: Department for Education.

Firth H. and Horrocks C. (1996) No home, no school, no future: exclusions and children who are "looked after", in Blyth E. and Milner J. (eds.) *Exclusion From School: Inter-Professional Issues for Policy and Practice*. London: Routledge.

Galloway D., Ball T., Blomfield D. and Seyd R. (1982) *Schools and Disruptive Pupils*. London and New York: Longman.

Gillborn D. and Gipps C. (1996) *Recent Research on the Achievements of Ethnic Minority Pupils*. London: HMSO.

Gillborn D. (1992) *'Race', Ethnicity and Education: Teaching and Learning in Multi-Ethnic Schools*. London: Unwin Hyman/Routledge.

Hayden C. (1994) Primary age children excluded from school: a multi agency focus for concern, *Children and Society*, 8, 3, 132–148.

Hayden C., Sheppard C. and Ward D. (1996) *Primary Age Children Excluded From School. Report No. 33*. Portsmouth: University of Plymouth.

Hayden C. (1997) *Children Excluded From Primary School.* Buckingham: Open University Press.

Home Office (1995) *Young People and Crime. Research Study 145.* London: Home Office.

Parsons C. (1996) Permanent exclusions from schools in the 1990s: trends, causes and responses, *Children and Society*, 10, 3, 177–186.

Parsons C. with Benns L., Hailes J. and Howlett K. (1994) *Excluding Primary School Children.* London: Family Policy Studies Centre.

Pitts J. (1997) Youth crime, social change and social class in Britain and France in the 1980s and 1990s, in Jones H. (ed.) Towards a Classless Society. London: Routledge.

Roaf C. and Lloyd C. (1995) *The Welfare Network: How Well Does the Net Work?* Occasional Paper 6. Oxford: Oxford Brookes University.

Squire R. (1996) The Government Perspective on School Exclusions, *National Children's Bureau Conference*, 9 July.

Social Services Inspectorate and Office For Standards In Education (1995) *The Education of Children Who Are Looked After By Local Authorities.* London: Department of Health and OFSTED.

Steinberg L. (1986) Latchkey children and susceptibility to peer pressure: an ecological analysis, *Developmental Psychology*, 22, 433–439.

Stirling M. (1992) How many pupils are being excluded?, *British Journal of Special Education*, 19, 4, 128–130.

CHAPTER 12

Young People's Experience of Crime and Violence: Findings from a Survey of School Pupils

David Porteous

Introduction

Official statistics on the victimisation of young people are of limited use in assessing the true nature of the problem. Even the British Crime Survey does not access respondents under the age of 16 years. Only the most serious offences are reported and more often than not the focus is upon young people as perpetrators and therefore 'problems' for the community. The nature and extent of victimisation involving young people within the wider community and the factors which contribute towards it are therefore effectively overlooked. Once the immediate perpetrator has been identified and dealt with, the media and indeed the legal system are sated. Identifying and addressing their social origins is an infinitely more time consuming and more difficult task.

The origins of much youth victimisation are to be found within schools and in the other spaces which they occupy within the neighbourhood. If we wish to understand the 'natural history' of specific incidents of youth violence therefore, we should turn to these sites of conflict and, more importantly, to young people's experiences within them. Information derived from such analysis should allow us to make sense of the more serious incidents that can otherwise seem inexplicable. It should also provide a basis for developing community safety strategies aimed at reducing the victimisation of young people since it is only logical that these will work best when they operate at the lowest level of escalation.

This chapter presents the findings from a survey of pupils concerning their experience of conflict and violence inside and outside of their school in North London. It reveals the nature and extent of these experiences, where and when violence takes place and how it affects different groups of young people. It describes the pupils' familiarity with weapons and drugs and the incidence of racial and sexual harassment.

The area in which the pupils' school is located has witnessed a number of serious violent incidents in the last three years in which young people have been both aggressors and victims. In 1994, a Bengali youth was brain damaged having been struck over the head with a snooker cue. The fatal stabbing of the head teacher Philip Lawrence made national headlines the following year, as did the death of local teenager Richard Everitt, also from a knife wound. Then in 1996 an Austrian tourist was repeatedly raped and thrown into a canal by a group of young men. Within the school, a fairly typical comprehensive in an inner London Borough, staff report that they are having increasingly to manage conflict which inevitably undermines their educational role. It appears as if tension on the streets is being imported into the playground, corridors and classrooms.

In this context the Vauxhall Centre for the Study of Crime, at the University of Luton began, in late 1996, a two year research programme aimed at better understanding the dynamics of youth violence in the area and developing strategies to reduce conflict. The school and its pupils and staff have been the initial focus of the research for many reasons. The institution is in some ways a microcosm of the wider community bringing together young people from around a cosmopolitan borough. It is a point of access for researchers providing us with a gateway to groups of young people and their families in the neighbourhood. And as suggested above, it is in itself a site of conflict. As the survey reveals with 46 per cent of incidents reported by the young people involved took place within the school.

The project began with a period of broad consultation in which the research team met with staff and students, individually and in groups, to explain the purpose of the research and to enable them to voice their concerns and anxieties. With the school we established a staff–student steering group which we report to and which guides and advises us as it did, for example, in the design and administration of the questionnaire survey. The survey focused on issues which emerged as important in our earlier informal discussions and it will inform the next stages of the research in ways which we describe in the concluding section. We now briefly describe the survey methodology before turning to its findings, outlining first the overall responses and then considering the differences that emerged between groups of pupils. Finally, we discuss the implications of our findings for the development of the action research project.

Survey methodology

The questionnaires were distributed to pupils in years 7–11 (ages 11–16) in their form groups in a session that is normally given over to personal and social education. All tutors were provided with guidelines for the administration of the questionnaires which explained its purpose and gave an assurance to pupils of confidentiality. The research team and some pupils from the steering group assisted form tutors in this process. It was made clear that completion of the questionnaire was voluntary and that any questions could be missed out if pupils so wished. At the end of the session, the questionnaires were collected in blank envelopes and returned to the school office.

Five hundred and forty-three questionnaires were completed, representing a response rate of approximately 60 per cent. Although this is a relatively large sample of young people, it cannot be assumed that it is representative of the school as a whole, at least not in every way. For example, amongst the significant minority of pupils who did not complete questionnaires may well have been a disproportionate number of truants who's experiences may significantly differ from those of the majority. On the other hand, we did receive approximately proportionate numbers of questionnaires in terms of age, gender and ethnicity.

We should also qualify the significance placed on our findings by noting the relatively crude nature of the questionnaire method. Clearly we could not expect to capture the range or depth of meaning attached by respondents to the questions we asked. For example, various interpretations of the term 'threatened with violence' were possible. Nonetheless, the method was the most effective way of quantifying a large number of pupils' experiences. Understanding these experiences in more depth will be the aim of next stage of the fieldwork.

Survey findings

Based on our initial discussions with students and staff, the questionnaire asked pupils about their experience of different forms of anti-social behaviour and violence inside or outside of school within the current year (i.e. 1996/97). Their responses, presented in Table 1, reveal that name

Table 1.   **Pupils experience of anti-social behaviour and violence**

	A few times	Often	Total	(No.)
Called names and cussed	66%	20%	86%	(463)
Threatened with violence	42%	5%	47%	(251)
Had belongings taken	38%	5%	43%	(230)
Hit, kicked, pushed about	36%	7%	43%	(228)
Touched up	8%	4%	12%	(63)

calling in general and racist name calling in particular is commonplace and that a substantial minority of pupils had been threatened, had things taken from them and been involved in physical skirmishes.

With the exception of name calling and in a different way, sexual harassment, however, it is notable that only a relatively small proportion of students had been frequently victimised. Whilst being threatened with violence once or twice, for example, could almost be expected in this context, being persistently threatened is very unusual.

In addition to these general indicators of conflict, the questionnaire also asked pupils about their experiences in relation to weapons, drugs and racism. Eleven per cent of our sample said that the people who had victimised them had been carrying weapons. Knives were the most commonly cited implements, but sticks and poles, bottles, metal bars, bats and guns were also reported as having been used. Drugs had been offered to 28 per cent of respondents. Cannabis (described variously as weed, marijuana, puff, joints, grass, pot, hash, spliff and draw) accounted for three quarters of what was said to be available, but a wide range of illicit substances were mentioned. One in four pupils said they had been a victim of racism. This was usually in the form of name calling but 20 respondents said they had been beaten up in a racist attack.

The questionnaire asked: Of all these things, what was the worst thing that happened to you in the past year? Two hundred and ninety-two pupils answered the question, 54 per cent of the sample overall. For a third of respondents, being the victim of or involved in physical violence had been the worst thing. One in five cited cussing and name calling, one in six being threatened with violence and just under 10 per cent having their belongings taken or stolen. Eleven per cent of these responses specifically referred to racism or identified the ethnicity of their 'attackers', suggesting a racist motive. Pupils described these incidents in their own words (see below) and the above categorisation does not accurately reflect the variety of experiences. These comments may not be typical but they do reveal the real dangers that some pupils face.

Slightly more than half of all these incidents were reported to have taken place outside of school although this includes locations nearby as is evidenced by the fact that over 50 per cent of them occurred during school hours. Beyond the gates, 11 per cent of incidents were said to have happened on the way home but the majority took place in the evening or most commonly over the weekend. Whereas incidents of name calling were generally reported as having taken place at school, the more extreme instances of physical violence had occurred outside. This was to be expected. Our initial discussions with staff and students had suggested that, although the school is a noisy place, where a lot of bullying of

Pupils descriptions of the worst thing to have happened to them

"I had a gun put to my head" (15 year old Bengali male)

"They tell me that I don't have the right to stay in this country because I am an Asian" (15 year old Bengali female)

"My ring was nicked and sold for draw" (16 year old white female)

"The bricks and belts and racism" (12 year old Afro-Caribbean male)

"They kicked me and hit me and pulled my hair and punched me" (17 year old Bengali female)

"Being offered cocaine" (11 year old white male)

"I've only been threatened with violence. It's by someone that fancied me and wanted my attention" (15 year old Colombian female)

"Being slapped once because I was Asian and I stood up for myself and my other Asian friends" (14 year old Bengali female)

"I was beaten up by a large gang and had to sleep in an alleyway" (14 year old white male)

"People call me fat and other names like Spot the dog" (12 year old white female)

"When a Bengali gang about 16 years old rushed me and my mates" (12 year old Somali male)

"Bullied everyday" (14 year old Somali female)

"A black man was asking me rude things to do with sex" (15 year old white female)

"A group of kids tried to mug me for my money with weapons" (14 year old white male)

"West Ham getting knocked out of the cup" (15 year old white male)

different kinds goes on, it is also for most pupils a relatively safe environment compared to the streets.

We asked respondents to say who had done these things to them. They were most likely to be male and were in the majority of instances known to the pupil, although one in five were said to be strangers and a further 16 per cent to be from another school. There was usually more than one person involved, especially in incidents of racism and where the victim had been threatened with violence.

The final section of the questionnaire asked respondents about their own behaviour to others. As Table 2 shows, pupils were not slow to admit name calling and cussing themselves, nor indeed hitting, kicking and pushing

Table 2. Pupils' own behaviour and use of violence

	A few times	Often	Total	(No.)
Called names and cussed	64%	12%	76%	(396)
Hit, kicked or pushed about	38%	6%	44%	(226)
Threatened with violence	32%	2%	34%	(175)
Touched up	7%	2%	9%	(63)
Taken belongings	8%	0.4%	8%	(44)

others about. However, the numbers of pupils who had threatened others with violence, taken belongings or (to a lesser extent) touched someone up were noticeably smaller than the number who had had these things done to them (see Table 1 for comparison).

The proportion who said they had used weapons, offered drugs or used racist abuse or violence were also smaller, although 14 per cent of pupils said they had done the latter.

The survey results confirm that most young people at the school are at some time likely to be involved in some form of physical and verbal violence, as victims and/or perpetrators. However, the survey also revealed notable differences in the experiences of pupils according to their gender, age and ethnicity.

We have already seen that most perpetrators of the violence experienced by pupils were male – in approximately four out of five of the cases reported. Where physical violence is concerned, boys are also more likely to have been a victim. For example, just over a half of male respondents had been threatened with violence compared to a third of females and 46 per cent against 34 per cent had been hit, kicked or pushed about. Fifty-three boys (15 per cent) said their 'attackers' had weapons compared to four of the girls (2 per cent). They were also more likely to have experienced racism. Reflecting on these figures, we may note that 65 per cent of the school roll is male.

The situation is however reversed when we consider sexual harassment. Twenty-two per cent of female respondents said they had been 'touched up' compared to 7 per cent of males. Thirteen- and fourteen-year-old girls seem particularly vulnerable, as pupils of that age were also more likely to report being touched up. The perpetrators were normally male, on their own and likely to be strangers.

Figure 1. shows how experiences vary between pupils of different ages. It illustrates how cussing, though commonplace throughout the school population, declines as pupils grew older as does the likelihood of having one's belongings taken. By contrast, being confronted with weapons and

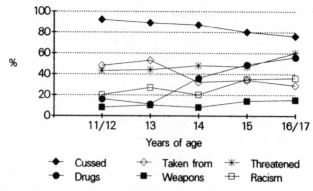

%

Years of age

◆ Cussed   ◇ Taken from   ✳ Threatened
● Drugs   ■ Weapons   ☐ Racism

Figure 1.   How pupils' experiences change with age

drugs and being threatened with violence becomes more likely as one becomes older, as does racism which one in five 11/12 year old pupils said they had experienced compared to one in three 16/17 year olds.

Although a higher proportion of older students reported being threatened with violence, the proportion of this age group who said they themselves had threatened others was not noticeably higher. In fact the survey suggests that it is their vulnerability to violence outside of school which increases. Thus, around 30 per cent of 15 and 16 year olds identified the perpetrators of violence against them as being strangers compared to 13 per cent of 11 and 12 year olds.

Many more pupils from ethnic minorities reported that they had experienced racist abuse or violence, 35 per cent of all 'non-white' respondents compared to 16 per cent of whites. Bengali pupils, 46 per cent of whom said they had experienced racism seem particularly vulnerable. They were more likely than any other ethnic group to have been threatened with violence and to have been hit, kicked or pushed about but less likely to have done these things themselves.

One final, important distinction can be made between groups of students. If we cross-tabulate the responses to the questions about using violence with those about the experience of violence, a clear pattern emerges.

What these data show is that those pupils who reported having abused or threatened others were more likely to have been abused or threatened themselves, that the perpetrators of violence are more likely to be victims as well. It is important to note that being a victim does not however make one more likely to be a perpetrator. So whilst 20 of the 23 pupils who said they had offered drugs to someone had been offered drugs themselves, they only represent 14 per cent of those offered drugs overall.

Table 3. Association between using violence and being a victim of violence

Have been hit, kicked or pushed about	*Have hit, kicked or pushed others about*	
Yes	No	Yes
	35%	52%
Have been threatened with violence	*Have threatened others with violence*	
Yes	No	Yes
	37%	66%
Have been victim of racism	*Have used racist abuse or violence*	
Yes	No	Yes
	23%	40%

It is also important not to exaggerate the causal significance of this association between pupils' behaviour and their likelihood of being victimised. For one thing, hitting or kicking someone may literally mean fighting back. For another, other factors such as one's sex and age are as likely to be determinant. Girls were less likely in general than boys to have threatened others with violence but of those that had, a higher proportion had been threatened themselves. In fact our data suggest that no one single factor can be used to 'explain' or 'predict' an individual pupil's experiences. Gender, age ethnicity and pupils' own behaviour all appear to matter but none can be said to be the most important. Most of the pupils had had at least some experience of violence and intimidation of some kind even if few reported being persistently subject to it. This of course makes finding ways of changing the environment and increasing the safety of pupils all the more challenging, since the process has to involve the whole school and not just some students.

Conclusion

The survey shows that anti-social behaviour, especially name calling, but including incidents of violence and racism are experienced by most of the pupils in the school. Much of this could be said to be the stuff of growing up – all schools bring together large numbers of energetic children and adolescents vying to assert their identity and that youthful exuberance frequently manifests itself in shouting, cussing and fighting is hardly a major new finding. However, many of these experiences constitute real threats to the well-being of the young people involved. They include bullying by classmates at school and attacks on individuals by groups outside of school time. The survey results illuminate these dangers and provide an insight into different patterns of victimisation.

We have clear evidence that anti-social behaviour and violence affects different groups disproportionately so some, such as Bengali pupils, are subject to greater victimisation than others. We see that the nature of pupils' experience changes as they get older. With age comes a certain maturity but also the temptation of drugs, the threat of weapons and greater vulnerability to attack outside of school. The survey shows that boys are more likely to be perpetrators and victims but also that their numerical domination in the school has the effect of increasing the 'net' victimisation of girls since those who bully or intimidate them are more likely to be male than female. And we find that to some extent, it is the pupils' own behaviour which affects their chances of being victimised. Those who abstain from anti-social behaviour improve their chances of being left alone.

One of the objectives of the next stage of the research will be to discuss messages such as this last one with groups of pupils. We could learn from those who manage to avoid conflict how much this is because they consciously do so and how they go about it. And we can ask those who have used violence themselves what they think might have prevented them from doing so. Similarly, we need to work with groups and individuals who have been particularly victimised to understand better how and why this happens and how these issues should be addressed.

There is a need to clarify the meaning of the findings with staff and students. Partly this is about identifying parameters for acceptable behaviour. How much of what goes on should we accept as 'normal' youthful exuberance. How could sanctions against certain behaviour be made more effective? It also involves talking through incidents in greater depth to see how they develop. We need to find out how group violence and intimidation operates, whether it is structured and regular or spontaneous and sporadic.

Similar work undertaken by one of the project team previously (Pitts J and Smith P 1995) allows us to speculate about some possible strategies for reducing victimisation. These include surveillance of 'hot spots' in and around the school, changing the physical environment in order to facilitate such surveillance and developing systems through which pupils can report incidents without fear of reprisal and with greater expectation that action will be taken.

Many of the issues relate to what goes on outside the school and there is a need to talk to parents and local agency professionals both to obtain their perspective and to involve them in developing strategies to reduce conflict and enhance the safety of young people in the neighbourhood. Whilst this takes the project well beyond the school gate, much of the violence encountered by pupils took place away from the school in the evenings and at weekends. In any case what occurs in the school is already influenced by external factors. One such is the rapid population change in the neighbourhood. At the time of the survey, two thirds of year 11 pupils had started their secondary school careers at other schools.

In line with current developments in community safety, a multi-agency approach is therefore required. The education department has a role in addressing issues such as the allocation of pupils with special behavioural needs and the resources which need to follow such pupils – this school has a disproportionately high number of statemented children. Education social workers should be involved in efforts to resettle excluded pupils within this school and others in a more structured and supportive manner than is currently the case. The police and the transport department need to work with the school on increasing the safety of pupils travelling to and from school. Local voluntary agencies with expertise in, for instance, drug and alcohol use, may be invited into the school to work with pupils on such matters.

The survey findings do not suggest easy solutions to the problems encountered by pupils. We cannot, for example, turn boys into girls or stop 11 year olds from growing up and even if we could we might find ourselves faced with higher rates of petty theft. And whilst certain pupils appear more vulnerable than others at certain times in their school careers, conflict in various forms affects everyone. Efforts to increase the safety and well-being of those at the school need to involve all pupils and other members of the community beyond. It is a collective responsibility.

CHAPTER 13

Youth Conflict in a London Neighbourhood

Philly Desai

Introduction

This chapter is an account of a study carried out in North London in 1996 among Bangladeshi young men[1]. The study came about as the result of concern among local schools, youth workers and the police about a series of conflicts which had taken place between groups of Bangladeshi young men from Stationville and Park Town[2], two North London boroughs which are next to each other. It is a short bus ride from one to the other or about a twenty minute walk. Stationville has a long history of racial conflict between white and Bangladeshi young people, and Park Town too has seen conflicts between Bangladeshi and black youths. However, on-going conflicts between groups of Bangladeshi young men was a relatively new phenomenon, which did not appear to fit the previous pattern of racialised conflict. This research was commissioned to explore the reasons for this hostility and to make recommendations to the relevant agencies in the light of our findings.

The research was relatively small scale and entirely qualitative in nature, focusing specifically on the perspectives of the young people involved and on their own explanations for the conflict. The research comprised qualitative interviews with young Bangladeshi men from Stationville and Park Town, as well as more informal discussions with young people and youth workers in the areas. In total, the research probably covered the views of about twenty young men in detail (those most closely involved with the conflict) but also included shorter conversations with a much wider range of young people.

[1]This chapter is based on research requested by Mr Michael Marland and funded by the Calouste Gulbenkian Foundation. The research team was Gulam Akbar, Akik Najeeb Ali, Philly Desai and Mukith Miah. This chapter was written by Philly Desai but was agreed by all the researchers. The researchers would like to acknowledge the support of the Marylebone Bangladesh Society and the Bengali Workers Action Group in carrying out this project.
[2]All locations and names have been changed.

Before discussing the findings of our research in detail, we would like to put this project within a broader social context. First, it is well established from various statistical sources (e.g., the 1991 Census, the recent PSI survey *Ethnic Minorities in Britain*, and the *Camden Bangladeshi Residents Survey*) that Britain's Bangladeshi population is one of the most deprived ethnic groups in the country. Bangladeshi people suffer from higher rates of unemployment, overcrowded housing, ill health and racial attacks than most other ethnic groups. Young Bangladeshi people's average levels of educational attainment in Britain's schools are much lower than the national average, although they are improving. It is beyond the remit of this research to assess the influence of these social and economic factors upon the behaviour of young people. However, the fact that the community suffers such high levels of deprivation is an important backdrop to the behaviour of these young people and should not be forgotten.

Second, we want to point out that this conflict involved only a minority of young people from each area, and that the majority of Bangladeshi young people were not involved and probably not interested in these hostilities. Many young people from Stationville have friends and relations in Park Town, and *vice versa,* and they visit each other without suffering attacks or hostility.

Third, whatever the reasons for the conflicts, we do not believe that they are explained by 'Bangladeshi culture', whatever that term may mean. It has been suggested in press coverage of these events that poor parental supervision is somehow intrinsic to the Bangladeshi community, but we do not agree with this. Certainly, there may be some Bangladeshi families where relations between parents and children are weak, as is the case with any ethnic group: however, we do not see any reason to attribute this to aspects of Bangladeshi or Asian culture. In fact, statistical evidence suggests that Asian young people are less likely than white or black young people to commit any sort of crime, and that Bangladeshi young people are the most law-abiding of all (Office for National Statistics, 1996).

Thus, whilst there is no reason for complacency about the criminal and anti-social activity which is taking place, there is no evidence of a large-scale breakdown of order within the Bangladeshi community, nor of a crisis among Asian youth in general. In fact, when one looks at the much younger age profile of the Bangladeshi and Pakistani communities compared with the white population, one might wonder about the relative infrequency of criminal activity among the Asian communities.

Background

The areas

In order to understand the nature of the conflict between the groups of young Bangladeshi men from Stationville and Park Town, it is important to outline the nature of the two areas concerned. Much of the conflict centres around the territorial loyalties and pride of these young men, so it will be useful to start with a brief description of the areas.

Although it is accurate to talk about the conflict in terms of Stationville and Park Town, the young people usually define the areas as 'Station Street' and 'Park Estate', sometimes also including an area slightly to the west of Park Town called West City Road. The young people from Stationville do not all live in Station Street and the young people from Park Town do not all live on the Park Estate, but these are the names and the areas with which they identify.

Station Street

Station Street is often seen as the centre of the Stationville Bangladeshi community, both geographically and emotionally. Over the last ten to fifteen years the area has shifted from being regularly subjected to racially motivated attack by white youths, to being an area which is now seen as safe for the Bangladeshi population. This change has been achieved by the community defending itself from racial attacks and becoming less accepting of aggression and insults. The younger men of the community have played an important role in this process, as they have taken to banding together in groups both to resist racial hostility and simply to socialise. The area is now seen by many young men as a place where 'Bengalis Rule', and they feel a great sense of pride and allegiance to what they think of as 'their area'. There is a strong sense of the hierarchy of age groups, with younger groups relying upon the older groups for back up if they have a problem they cannot resolve.

Park Estate

The Park Estate is a residential area in Park Town where many Bangladeshi families live. However, in contrast to Station Street, Bangladeshis are not the dominant ethnic group there. In fact, there is a large black community on the estate and according to some young people it is the black young men who 'rule the area'. Bangladeshi people complain that they are attacked and robbed by young black people and there is little satisfaction with the police response. This reached its peak in 1996 with the murder of a Bangladeshi young men, allegedly killed by a black man. The Bangladeshi young man, aged 27, was seen as a role model for Bangladeshi youth in the area and his murder greatly shocked the community. No-one has been convicted of this crime and this has contributed to the community's lack of faith in the police and in the criminal justice system more broadly.

In the late 1980s there were a series of conflicts between groups of Bangladeshi young people and Moroccan young people on the estate. Reportedly, at this time the young people of Stationville and those of Park Estate would back each other up, and Bangladeshi young men from Station Street came to help the Park Estate youths in these conflicts. Also, young men from Stationville and Park Town used to back each other up in their various conflicts with Bangladeshi young men from East London, in a kind of 'East versus West' rivalry.

I used to think they were all right, especially when we went to fight the East London boys. At that time we would go and help them and they would help us.   Park Town resident

Unlike the young men of Stationville, there does not appear to be a tradition of older boys supporting younger boys in conflicts in Park Estate. Indeed, the younger boys from this area are reported to criticise the older men (aged 20+) for being cowardly and for refusing to back them up in their fights against the Stationville boys.

If the Park Estate older ones involved themselves and supported us then the Station Street boys will be nothing. It's only because our older ones choose not to get themselves involved, that's why they (the Station Street boys) feel they've got more freedom.   Park Town resident

According to youth workers, the younger boys (14–17) like to think of themselves as having a 'posse' (a gang) and to call themselves the Park Estate Posse, but this sense of loyalty to one's area is not as strong or as visible as in Stationville.

Schools
The local schools in these areas also play a central role in the conflict, if only because they are often the site of the fights which take place. Fights may start in school and escalate outside the school gates, or incidents outside the school may have repercussions within the school.

West Park School and Queen's Wood School are the main schools attended by Bangladeshi young people in Park Town. They have also been the sites of two of the most serious incidents in the conflict we are discussing, as there have been stabbings of young men within both schools. In West Park School, there are a minority of boys from the Stationville area, with the majority of Bangladeshi young people from Park Town.

Some of the boys from Stationville have said that they are bullied and picked on in and around the school by Park Town boys, both from Park Estate and West City Road. They claim that this bullying is the reason for the conflict.

> *We were hearing rumours – "You're dead, were gonna kill you" – they could get us anytime, on the stairs . . .*
>
> Stationville resident, pupil at West Park School

However, others have suggested that these few boys, who are associated with the Station Street area, act in such a way as to bring trouble on themselves. They have been described as 'cocky' and acting as if they are 'hard' because they see themselves as Station Street boys with access to strong back up from their elders (17–20 year olds).

> *The Station Street boys are best at getting their older ones involved, they always go and ask for back up. We don't – we tackle it ourselves, even though we've got less people.*   Park Town resident

Regarding the attitudes of the authorities to the conflict, there is some suggestion that its potential seriousness was missed by both teachers and youth workers. The fact that the conflict was between groups of Bangladeshi young men, rather than Asian and white young men, meant that some assumed it was merely a question of playground arguments. Few thought that it would escalate and involve the use of weapons until these things were already taking place. It seems there was an assumption that intra-racial conflict did not need to be treated with the same vigorous discipline as might have been used in a case of inter-racial violence.

On the Stationville side, many of the young men involved in the conflict either attend or attended Stationville School, although there have not been any incidents in or around the school in connection with this conflict. Bangladeshi students form the single largest ethnic group in Stationville School but the school is culturally very diverse, with increasing numbers of African students from Somalia and Ethiopia, for example.

The History of the Conflict

The histories of on-going conflicts are often difficult to unravel and this situation was no exception. Asking 'who started it' rarely elicits the same story from both sides. People's memories fade and they may not tell the whole truth, wishing to make their side in the conflict look like the innocent party. Also, different people have different timescales, so whilst some of the younger people said the conflict started one or two years ago, older people cited events five or six years ago as the beginning of the hostility. In these contexts, people may genuinely not be certain 'what started it': what they do know is that their group of friends do not like another group of young people. Thus, we do not have an objective answer to the question "Why did this conflict start?" However, we do have a good understanding of why different people *think* it started and how they act in accordance with their ideas. In trying to explain what is happening now, this may be just as important as uncovering what actually *did* happen many years ago.

During our research we asked young people and youth workers what started this conflict between Bangladeshi young men from the two areas. It was generally agreed that prior to about 1990, Bangladeshi young people from Stationville and Park Estate got on well and were usually friends. There was a common football team, West End United, and they often socialised together and helped each other out if they needed support. Older youth workers felt that as the adolescent Bangladeshi populations in each area grew, they no longer needed each others help and support. They began to see each other as rivals rather than friends, as they developed locally based identities around the areas where they lived rather than around their common identity as Bangladeshis.[3] As one youth worker said:

We thought we were Bengalis, we did not symbolise ourselves as SSP.[4]
Youth worker, Stationville

Some people we spoke to attributed the conflict to an incident concerning the football team. We were told that Stationville fans of the West End team started a fight with the fans of the East London team. This resulted in the East London fans attacking the West End fans, including those from Park Estate. This created trouble between the Park Estate and the East London groups. The Park Estate fans blamed this on the behaviour of the fans from Stationville and the animosity between Stationville and Park Estate boys grew from there.

Another explanation we heard was that the conflict started as a result of an incident at the wedding at the Stationville Bengali Community Centre in 1996. Allegedly, during the reception for a wedding of a young man from Stationville, some boys from Park Estate started harassing the wife of one of the guests. This resulted in the Stationville boys taking offence and a fight ensued, which started the most recent series of hostilities. Youth workers have backed up these accounts and, indeed, a conflict between families can be taken very seriously.

---

[3]Claire Alexander (1996) found similar feelings of rivalry between black young men from Brixton and Harlesden.
[4]Station Street Posse, one of the names used by some young men from Stationville to describe their group.

Some Incidents

In order to help the reader to understand the analysis which follows, we want to outline some incidents of conflict which have taken place. This will show the kinds of motivations involved, how people are drawn into conflicts, and how school-boy skirmishes can escalate into far more serious incidents. These examples have been reconstructed from a variety of different sources, from what we were told by the young people involved, youth workers and from police records where these were available. We were not in a position to assess the validity of all the information we received. These accounts should therefore be treated as a version of events as told to us, not as the absolute truth.

Eid Day 1996
In a central London park on the Eid Day 1996 there was a fight between a group of Bangladeshi young men from the Stationville area and a group from the Park Estate area. A brief description of the events leading up to this will demonstrate some of the points made above.

Ali, from West City Road, had an argument with Mohammed, from Stationville, in Park Town school. Both boys were aged between 15 and 16. It was a trivial incident and quickly resolved. The next day one of Mohammed's friends, also from Stationville, put a drawing pin on Ali's chair during class. This resulted in a fight between the two boys. They both told their friends, from their respective areas, about this fight and their friends came to back them up. However, before the incident escalated further, an older boy from West City Road, respected by both sets of younger boys, intervened and told the younger ones to calm down and abandon the idea of a fight. They did this, but later in school one of Mohammed's friends, Rafiq, was beaten up by Ali and his friends.

Rafiq was temporarily excluded from school as a result of this fight. He then approached some of his friends and older relatives from the Stationville area and asked them to back him up in his attempt to seek revenge for being beaten up in school. He got together a group of 15-20 young men, some his age and some older. They intended to ambush the West City Road group at the mosque on Eid Day as they knew they would be there. When they saw the group of boys from West City Road they challenged them. According to one report, the older boys from Stationville demanded an explanation for the attack upon Rafiq, but the heated argument soon became a physical fight. The West City Road group were outnumbered in this fight, and some of the boys from Park Estate who were also there tried to stop the fight by physically separating the two groups. Not all the boys from Stationville knew which boys were from Park

Estate and which were from West City Road and in the fight which took place some of boys from Park Estate were also attacked by the Stationville boys. The Park Estate group were aggrieved at having been attacked when, by common consent, they had been trying to stop the fight. Rafiq apologised to them for the misunderstanding and they were temporarily pacified.

However, the West City Road boys still bore a grudge against Rafiq and his friends and, according to Rafiq, were keen to get the Park Estate group on their side. This tension rumbled on until the older boys (aged 18-20) from both sides decided to take things into their own hands. They brought the younger people from both sides together and, by a mixture of argument and physical discipline, tried to persuade them to abandon their conflict. This had the effect of damping down the immediate conflict, but only temporarily.

This shows how small incidents in school can escalate outside school, how younger boys can get their older friends and relatives involved in conflicts, and how young people feel an obligation to back each other up even when they are unaware of the nature of the conflict or who they are supposed to be fighting. Although involvement from the older boys within the Bangladeshi community can be useful in the short term, their influence cannot be relied upon to resolve these conflicts on a longer term basis.

The incident at Queen's Wood School
One of the Stationville resident boys in Queen's Wood School was beaten up by some older boys from the school. This boy's older brother was one of the key members of the group associated with Station Street and determined to exact revenge for his younger brother. The older brother, aged 17, gathered together a group of about 12 young men from the Stationville area, and returned to Queen's Wood School a few days later. He and his friends found the boys who allegedly beat up his brother taking a GCSE exam in the school gym. They entered the gym and attacked several students, one of whom was stabbed. One of the attackers was detained at the scene and three were arrested outside the school later. Later in the same day, one of the boys associated with the Station Street group but not involved in the Queen's Wood School incident was attacked with a bottle while walking in a nearby street.

A few days later, a group of year 10 Bangladeshi boys from Stationville who attend West Park School were beaten up by a group of boys resident in Park Town. These Stationville boys were not involved in the incident at Queen's Wood School but were seen as legitimate targets as they were from Station Street. When we spoke with these boys, they said the Park Estate boys had later apologised to them for beating them up. The reason they were attacked, apparently, was to oblige the older boys responsible for the Queen's Wood School incident to come back to Park Estate and thus give them a chance to take revenge.

This shows again how small school incidents can escalate to a dangerous extent, and also how people not directly involved but associated with a particular group or area can be targeted after an incident.

Possible explanations for the conflict

Providing explanations for any kind of human behaviour is a difficult and complex task. People are influenced by a wide range of factors, some of which they themselves may not be aware of, and one can rarely predict what combinations of factors will produce particular outcomes in individual situations. What we can do is to describe which factors make conflict of this kind more likely to occur, and this is what we aim to do here.

Social context

Clearly, explanations exist at different levels in society, ranging from the wider social and economic context in which people live to the individual decisions they make in particular circumstances. We know that the Bangladeshi population is characterised by high levels of deprivation, including unemployment, overcrowding, poor achievement in schools and a high incidence of racial attacks. These factors are important in providing the context for young people's behaviour. It goes beyond the scope of this research to assess the influence of these wider social issues, but we believe they are important and should not be overlooked.

The values of young men

When we spoke with the young people we gained a strong sense of the system of values which influences their behaviour, especially when they are in groups. Although not all young men have the same set of values and they may disagree, there is a strong pressure on young people when in groups to conform to the expectations created by peer pressure.

Areas and identities

Research looking at conflict and hostility between groups of young men has almost always emphasised the importance of area-based loyalties. For as long as there have been sociologists to investigate, groups of young men have been in conflict with other groups, whether they were from the other side of the railway tracks, the school in the next town, the local college or the next estate[5]. Thus, it is not surprising to find similar processes in the Bangladeshi population.

---

[5]Frederick Thrasher noted similar processes in operation in America in the early 1920s.

The young men we spoke with had a strong sense of loyalty to the areas where they lived, Station Street and Park Estate. This was particularly true of the young men from Stationville, for whom Station Street had a central place in their self image and sense of worth. It was important to them that they had created a safe space for the Bangladeshi community of Stationville against the backdrop of racism and hostility. Any implied threat or insult to 'their area' was taken as an insult to their group as a whole, whether this came from white people or from other Bangladeshis.

They never had the guts to come down, Park Estate, white boys, anyone, they never had the guts to come to our area. Stationville resident

The young men we spoke to from Park Estate clearly resented those from Station Street. They felt that the young men who associated with this area had an inflated image of their self importance and toughness and, although this is only a guess, they may have felt the need to take them down a peg or two. Certainly, they resented the way that young people from Station Street behaved when in the Park Estate area, which they described as deliberately provocative.

They were walking through our area saying "We could pull you out of your houses", even their older ones. Park Town resident

Going into another group's area is often taken as a mark of courage or daring among these young men. Some young men from Station Street claim that they have often been into the estates and schools where their opponents live and attacked them 'on their own turf' and they see this as proof of their bravery and superiority. This may be one explanation for the frequency of incidents within schools in Park Town. They bolster their claim by observing that no one from Park Estate has ever attacked them in Station Street.

We went to their estate (Park Estate), just seven of us, and we went to the middle of the estate and beat them up. We went right in the middle, you know there's a club and a little green in the middle? We went right in there and beat them up and they didn't dare touch us! They could have battered us but they didn't dare touch us. Stationville resident

It's the whole school [West Park School] against him, 200 against him, and six of us just went down and sorted them out, that's how pussy hole they are . . . It's just, they think if they see six of us coming up and giving it, they know, they think "They're ready for it", we don't give a fuck. Stationville resident

This strong identification with areas gives some groups of young men a sense of pride and of identity. It provides a way for them to place themselves in their local world. However, this pride is very sensitive to insults and there are many ways in which one can take offence. If someone from a particular group is assaulted by a rival group, the rivals may feel that anyone associated with their opponents is a legitimate target. This is illustrated by the aftermath of the attack at Queen's Wood School. If they cannot find the people who actually carried out the assault, they may choose to attack that person's friends or brother, for example. Among some young people, their sense of pride requires them to retaliate quickly and they feel humiliated and shamed if they fail to do this.

Loyalty to your friends/your 'posse'
Groups of young men are often expected by their peers to back up their mates unless there is a good reason not to do so. They may not always do so, of course, but they often do and this is one way in which conflicts escalate and involve larger groups. These loyalties have various sources, including a common area of residence, going to the same school, attending the same youth club, having brothers or cousins who are friends, or simply socialising and spending time together. Adolescence is a time when the peer group is a very important source of support and identity for young people, and therefore the values of the peer group can exert a considerable influence on behaviour. Again, this is true of young people from all ethnic groups, not just the Bangladeshi population.

We must remember that these young men live in areas which are not always safe. In Park Estate the young Bangladeshis feel under threat from black young people and in Stationville from white youth. In both areas, there is little faith in the effectiveness of the police and the criminal justice system to protect people or apprehend and punish wrong doers. Thus, it is important in both areas to feel that one can rely upon one's friends for help, protection and retribution. Young men who live in the same area will often therefore feel an obligation to back each other up. They feel a common sense of belonging and an attack on one member of their group can be seen as an insult to everyone associated with the group. As the Eid Day account shows, a very minor incident can escalate out of all proportion if the two boys involved are from different areas as they may see the conflict as concerning their areas rather than them as individuals.

The first line of back up in these situations is from one's peers, i.e., friends of roughly the same age. However, if the incident cannot be resolved in this way or if one side cannot muster large enough numbers, they may call for help from their older brothers or friends. This is particularly true if the attackers are older than the people who get attacked, as this conflicts with the theoretical principle that it is only legitimate to fight with one's peers. In these situations it is seen as right and fair to involve older men and it is in this sort of incident that there is the potential for real danger. According to some reports, one of the key factors in the Queen's Wood School incident was that the boy from Station Street was attacked by West Park School boys who were older than him, and it was this which legitimated the involvement of older people from Station Street.

They beat up our younger ones, if it was all the same age we would leave it, but they beat our younger ones . . .   Stationville resident

Again, research among groups of white young men involved in racial violence has shown similar processes and loyalties taking place[6]. The fact that some young people see each other not as individuals but as members of groups associated with areas is one of the key factors underlying this conflict. Small incidents escalate quickly if the participants see events as part of a broader conflict rather than as one-off fights, and this behaviour reinforces itself as young people learn from experience that they are indeed seen as legitimate targets by their rivals by virtue of their association with particular areas or groups of people.

Individual variations
So far we have discussed the behaviour and values of young men in groups. We have looked at the importance of peer pressure and at how people behave when they are together. However, it would be wrong to imply that all young people subscribe to the same value system, or that values always convert themselves into action. The groups of young people we are discussing are not organised gangs with formal membership criteria and consistent codes of behaviour, but rather a collection of friends and acquaintances who sometimes agree on a common response to their situation and on other occasions may disagree.

In fact, many young Bangladeshi males are not involved at all in the conflicts described and if conflict comes their way they take steps to avoid it. Here, for example, is a young man from Stationville describing how he frequently goes to Park Town Estate to visit his relatives.

I've been there, never had any trouble. Obviously, if someone comes up to you and says "Where are you from?", if you say "Yeah, I'm from Station Street, why, what's the matter, are you giving it. . .?" then they will batter you. But if you just say, "Yeah, I'm from Station Street but I don't want no trouble, no, I'm not giving it", then they ain't gonna do nothing. It's just some people are like, "Yeah, I'm from Station Street, what's the matter?"   Stationville resident

---

[6]For example, Roger Hewitt found similar processes in his study of racist ideologies in South London, documented in *Sagaland*.

This young man knows the codes of behaviour which are likely to create problems for himself and he avoids them. If challenged, he adopts a calm and even submissive demeanour and goes on his way. He contrasts this with the behaviour of other friends of his when they go to the Park Town area, and he implies that their attitude may be construed as deliberate provocation by the Park Town residents.

Another young man describes how he avoids racial conflicts in the Stationville area, where conflicts between white and Bengali young men have been frequent in the recent past:

> *Two years ago what happened, me and my mates were going to Station Street and about five white kids, big, in their 20s they come up and said "Are you from Station Street?" So I give it, "They know about Station Street as well!" And I said "No" and the other two said "Yes", and they got battered and I did a runner!*

In both of the cases, the young people are principally concerned to avoid trouble. They do not identify with 'their area' so strongly that they are willing to get beaten up in order to avoid losing face, and by using these tactics both of these young men minimise their involvement in violent conflict.

There is also a variety of attitudes within the groups of young people who are involved in the conflicts. Young people in these groups play different roles, with some ready to start a fight with only slight provocation and others more willing to 'live and let live'. For some young men, their identification with 'their group' and 'their area' is so strong that the slightest perceived insult requires some form of retaliation, whilst others within the group have a more moderating influence and can suggest other ways of resolving potential conflicts. Here is one young man, known for his enjoyment of a good fight, describing two other members of his group of friends:

> *Well, you know what they are like, they are in the gang, but they will not go out and look for trouble. If trouble comes to them they will fight, but they will not go and look for it. Like, say someone is being mouthy over there, me I would go over and say, "Yeah, are you talking to us?" But they would say, "They are over there, leave them, ignore it. Wait for them to come over here and do something, and then batter them."*

These differences of behaviour relate in part to the self-confidence of the young people concerned. It requires considerable confidence to go against the normal behaviour of the peer group. Those young people who do this usually have better powers of self expression and a more persuasive personality. They may, of course, use these interpersonal skills to deter other members of their group of friends from involvement in violence or to encourage them to take part. Clearly, if youth services and other agencies can work with these key young people to exercise their influence in a positive way, this could have a real effect on the ground.

The police
We did not set out to interview members of the police force as part of this project, but the police are clearly central to any discussion of young people's involvement in violence and crime. The police are the front line agency, both for victims and perpetrators of crime, and therefore their relationship with young people is likely to have a strong influence on young people's attitudes to the criminal justice system as a whole. So what is the nature of the relationship between the police and the young people involved in these conflicts, and what is the effect of policing upon young people's behaviour?

The picture we got from talking to young people was predominantly, although not entirely, negative. Whilst some community police officers were seen as reasonable, few young people or youth workers in the area had much faith in the police force as an institution.

> *I would say there is no faith at all in the police. I have no faith in the police.*   Bengali youth worker, Park Town

There were various reasons for this lack of faith, some to do with the perceived effectiveness of police responses and others with the way in which young people were treated by the police. Response times were a common cause of complaint, with many young people suggesting that it was simply not worth calling the police if they were threatened or assaulted. They felt that the police would arrive some time later and would be unable to take any action by then. Better, many thought, to get some reliable friends together and sort the problems out oneself. Indeed, various young people commented that it was the failure of the police to act effectively which had prompted them to take matters into their own hands.

> *They (a rival group of Bengali young men who wanted to beat him up) phoned me on the mobile and said "Look out of your window." I looked and there were about 15 of them standing there outside my door. I thought "Shall I call the police?" Then I thought "We are always calling the police, they come half an hour later." I just grabbed a knife and went out – they all ran.*   Park Town resident

The following quotation is from a young man from Station Street, describing how he came to lose faith in the police and decided to take matters into his own hands. He is talking about a fight against a group of white young men from a nearby area.

> *If you go to the police nothing happens. You know Jehangir, he got beaten up he went to the police and nothing happened. He got a fracture. We know who done it. White boys . . . they live round here. After that you feel angry. The police don't do nothing, we've got proof, everything's happened and no-one gives a shit. Like in our group, I was beaten up once so my dad said "Go to the police." I went to the police, he came and looked at me and he said, "Well, that's not enough." I had bruises and he said "That's not enough, I can't do nothing." From that day in my family no-one believes the police no matter what happens, we'd rather solve it. And then we sorted in out in a fight. We felt better after that, "All right, I got beaten up, I got you back". You tell the police, they go "All right then, we'll do something", you wait two years, nothing happened. These days no one really believes the police. I would never believe the police. . .*

Most young Bengali people in the area also believed that the police responded less quickly to crimes committed against Bengali people than to crimes against the white population. They had formed this opinion over many years, often as a result of what they considered to be police inaction over racist attacks in the past. We cannot assess whether or not this is objectively true, but it is certainly a common belief among the young people, especially in Stationville which has a long history or racial conflict. The previous quotation shows this effect, where police ineffectiveness in cases of racial attacks is taken as indicative of how the police respond overall.

This quotation also raises the final issue which we want to address here in the context of policing. The young man says that "you wait two years and nothing happens". There are two possible explanations for this: either nothing is happening, or the crime is being investigated but the investigation takes a long time. If crimes are being investigated, the police appear not to keep young people informed of progress and this leads the victims to believe that nothing is happening. If people were told what was happening, what the next step was, and why things take as long as they do, then young people might have more faith in the official system of justice and not feel the need to seek their own forms of redress.

Overview and recommendations

We have tried to describe the factors which have led to the series of conflicts between these two groups of young men, and to suggest that social factors, the values of young people and individual variations all need to be taken into account in understanding the situation. At the time of writing, the situation appears to have calmed down, possibly due to the convictions of some of the young people from Stationville and also the transfer of others away from West Park School to schools nearer their homes.

This is a small-scale research project but we believe its findings have important implications for a variety of agencies. We have decided to limit our recommendations to those which directly concern the conflicts we have discussed. Clearly, there are also implications for local careers services and colleges, community safety teams, economic regeneration projects. There are also a variety of issues concerning the relationships between young people, their families and schools, but these have been more fully considered elsewhere (e.g. Marland 1996a and 1996b).

Some of our recommendations involve changes in practices which can be implemented relatively quickly and which do not involve any additional resources. Others do have resource implications and local authorities will need to assess the likely cost of implementing some of these ideas, against the social costs of not doing so. We urge the relevant authorities to consider the recommendations below.

The Youth Service is in many cases the only agency which some of these young people come into contact with voluntarily. Excluded from school or regularly truanting, they have a sometimes tenuous relationship with schools and teachers[7]. They may come into contact with the police quite frequently, but this is rarely a positive or helpful experience. Thus, the youth service is an important and unique access point to some of the most vulnerable young people.

The following are recommended courses of action for the youth service:

- Joint activities involving young men from both areas. Stationville has conducted successful work among white and Bangladeshi youths using football as a way to get young people together, and this could be tried in this context too.

- Social education and, possibly, role play activities, suggesting ways for young men to deal with conflict situations without resorting to violence. This could be via youth clubs or in association with local schools. Key young people could then become "peer educators", helping other youngsters to find alternative ways to solve their disagreements.

---

[7] *Young People and Crime*, a large Home Office Study, found that weak relationships with school, regular truanting and being excluded from school were among the key factors which pre-disposed young men to become young offenders. Weak relationships with their families was the other most important factor.

- Exploring the ways in which young men can feel a sense of pride in the area where they live without this necessarily leading to hostility towards those from other areas.

- Increased outreach work with the most vulnerable young people, who are quite likely to be excluded from schools and youth clubs, and therefore lack responsible adult role models.

The following are recommended to schools:

- To review disciplinary procedures to ensure that swift and effective action is taken to resolve minor arguments within the school, thus avoiding their escalation outside school.

- To consider the seriousness with which non-racist conflicts are taken, and to ensure that teachers are aware of local hostilities between groups of young people whatever their ethnic origins.

- To try to avoid the segregation in classes and friendship groups between young people from one area and those from another.

- To consider ways of working with the youth services as discussed above.

The following are recommended to the police and youth justice systems[8]:

- To work to improve relations between the police and ethnic minority communities, particularly the younger generation.

- To work to restore faith in the effectiveness of police responses to calls for help from members of minority communities. This could involve:
  - improving response times, ensuring that young people are treated with due professional courtesy and taking steps to eradicate the common belief that ethnic minority young people are treated less politely and less fairly than their white peers;
  - keeping people informed of progress in investigations, and ensuring that if no prosecutions are to take place people fully understand the reasons for this.

---

[8]There are many other reports which have looked at how young people from minority communities view the police and what reaction the police might take to improve relations, e.g., the Policy Studies Institute reports *Changing Lives (1994)*, and *Police and People in London* (1984), as well as the Scarman Report, of course. These recommendations are therefore not exhaustive but are those which seem to us to be the most pressing in this context.

- The courts need to speed up the process from charging to trial. Lengthy delays only allow for resentment to fester and create the assumption that young people are "getting away with it". For the young people concerned, they may also make the relationship between punishment and crime appear rather tenuous.

References

Alexandre, C. 1996. *The Art of Being Black: The Creation of Black British Youth Identities.* Oxford: Oxford University Press.
Dhaliwal, P. 1996. *Camden Bangladeshi Residents Survey.* London: London Borough of Camden/ Institute of Education.
Graham, J. and Bowling, B. 1995. *Young People and Crime.* London: Home Office Research and Statistics Directorate: Research Study 145.
Hewitt, R., and Institute of Education 1992. *Sagaland: Youth Culture, Racism and Education. A Report on Research Carried out in Thamesmead.* London: The Centre for Multi-Cultural Education, Institute of Education, University of London.
Marland, M. 1996a. *Intra-Bangladeshi Male Violence.* Unpublished Paper, North Westminster Community School.
Marland, M. 1996b. *School Perspective: The Barriers to Learning for Bengali Young People.* Unpublished conference paper, from Developing Opportunities for Bengali Young People, Education and Leisure Services, Westminster Council.
Modood, T. et al. 1997. *Ethnic Minorities in Britain.* London: Policy Studies Inst.
Office for National Statistics. 1996. *Social Focus on Ethnic Minorities.* London: HMSO.
Shaw, C. 1994. *Changing Lives: Volumes 1/2/3.* London: Policy Studies Institute.
Thrasher, F. M. 1927. *The Gang.* Chicago: University of Chicago Press.
Utting, D. 1996. *Reducing criminality among young people: a sample of relevant programmes in the United Kingdom.* London: Home Office Research and Statistics Directorate: Research Study 161.

CHAPTER 14

Youth Prostitution and Planning for Safer Communities

Lana Burroughs and David Barrett

Introduction

The involvement of young people in prostitution is not new, but what we have seen in recent years within the UK has been youth prostitution receiving increasing attention from a variety of sources. These include the media, the children's charities, some parts of the child protection system and academics. Others have been notable by their silence, namely, government ministers and the DHSS in cases where youth prostitution occurs within the care system or amongst children who are the responsibility of statutory services. However, even they have recently shifted their attention to young people and prostitution, largely as a result of several years of intense lobbying by the children's charities.

Even though there has been a recent shift in understanding, and thus recognition that young people are involved in prostitution on our streets in this country (this chapter is largely concerned with street prostitution rather than off-street saunas, clubs etc.) government ministers have been very slow to acknowledge the problem. That said, it was the Home Office junior minister, Timothy Kirkhope, who highlighted the issue in 1996.

The long term denial of youth prostitution in the UK has been apparent, at the same time as growing attention has been paid to the issue in many third world countries. As a result, little research has been undertaken in the area of youth prostitution in the UK. Some local project-based research has been undertaken but it is not possible to construct a national picture of the prevalence of youth prostitution on the basis of these studies. National data is therefore largely unavailable. However, more and more projects have been undertaken in recent years and they are beginning to give us a sketch of national trends (Barrett, 1997).

Youth, in this context, is a fairly flexible term but is most usefully viewed as referring to people who are under 18, and fall within the definition of a 'child' in the Children Act, 1989. Those people aged eighteen or under who are involved in street prostitution are deemed by the Act to be 'children in need' who are 'at risk' of 'significant harm'. In recent years it has become more generally accepted that young people involved in prostitution should be responded to by the child protection system.

One of the most frequently used definitions of prostitution is: 'the provision of sexual services in exchange for some form of payment, such as money, drink, drugs, other consumer goods or even a bed and a roof over one's head for the night' (Green, 1992). This definition offers a broader and more realistic view of youth prostitution than one which focuses only on financial transactions.

The origins of youth prostitution

What are the origins of youth prostitution? There are many factors contributing to a young person's involvement in prostitution. There are both 'push' and 'pull' factors (Hayes and Trafford, 1997). Conditions at home, family conflict, violent or sexual abuse, may 'push' young people to run away or move on, and this may make the 'pull' of 'street life' more attractive. The links between poverty and abuse are clear (Pitts, 1997). Children who live in neighbourhoods that are in decline may drift into self-destructive behaviour which is unlikely to stop once it has started. Some children point to family strain as a key factor in their decision to take to the streets. These strains include economic shortfalls contributed to by recent changes in benefit levels, or child abuse within a family which forces the child to escape. There are, of course, other perpetrators of abuse, like the pimps, who are particularly skilled at identifying vulnerable young people and filling emotional and material voids in their lives, and the 'punters', apparently 'ordinary' men going about their daily business, but willing to pay an additional premium for sex with children.

The ingredients of youth prostitution include violence, invisibility, denial, harassment, ghettoisation, health risks and the selective use of the law which, in effect, ignores the reality that, more than most other groups, young prostitutes are 'at risk' or in danger of 'significant harm' as defined by current child care legislation. This arena of work is therefore, under-standably, very intimidating for the helping professionals involved.

As with the growing acknowledgement that young people involved in prostitution are being abused, similar changes are taking place in official perceptions of the offences involved in the encounter between the young prostitute and his or her 'client'. It is now more widely accepted that the young people involved are victims of sexual exploitation and not perpetrators of, or accomplices in, criminal offences. This helpfully acknowledges the powerlessness of those young people involved in prostitution, many of whom have been on the receiving end of dis-crimination, poverty, disproportionate health risks or simply services which have, in effect, let them down. This amounts to children being left out and excluded from what is rightfully theirs, an ordinary childhood – a childhood which promotes their welfare and healthy development emotionally, physically and intellectually. To those who argue that some young people 'choose' prostitution, we pose the question 'what other choices did they have?'

Many aspects of professional practice with young prostitutes are contradictory and confused. For example, the criminal and administrative law are applied erratically, some Area Child Protection Committees (ACPC's), do not appear to view child prostitution as child abuse (although this appears to be changing after pressure from the children's charities), and professionals who do engage with the issue feel insecure about their roles. Recent research has given us a far clearer view of the nature of these issues and the ways in which, key agencies might work with the problem (c.f. Bernardos, 1996).

Enhancing our capacity to help

Good ideas for practitioners and government that include practice models, insights and ideas have been offered, recently (Barrett, 1997) Some examples from this source, include, two workers from The Children's Society project in Manchester discussing the skills required for effective street work with young prostitutes; the chapter by a lawyer offers useful guidance to solicitors working with vulnerable and frightened children, while the chapter on health has many creative ideas for health practitioners, including harm minimisation strategies.

What can the government do? It could, de-criminalise youth prostitution, overhaul the Sexual Offences Acts, utilise the Department of Health (DoH) to give proper leadership on the issues via ACPC's etc. These same issues will doubtless be around for some years to come, while young people continue to be exploited. Other proposals emphasise that, those involved in child prostitution have often, slipped through one type of 'safety net' or another, many are from 'in-care' backgrounds and, often, the post-care duties of their local authority have not been fulfilled. Therefore, central government should give urgent consideration to the establishment of a network of foyers in which young people could live and receive support and advice, into their early 20s if necessary. These foyers could, if necessary, be commissioned by central government and run and co-ordinated by the children's charities who, after all, have considerable expertise in this area.

Many individuals and agencies with formal responsibility for their well-being have, nonetheless, consistently let down young people who become involved in prostitution. This is a sad indictment of our child care services.

The young people themselves argue that prostitution is often the best of a bad set of choices available to them and that they remain powerless to make other, real, choices. Some families abuse children and some local and central government departments are not fulfilling their legal responsibilities. Previous denials by statutory agencies about the existence of child prostitution in their areas have looked increasingly dubious and untenable. However, there is some room for optimism. Last year, at the instigation of the children's charities, a multi-agency, national working group was set up. It is heartening, to see that the Association of Directors of Social Services (ADSS), the Association of (Chief Police Officers (ACOP), the DoH, the Crown Prosecution Service (CPS) and the children's charities are meeting to increase the emphasis on the protection of the children involved in prostitution and the prosecution of the adults who abuse them, or profit from exploiting them. The ADSS and ACOP now have position statements on young people and prostitution and they are obtainable from these organisations.

The way ahead

The recommendations below could help to alleviate the problem of youth prostitution and some of the factors associated, with it. They are:

- Local services, including the police and the Crown Prosecution Service, must not be selective in the exercise of their statutory duties and the implementation of their mandatory obligations under the criminal and civil law.

- The Sexual Offences Acts should be amended to be consistent with the Children Act, 1989.

- The criminal law should not be utilised to criminalise young people involved in prostitution; the use of minors as prostitutes should be regarded as child abuse and sentencing should reflect this.

- The statutory responsibilities of local authorities for the post-care support of young people should be observed universally and interpreted generously.

- Helping professionals who work, with young prostitutes should receive additional, specialised, multi-agency education and training in order that they can more effectively mobilise services and resources.

- The school curriculum should be proactive in dealing with questions of sexuality, sexual behaviour and health, recognising that schools can often be a crucial source of support and information for young people involved in prostitution.

- The DoH should take the lead on every aspect of youth prostitution, co-ordinating the activities of other agencies where necessary.

- Extreme social disadvantage should be compensated by targeted benefits aimed at preventing young people entering prostitution out of economic necessity.

- Agencies involved with youth prostitution should recognise the contribution of economic decline and neighbourhood destabilisation to family breakdown, running away and youth prostitution.

- Central government and the voluntary sector should establish a national network of foyers where vulnerable young people can stay and receive advice and support, into their early twenties if necessary.

Youth prostitution on the streets: making it safer

The main players in making the streets safer for young prostitutes are the young people themselves, the local community, the helping professionals including the police, and local and national government. Each of these groups has a clearly demarcated role to discharge but to be effective they must work together.

Young prostitutes can themselves, and sometimes do, work in pairs looking out for one another, especially, where they do not have pimps. They can also practice safe sex and develop this into a harm minimisation strategy, a concept approach used commonly in the drugs field, that includes leaving used condoms or syringes in safe locations such as disposal boxes. These can be a serious health hazard to local adults and children.

Community safety officers can co-ordinate street-level safe sex strategies and/or harm minimisation strategies, used condoms and syringes need collecting, new ones need to be available. Other professionals, for example outreach workers employed by a variety of agencies, can work in pairs with mobile phones, radios or other means of communication (for a fuller discussion of safer professional strategies see Hayes and Trafford 1997).

Punters, whether kerb crawling in cars or on foot are a mixture of voyeurs, 'prospects' and those who are actively seeking sex. Together with the presence of pimps, these men can make an area feel very intimidating, especially after dark. Good street lighting, the recording of car numbers, sometimes by covert video cameras, and the confident presence of helping professionals can counter that feeling. Pimps and punters are dangerous, pimps are notoriously violent and some punters murder prostitutes.

Entire communities can feel intimidated. But spontaneous community action may simply move youth prostitution up the road or into the next square. 'Tolerance zones' or just moving young prostitutes on, is an overly simplistic and ineffective approach to a complex problem. To be effective, the responses of local residents must be fully integrated with those of the professionals operating in the area. These strategies must manage the street culture but provide exit points for those just entering the 'life' and those seeking a way out of it and support of those who feel trapped in it. In addition, such strategies must accord with the ethos of the 1989 Children Act which promotes child welfare and protection rather than punishment or the criminalisation of the behaviour.

The minimum sufficient network for effective implementation

The decriminalisation of youth prostitution, increasing the tariff for those caught abusing children and the consistent implementation and application of both the civil law (for young people), and the criminal law (for the perpetrators), has been consistently argued for. Similarly, an integrated, collaborative inter-agency approach to youth prostitution has been recognised as essential for many years. Perhaps, in some areas, inter-agency cooperation is simply out of the reach of service providers in the face of professional rivalry and competition for scarce resources. However, more optimistically, the mental health field and some parts of the child protection system provide positive examples of how agencies can work well together. Additionally, of course, as we have noted above, the recent period has seen significant collaboration, and a marked change of attitude amongst some of the agencies concerned with youth prostitution.

The demand for integrated services and closer partnership has met with a positive response and with continued positive leadership on the part of the DoH, in particular, further progress seems likely. This will serve to mobilise the multi-agency ACPC's on the issue of youth prostitution in the spirit of the DoH's *Working Together* document. It will also fuel the debate about how local authorities will discharge their responsibilities in relation to the section of the Children Act, 1989, which allows them to provide financial support to vulnerable young people from 'care' beyond the age of 16.

The administrative implications of implementation

As we have already noted, there are many players who should be involved in working with the issue of youth prostitution; some are large organisations like health and education authorities, others can be small like a very small charity or a group of volunteers.

If we take the example of health as an organisational 'case study' we see that young prostitutes have multiple health care needs that are generally poorly addressed by providers. Intervention must be based on a real understanding of the effects of early abuse and deprivation, running away, being in care, illicit drug use and risk behaviour, together with a consideration of young people's views and a frank examination of the worker's own feelings and skills. As we have noted, the statutory framework for child protection can work well but problems exist with the referral process, particularly in relation, to youth prostitution. Outreach and peer education work in which client's needs set the agenda have been successful but they also have limitations. Uptake of health care by drug users, including some young mothers, who are engaged in prostitution, has been poor. For a health authority to meet the needs of these young people is a complex task which will make significant demands upon resources.

The economic implications of implementation

There is evidence that poverty and sexual abuse together, correlate very closely with young people's involvement in prostitution (Pitts, 1997). Youth prostitution is both a survival strategy and a way of exerting control albeit one which requires the neutralisation of formal moral controls and a denial of risk. The period since 1979 has seen neighbourhood decline (Hutton, 1995), a substantial increase in social disadvantage, paralleled by a reduction in residential accommodation, housing and state benefit entitlements for young people (Pitts, 1997). The resultant erosion of citizenship requires development of new forms of social solidarity which include a welfare system characterised by a high degree of social protection as an expression of that solidarity (Hutton, 1995, and Pitts J. in this volume). At the heart of such a welfare approach lies a conception of a just society which combats disadvantage, and offers and educational experience which equips citizens for full economic, social and cultural participation. Such a society confers both rights and obligations which are the cornerstone of social citizenship (Hutton, 1995, 1997).

Current law and policy on youth prostitution

Between 1989 and 1995 the police used criminal legislation to issue 2,380 cautions and 1,730 convictions to young people under 18 for prostitution-related activities. But the existing legislation available to convict adults who use prostitutes requires re-drafting to underscore the seriousness of attempting to have sexual relations with a minor. If young people are regarded as victims, as opposed to perpetrators in these encounters, however, there is ample scope for prosecution under the 1989 Children Act, and established inter-agency child protection procedures are already in place to investigate allegations. However, Alan Levy (1997), argues that the 1989 Act is significantly under-used and that the criminal law is being wrongly targeted at the children, rather than those who are exploiting them. Put simply, administrative law is being under-used and the criminal law is being wrongly used.

Generally, the law relating to prostitution has developed piecemeal and it is often ineffective for the 'policing' of prostitution For example, many argue that cautioning is counter-productive in relation to young people involved in prostitution that prosecution is no deterrent. The challenge to services like the police, health and social services is to develop forms of timely intervention which, without being either oppressive or coercive, investigate a young person's circumstances and develop realistic exit strategies for them (and some punters too). Models of cooperation developed in child abuse cases can be applied, with only slight modification, to young prostitutes, but a comprehensive legislative review is also required. Importantly all of those who have examined the issue of youth prostitution in depth, although they are few in number, are agreed upon the characteristics of an effective legal response to youth prostitution. They are that:

- The criminal law should be reformed and updated.

- Implementation of the criminal law should be consistent and targeted upon punters rather than young people.

- Administrative law should be utilised wherever feasible to protect young people engaged in prostitution.

The implications for professionals working with young prostitutes

Many of the professionals who work on the streets with young prostitutes have received little or no specialist training for the job. Many of the skills developed are a product of experience or borrowed from other, more established, areas of work like youth work and the harm minimisation strategies developed in the drugs field. Some children's charities have made further progress by developing their own models of in-house training (Hayes and Trafford, 1997). Inter-agency and multi-agency training, similar to that developed in child protection, could be utilised or, indeed, that system could be extended to include youth prostitution. Survivors of youth prostitution could assist in any such training, to offer new insights and perspectives from their own experiences.

New initiatives

At the macro-level of government departments and national children's charities we await the outcome of their current deliberations. At the micro-level, local projects and children's charities have, again, been leading the way aided by health promotion projects and other local initiatives. But these are mostly short term and reactive interventions rather than pro-active, long term strategies. However, both Barnardos and the Children's Society have several years experience of monitoring, evaluation and review of the quality and relevance of their youth prostitution services. Consulting young people, the local community and other professional groups; collecting statistical data and fund-raising, are all ingredients of such a longer term strategy. There, is much that other service providers could learn from them.

Conclusion

Developing a community safety strategy for intervention with young prostitutes is unlikely to find many dissenters, but how does it link with strategies to counter other forms of crime and victimisation?

In Luton we have seen the local Crime Reduction Partnership making important connections between crime and adult unemployment, youth unemployment, overcrowded housing and one parent families (Blowers et al. 1992 and Elvin and Marlow in this volume). It also noted the problem of local youth which was summed up as 'Many young people have nowhere to go and no one to care'. The connection with problematic schooling was also made. All these factors are closely associated with youth prostitution. At national level too, debates about crime and safer communities in general are converging with debates about young prostitutes. This congruence of perspective is significant, but no less alarming for that. The concern about youth prostitution must be fully integrated into the mainstream of the national debate if effective long-term solutions are to be devised.

Bibliography

Audit Commission, (1996), *Misspent Youth, Young People and Crime*, Audit Commission, London.

Barnardos (1996) *Streets and Lanes (SAL's) Annual Report* April 1995, Barnardos, London.

Barrett, D. (ed.) (1997) *Child Prostitution in Britain: Dilemmas and Practical Responses*, The Children's Society, London.

Blowers, G. Southwell, C. and Marlow, A. (1992), *The Luton Partnership*, Luton Borough Council.

Farrington D. (1996) *Understanding and Preventing Youth Crime*, Joseph, Rowntree Foundation, York.

Green, J. (1992) *It's No Game*, National Youth Agency, Leicester.

Hayes, C. and Trafford, I. (1997) 'Issues for voluntary sector detached work agencies', Barrett D (ed.), *Child Prostitution in Britain: Dilemmas and Practical Responses*, The Children's Society, London.

Hutton, W. (1995) *The State We're In*, Jonathan Cape, London.

Hutton, W. (1997) *The State To Come*, Vintage, London.

Levy, A. (1997) Abused and Exploited, *The Times*, 29 April, p 41.

Liddel, A. and Gelsthorpe, L. (1994) *Inter-Agency Crime Prevention: Organising Local Delivery*, Police Research Group Crime Prevention Unit Series, Paper 52, London, The Home Office.

Pitts, J. (1997) Causes of youth prostitution, new forms of practice and political responses, Barrett D. (ed.) *Child Prostitution in Britain: Dilemmas and Practical Responses*, The Children's Society, London.

Tilley, N. (1992) *Safe Cities and Community Safety Strategies*, Police Research Group Crime Prevention Unit Series, Paper 38, The Home Office.

CHAPTER 15

Community Safety, Crime and Disorder

Tim Hope

Is 'crime prevention' an end in itself or a means to the end of achieving community safety – and if so, what is community safety? Obviously, in as much as victimisation, criminality and disorder threaten people's well-being, life-style and life-chances then the prevention of crime will create community safety. But are the interests of the various parties to crime – the State, victims, the community and potential offenders – always the same; is 'community safety' the aggregation of these interests into a 'common good' acceptable to all – or is the construction of community safety contestable, involving sometimes incompatible ends and conflicts of interest?

In some way related to this is another issue: since crime prevention has not been seen hitherto as an explicit purpose of government – at least not in the same way as health-care, education, social security or personal social services – we do not have a specific set of services and practices in place to pursue crime prevention. So, do we seek to design *new* institutions, programmes and practices to address specific manifestations of crime and disorder; or should we rather look at the way we presently govern and administer our services and interventions and seek reform where such activities seem manifestly criminogenic? If local government is to have a statutory responsibility for community safety – if community safety is to become acknowledged as a public good – community safety officers and committees in local government administration will need to ask themselves such questions.

Crime prevention covers a considerable range of activities. Likewise, the term 'community safety' means many things. However, I want to take the term literally – and to look at safety in communities, especially those which seem unsafe. When we look at a community – or a school – with a high degree of crime or disorder, is this because it contains a large number of 'individual risky people' – so that, say, if some of those people were 'treated' within, or removed from, the community then the community's problems would diminish proportionately. Or are high community crime rates a consequence of the 'social structural position of the community' relative to others, and of the pattern of relationships within them – so that it is necessary to change the structure of the community itself – or its position within society – in order to reduce its high crime risk. In other words, when we are striving for community safety, are we seeking to change individuals or to change communities and institutions?

To illustrate these issues, it may be helpful to go over some of the history of 'disorder' in the past twenty-five years – at least so we might see where we are coming from.

Disorder, prevention and community

Currently, disorder is in the news: anti-disorder, 'zero tolerance' policing is claimed to be a raging success from New York to Middlesbrough – and the police can hold their heads and truncheons high once more. For the first time, the forthcoming Bill from the Government will be entitled the *Crime and Disorder Bill* – and it will also provide local authorities with a battery of civil powers, including a new Community Safety Order, which will allow civil courts to issue orders at local authority behest which might potentially exclude or ban people from particular communities; an approach pioneered in the London Borough of Hackney and seen as a means of protecting people from their neighbours' predations[1]. So, what is this disorder?

Actually, the problem of 'disorder' has been with us for quite a time. Indeed, in one way or another, it can be seen as the exemplary case for the development of crime prevention theory and practice (Clarke and Mayhew, 1980). And it is instructive to look back over its short history to illustrate how messages about community safety move back and forth between research and practice. Back in the early 1970s, disorder was called 'vandalism'. Almost before the last slab of preformed concrete had been placed upon the last tower-block – and the last tile stuck precariously onto the last city centre shopping precinct – the newly created urban environment was being marked by what we have now learnt to call 'signs of disorder' – especially damaged public property and graffiti. Right from the start 'vandalism' came to symbolise a variety of public issues. Initially, there were those who wanted to *individualise* the problem – to find the 'mindless vandal', the anti-social element responsible for public despoliation and, according to their proclivity, punish or correct them (cf. Kellmer-Pringle, 1973). Yet this view was soon overtaken by other messages from the world of research.

Perhaps because of its mundanity, its visibility, and its seeming inseparability from the routines and locales of everyday life, sociologists began to see vandalism as an exemplar of what might be called the 'normalization of deviance' – rather than being an exceptional behaviour, vandalism could be understood as a consequence of routines and activities of everyday life – especially those concerning the play and leisure opportunities of the youthful inhabitants of the new public environment[2.]

Yet vandalism has always played a powerful symbolic role. In the 1970s, it stood as a symptom – or indictment – of the processes of urban planning and design which had been created – largely by public authorities – out of the massive post-war programme of urban change and redevelopment. Thus, vandalism was not to be seen as a 'youth problem' – certainly not in any culture of mindless destruction amongst anti-social youth – but as an 'environmental problem'. Consequently, the remedy for vandalism was to be found in changing the environment – to bring about a better fit between the built environment and those who inhabited it. And there were various approaches which emerged. Oscar Newman's book *Defensible Space* (1973) captured the public imagination because it seemed to point directly to ways in which physical design might be implicated, not least in articulating a public mood which had already begun to become disenchanted with modernism – in architecture, social planning, and so on[3].

The environmentalism of *Defensible Space* also helped usher-in an approach rooted in behavioural psychology – now known as 'situational crime prevention' – which saw the best prospects for crime prevention as seeking to alter the physical environment so as to reduce opportunities for crime and to increase risks (Clarke and Mayhew, 1980). Again, this was an approach which saw the criminal employing an understandable, everyday calculus of decision-making – obviating the need for any special motivation or background circumstance (Clarke and Cornish, 1986). Yet whatever the behavioural basis for this explanation of crime, it had an important practical advantage: it offered the prospect of 'designing out crime' through the employment of relatively cheap, seemingly uncontentious and above all 'technical' remedies for social problems. Moreover, unlike the purely physical and mechanistic approaches of conventional security measures – of locks, bars and alarms – these remedies were to be firmly grounded in a sophisticated 'behavioural science', promising greater efficiency and effectiveness.

Situational crime prevention did not emerge in a vacuum, nor was it the first time that social scientists had offered solutions to the problems of crime. Indeed, situational crime prevention was seized upon by many as a solution to the previous solutions, offering an alternative to what had been seen as the previous decades' failures of prevention. In particular, this included the efforts at change through community action and development – the 'Great Society' Programmes in America, the Community Development Projects in Britain, all of which had become mired in conflict[4]. Community activists – whose diagnosis of delinquency became entwined with a broader critique of inequality and what seemed then to be the new phenomenon of de-industrialisation – stepped into irreconcilable conflict with local politicians, essentially over the legitimacy of local politics[5]. The Home Office and the 1970s Labour Government were traumatised (Loney, 1983) – if the solution to the crime problems could not be found in criminal justice, it would certainly not be found in local political activism.

Situational crime prevention offered a way out – it was both technical and managerial. It involved rational planning and would hopefully require the minimum of human agency in its implementation. Done properly it could avoid the fortress society and provide a means whereby crime would simply not emerge. And it offered a means of doing more while spending less (Hope, 1995a). Local authorities were to be in the forefront of much of this activity. Many of the problems of disorder, vandalism, and so on were seen as problems of the 'public sphere' – they occurred in public and were thought to symbolise something about public life. And local authorities still retained ownership and statutory authority for much of the public sphere as well. The general mood at the time was one of caution – we might have made some mistakes with the public environment but with careful attention to detail we could begin to correct them; above all, 'there was no need to worry about crime' – there may seem to be a lot of it around but this was mostly trivial vandalism which could be cleaned-up; there were no serious social or community problems behind it, nor were those involved in it exceptional, worrying or threatening people[6].

Yet, there was also a growing sense of unease – for what had also begun to emerge by the late 1970s was the phenomenon of the 'problem estate'. These were places which, despite often having only recently been established, were tremendously unpopular with their present and prospective residents. Again, the problem was seen as one of 'image' – these were places which looked uncared for, and where no one had much incentive to exercise concern or maintain standards. Many argued that along with the great expansion of mass public housing there had grown up a bureaucracy of housing management which was remote and inefficient. Repair services, cleaning and estate maintenance were not being delivered, children's play spilled over into vandalism, residents became disempowered and demoralised – and voted with their feet to get out of these places if they could[7].

The solution was to devolve local services – to make housing management more sensitive to the needs and demands of residents – literally, to repair the 'broken windows' as soon as they got broken lest they encouraged more damage, to clean-up estates and to create symbols that estates were well-cared for, and that residents were concerned and would exercise control over their home environment. Much of this may now seem common place in local authorities but it formed the basis for the drive towards estate improvement schemes throughout the 1980s – some of it encouraged by the Department of the Environment and carried out by local authorities on their own properties, though with the guidance and stimulus of external change agents including NACRO, Safe Neighbourhoods Unit, and the Priority Estates Project[8].

For a while, there seemed to be some successes, especially amongst the high-rise tower blocks which had been the sites of disorder in the 1970s: families with young children were no longer housed in them – a prevention policy, by the way, clearly supported by research[9], their common areas had been cleaned, a variety of entry-phone and concierge systems installed to protect residents, and they were popular with older people[10]. Estates were better maintained, and the worst designed sites for vandalism removed. Moreover, tenant involvement schemes also seemed to be pointing the way – especially in the procedures developed for consultation and resident management. And they also unlocked considerable potential for community leadership – especially amongst local women (Campbell, 1993; Rock, 1988).

In all this effort, the central theme was that residents and local authorities could be brought together to participate in the common purpose of making their environments a better place to live. And although crime prevention was never acknowledged as the primary aim of this work, the underlying belief was that the quality of life on these estates – including their community safety – could be enhanced by making them worthwhile and valuable environments. *And that still meant, primarily, improving the material environment of dwelling and estate.* Still, by tackling the signs of vandalism and disorder, an incentive would be developed for community life. Through both the practice of tenant management and in taking greater pride in their environments, the estates would increase in value in the eyes of their tenants who would then be encouraged to stay. The communities on such estates would thus begin to *stabilise*: and out of this stability could grow the kinds of 'informal social controls' which would sustain harmonious relations amongst residents and low rates of internecine victimisation[11].

The concentration of crime and poverty

Yet things started to go wrong during the 1980s on the public estates. It is now apparent, from research evidence assembled by the Joseph Rowntree Foundation *Inquiry into Income and Wealth* that we have seen a substantial concentration of poverty in local communities, particularly in the public housing sector. And because of the way that the new public environment was constructed, this showed up as a 'substantial overlap between areas with high dependence on Income Support and areas predominantly of council estates' (JRF, 1995; Vol. 2, p 93).

Writing about the growth and concentration of poverty in the ghettos of America, William Julius Wilson has pointed to three contributory factors (Wilson, 1987). Similar processes can be seen in this country (Hope, 1996):

Concentration of socially-vulnerable groups
In general, the combination of economic restructuring and the residualisation of public housing has concentrated low income groups together, creating particularly a gender/age mix of poverty – involving unemployed young men, female-headed lone parent households, and the elderly. What might be thought of as the structure of the 'new poverty'.

Political isolation
Those with more personal resources are the ones who sustain voluntary community activities. Amongst other things, right-to-buy and transfer schemes may have served as a mechanism for siphoning-off from the worst estates those families who may otherwise have formed the pool of political and community leadership or voluntary activism – not only serving through local residents' associations but also acting as a conduit to local political leadership in articulating the needs of their communities.

Economic isolation
The spatial isolation of these estates on the periphery – and the departure of employment opportunities from inner city locations – has not only reduced employment opportunities generally but severed young people's informal networks leading towards sustained permanent employment that so much characterised industrial life. In particular this has problematised entry into the labour market[12].

But how has this resulted in crime and disorder? Our recent analysis of the *British Crime Survey* shows that victimisation from crime is highly unequally distributed amongst residential communities in England and Wales[13]. Areas with the top 10 per cent of crime rates have *over a third* of all property crime. Over half of all property crime is distributed amongst 20 per cent of communities. Conversely, the least affected half of the country only experiences 15 per cent of the crime. Respective shares of violent criminal victimisation are even more sharply drawn (Hope, 1997). And during the 1980s, regional and area inequalities in crime victimisation increased (Trickett et al., 1995). The risk of victimisation – especially of repeat victimisation – became much more unequal between communities.

Further, our analysis shows that the key characteristics of the highest crime communities are:

1. the lack of economic resources of neighbourhood residents:
2. the predominance of rental housing tenure; and
3. their demographic structure, including above average concentrations of people under 25 years, lone-parent households, and single-person households.

Importantly, the risk of victimisation is increased for individual households not only if they live in areas with these characteristics but also additionally if they possess them themselves. Both the distribution of victimisation and the characteristics of high crime communities, also suggest that 'crime victimisation may be concentrating in residential areas alongside the concentration of poverty and deprivation'.

But what implications has all this for the practice of community safety? The survey data also reveal that the high crime rates in these areas are accompanied by other things:

* the greater likelihood of repeat victimisation in high crime areas

* the greater worry amongst residents about their risk of crime victimisation

* their greater likelihood of reporting a range of disorders as 'big problems' in their communities

* their greater likelihood of thinking that most crimes in their neighbourhood are committed by local people rather than outsiders

The data just reviewed suggest two possibilities:

* that the concentration of the 'new poverty' in particular communities is related – indeed, may even be 'causing' – the concentration of crime and victimisation

- that these are being accompanied by an increase in more visible signs of 'social dislocation' (Wilson, 1987), chief amongst these being the salience of 'disorder'.

Crudely, the emerging public policy response to these twin manifestations seems to be involving a choice of emphasis between, to use a well-worn but successful slogan, being 'tough on crime' or 'tough on the cause of crime'. What we may now be seeing in public policy is a marked shift in the way that disorder in communities is being thought about and acted upon. As I have described, the earlier phase of thinking about disorder saw it as primarily an 'environmental problem' – one that placed responsibility on the environment in which people lived. The remedy was thus to strengthen the environment – either directly by physical alterations, or indirectly through the process of community-participation. Either way, a better environment would lead to a stable community, and a stable community would lead to more order, more cohesion, more defended space, and less crime.

Yet the changes occurring in many communities since the 1980s, which I have just described, may also be the context for a new response to disorder emerging in public policy. In the Home Office legislation emerging from the recently-elected Labour Government, the choice of emphasis seems to be settling rather more upon toughness about crime than about its causes[14]. Here, the problem of disorder is being redefined as a 'problem of communities' – a problem of the social relations within communities.

Zero tolerance and democracy

Yet it makes a crucial difference whether the community problem itself is conceptualised as one which is primarily about *individuals* or one that is about *collectivities* – that is, about 'relationships between individuals'. A clear, unifying theme of current policy measures is the idea of 'internal predation' – the victimisation and harassment of residents by co-residents. And following from this, the evidence from research is being interpreted as supporting the idea that the problem of order in residential communities is one of individuals. This is evident both in the way in which policies about repeat victimisation and the Community Safety Order are developing.

Repeat victimisation
The findings from survey research seem to provide compelling evidence that the greatest preventive gains can be made by directing efforts towards repeat victims. If they are somehow protected, cocooned, or removed from risk, then this will have a substantial impact on community crime rates.

And the argument has compelling grounds that preventive resources are being targeted on the most deserving and those most in need[15].

However, for any resource to be targeted, there has to be some 'selection criteria' – some way of distinguishing those who should receive the targeted benefit. Yet so far, the only two things we know with much certainty from the research are:

1. that repeat victims are to be found in communities where there are a lot of victims; and
2. that the only predictor we have that someone will be a repeat victim is that they have already been victimised, and that this predictiveness wears-off quite rapidly over time.

Now, this could be seen in two ways: that communities are high-crime communities because they contain high-risk people, or that people are high risk because they live in particular communities. The present Home Office policy seems to think the former, and is thus seeking to bring down community crime rates by doing something about high-risk people. What is clear is that the rate of victimisation is higher in some communities than others – that is, victimisation is more likely and frequent – but it is certainly not clear whether the policy of cocooning individuals would bring about lasting reductions. Much depends on what one thinks is driving the rate of victimisation. Is it, for example, the persistent vulnerability of certain victims, the persistent determination of certain, repeat offenders, or the structure of the community – including persistent youth unemployment and drug use, which may be leading those involved to escalate their rate of offending? In all the research we are not at present much clearer as to which of these it might be.

Person-based disorder
Similarly, the issue of disorder is increasingly becoming one associated with *people* rather than the environment. At the end of the 1980s, Janet Foster and I studied the effects of the Priority Estates Project improvement schemes (Foster and Hope, 1993). On both of the estates which we studied, we found residents reporting fewer 'environmental disorders' – i.e. residents were ceasing to see vandalism, graffiti, litter, and so on as problems on their estate – presumably as a result of PEP's efforts including clean-up campaigns, better caretaking, tenant involvement, and so on. Yet there were also increases in residents' perceptions of 'disorders associated with people' including disturbances from youths, noisy neighbours, people hanging around drinking, and so on. However, it was not clear whether this collective change of perception signified a displacement of anxiety – or

shift in tolerance – towards those, primarily person-based, disorders which remained after the PEP improvements, or an actual increase in such disorders as a consequence of changes in the social mix of the estates which occurred simultaneously (Foster and Hope, 1993). Yet, on neither estate did residents' anxieties about being out on the estate increase, nor their worries about becoming victims of crime. And, overall, crime victimisation rates had not increased either. Certainly, these estates were going through a process of considerable de-stabilisation – including a concentration of the young poor, and an increasing concentration of victimisation amongst them (Hope, 1995b). However, the kind of dramatic rise in fear and deterioration had not occurred.

Recently, the American criminologist Ralph Taylor has argued that the research evidence suggests that 'the bulk of the causes of people's fear of crime arise from differences between residents responding to the same community conditions' (Taylor, 1997). People are certainly worried about crime victimisation, and may feel generally insecure and dissatisfied, but these feelings stem from more obvious sources – their actual recent experience of victimisation, or their reactions to the social instability of their community. But generally, there seems no uniformly fearful reaction to the signs of disorder.

These findings have two implications for the evolving debate about zero tolerance policing or Community Safety Orders:

1. that efforts to crack down on disorder – particularly focused on individuals' behaviour – may not have much effect on feelings of community safety unless they are accompanied by efforts also to address the 'material sources' of insecurity. The actual experience of crime victimisation may be one of them, but the destabilisation of communities would seem to be another powerful source of insecurity.

2. that 'tolerance' is not uni-directional. And this raises a complicated issue – though one which any policy of community safety may have to resolve, especially if it seeks to respond to the fear of 'internal predation'. On the one hand, it would not seem right to deny people protection from those who are directly disturbing or preying upon them. Yet on the other hand, it would neither be just to crack-down on people – especially the young – who have come to symbolise, in the minds of their fellow-residents, the social ills of their community, regardless of whether they are actually constituting much of a direct threat to others – even if they may be harming themselves.

And here, of course, we come back to a perennial issue which has exercised criminologists – the balance of justice, and the blaming and scapegoating of people for material conditions not of their choosing. This is also, of course, one of the litmus tests of governance and democracy. In taking on responsibility for ensuring community safety, local authorities are ultimately taking on responsibility for justice. The reality of crime victimisation on high crime estates involves the predation of one set of residents upon another. The criminal justice response is to exclude one from the other, through arrest and custody. Mirroring criminal justice, the hybrid power of the community safety order now also provides local authorities with an opportunity for exclusion. Yet, short of custody, local authorities may not be able to resolve the problem of justice on high crime estates so readily. For in as much as they are representative, democratic institutions, they are also custodians of the public good within their entire jurisdictions – and in practical terms have social and legal responsibilities not just for the victimised but for the victimisers – and their families – as well. The 'problem families', 'noisy neighbours', and 'delinquent youth' are residents and citizens as well, invoking both rights and statutory responsibilities from those who govern them locally. In this sense, then, the responsibility for community safety which local authorities now wish to take upon themselves, will also be a responsibility of governance and of justice. Perhaps as democratic institutions they are better placed than some within the criminal justice system. But there should also be no hiding from the fact that community safety is a *public duty* which is being placed upon them.

Notes

1. See LGA/LGMB, 1997, p 39.
2. See particularly contributions to Ward (1973).
3. See, especially, Jacobs (1962) and Harvey (1990).
4. For a discussion of the criminological significance of these programmes see Hope (1995).
5. There is a considerable literature on the politics of these programmes. See, inter alia, Marris and Rein (1972), Moynihan (1969), and Loney (1983).
6. For an example of this view see Hough and Mayhew, 1983; and for a critique see, inter alia, Young (1986).
7. See Power (1987a), Department of the Environment (1981).
8. See Power (1987a,b), NACRO (1989).
9. See Clarke (1978).
10. Safe Neighbourhoods Unit (1993).
11. For a discussion of this theory see Hope, 1995.
12. For interpretation of the criminogenic consequences of this transformation see McGahey (1986), Sullivan (1989), Hagan (1993).
13. Much of the following analysis – based on data from the British Crime Survey – has been carried out by the Quantitative Criminology Group, co-ordinated by Alan Trickett at the University of Manchester. References to research supporting the findings set out below can be found in Hope (1996, 1997).

14. At the time of writing, the Home Office White Paper (consultation document) for the forthcoming Crime and Disorder Bill, is awaiting publication; but see the Home Secretary's Address to a policing conference in June 1997 (Home Office Press Release, 149/97, 25 June 1997; available at http://www.homeoffice.gov.uk).
15. National Board for Crime Prevention (1994).

Bibliography

Campbell Beatrix (1993) *Goliath*. London: Methuen.

Clarke R. V. (ed.) (1978) *Tackling Vandalism*. Home Office Research Study No. 47. London: HMSO.

Clarke R. V. and Mayhew P. (1980) (eds.) *Designing out Crime*. London: HMSO.

Cornish D. B. and Clarke R. V. (1986) *The Reasoning Criminal*. New York: Springer-Verlag.

Department of the Environment (1981) *An Investigation of Difficult to Let Housing*. HDD Occasional Papers: 3/80 (Volume 1 – General Findings), 4/80 (Volume 2 – Case Studies of Post War Estates), 5/80 (Volume 3 – Case Studies of Pre-War Estates). London: HMSO.

Foster J. and Hope T. (1993) Housing, *Community and Crime: the Impact of the Priority Estates Project*. Home Office Research Study No. 131. London: HMSO.

Hagan J. (1993) 'The social embeddedness of crime and unemployment'. *Criminology*, 31, pp 465–491.

Harvey D. (1990) *The Condition of Postmodernity*. Oxford: Blackwell.

Hope T. (1997) Inequality and the Future of Community Crime Prevention, in Lab S. P. (ed.) *Crime Prevention at a Crossroads*. American Academy of Criminal Justice Sciences Monograph Series, Cincinnati, OH, Anderson Publishing.

Hope T. (1996) 'Communities, crime and inequality in England and Wales'. In T. Bennett (ed.) *Preventing Crime and Disorder: Targeting Strategies and Responsibilities*. Cambridge: Institute of Criminology.

Hope T. (1995a) 'Community Crime Prevention'. In M. Tonry and D. P. Farrington (eds.) *Building a Safer Society: Strategic Approaches to Crime Prevention*. Crime and Justice, vol. 19. Chicago: University of Chicago Press.

Hope T. (1995b) 'The flux of victimization'. *British Journal of Criminology*, 35, 327–342.

JRF (1995) *Joseph Rowntree Foundation Inquiry into Income and Wealth*. Volumes 1 and 2. York: Joseph Rowntree Foundation.

Kellmer-Pringle M. (1973) *The Roots of Violence and Vandalism*. London: National Children's Bureau.

Loney M. (1983) *Community Against Government*. London: Heinemann Educational Books.

Marris P. and Rein M. (1972) *Dilemmas of Social Reform*. Harmondsworth: Penguin Books.

McGahey R. M. (1986) 'Economic conditions, neighbourhood organization and urban crime'. In Reiss A. J. and Tonry M. (eds.) *Communities and Crime*. Chicago: University of Chicago Press.

Moynihan, D. P. (1969) *Maximum Feasible Misunderstanding*. New York: The Free Press.

NACRO (1989) *Crime Prevention and Community Safety: a Practical Guide for Local authorities*. London: National Association for the Care and Resettlement of Offenders.

National Board for Crime Prevention (1994). *Wise After the Event: Tackling Repeat victimisation*. London: Home Office.

Newman O. (1973) *Defensible Space*. London: Architectural Press.

Power A. (1987a) *Property Before People*. London: Allen and Unwin.

Power A. (1987b) *The PEP Guide to Local Management*. Volume 1: The PEP Model. Volume 2: The PEP Experience. Volume 3: Guidelines for Setting Up New Projects. London: Department of the Environment.

Rock P. (1988) 'Crime reduction initiatives on problem estates'. In Hope T. and Shaw M. (eds.) *Communities and Crime Reduction*. London: HMSO.

Sullivan M. L. (1989) *'Getting Paid': youth crime and work in the inner city*. Ithaca, NY: Cornell University Press.

Safe Neighbourhoods Unit (1993). *Crime Prevention on Council Estates*. Department of the Environment. London: HMSO.

Taylor R. (1997) 'Crime, grime and responses to crime: relative impacts of neighbourhood structure in *Crime Prevention at a Crossroads*. Academy of Criminal Justice Sciences, Monograph, Cincinatti, OH: Anderson Publishing.

Trickett A., Ellingworth D., Hope T. and Pease K. (1995) Crime victimization in the eighties. *British Journal of Criminology*, 35, 343–359.

Wilson W. J. (1987) *The Truly Disadvantaged*. Chicago: University of Chicago Press.

Young J. (1986) 'The failure of criminology: the need for radical realism'. In Matthews R. and Young J. (eds.) *Confronting Crime*. London: Sage.

CHAPTER 16

Community Safety in High Crime Neighbourhoods: a View from the Street

Karen Evans

Introduction

In 1997 the new Labour government made clear its commitment to ensuring that crime prevention would become a statutory duty of local government[1.] In the light of this commitment local authority personnel up and down Britain[2] were charged with the writing of corporate community safety strategies. The stated aim of these strategies will most probably be that of delivering planned reductions in their city's crime figures. At the same time recent research suggests that these personnel will be working in a context of comparatively high national rates of crime[3]. But should the focus of the community safety strategy be on crime or community? This paper is based on research[4] which suggests that, to be successful in achieving their overall aims and objectives, community safety strategies must take account of the specific dynamics operating within the communities to which they are to be applied[5].

Writing the community safety strategy

It is accepted practice, informed by previous examples and a variety of guidance pamphlets and manuals[6], that a city's or an area's community safety strategy should be informed by a local crime audit and the formation of a locally constituted multi-agency panel which can put into place the mechanisms by which the strategy can then be taken forward. The crime audit will typically be delivered by an organisation outside the local authority – either a national body such as Crime Concern or Safe Neighbourhoods Unit or a local research organisation or academic institution. The body of data so collected will then be used to help shape a locally relevant strategy for crime prevention which will be delivered over the ensuing years by local agencies working together with community groups and residents. Given this emphasis on local knowledge and experience and on local delivery mechanisms, it is somewhat surprising that the resulting strategies will often look so very similar.

Of course it is true that many of the issues which concern one inner-city neighbourhood will be faced by many others and that nationally felt problems are manifested at the local level. It is also inevitable that national concerns and priorities will affect local areas and will necessarily feed into local outlooks and attitudes. Furthermore, it is also increasingly recognised that problems which were once considered the preserve of the inner-city area can now affect other deprived areas in rural locations or out-of-town estates. In this respect, therefore, the similar nature and concerns of these strategies, especially when they relate to similarly structured areas, is not particularly noteworthy. However, it is important that these strategies do not miss the local dimension. In particular, delivery mechanisms must be effective at the local level and it is here, above all, that a community safety strategy must include an understanding of specific local relationships as well as being able to address the wider concerns of a local area. This emphasis on the locality may seem straightforward enough to local practitioners involved in the delivery services to a neighbourhood but in reality it entails getting to grips with an often complex set of interrelationships. I will argue here, that a focus on crime and crime reduction may obscure differences between communities, rather than illuminate them.

The centrality of crime or community?

Currently community safety strategies focus on the needs of the different client groups within a neighbourhood. The community safety gaze, and therefore subsequent practice, is informed by those debates which have emphasised the many different lived experiences which can coexist in an area at any one time and which are held by different social groups. So community safety strategies will acknowledge the different perceptions of an area's safety and differential levels of fear held by the elderly and the youthful population, for example, or the specific personal safety concerns of many women and ethnic minority groups.

The crime audits which inform local strategies are often based around a display and discussion of recorded crime statistics as they are presented over time and geographical location. There is a discussion of the prevalence and incidence of these and the more hidden and less well recorded crimes[7] and incidents which occur throughout the area. This data is then likely to be supplemented by a discussion of how crime and the fear of crime affect particular social groups. Problems are prioritised from a local perspective and possible solutions adopted and appraised.

The drawback of this audit-strategy-options model is that its focus has been on crime, rather than community, and it has thereby tended to define an area's problems from a partial and in many ways static viewpoint – for example this approach may demonstrate that an area is, or has become, a high crime area but may not lead to any greater understanding of the processes which contributed to this slide – and therefore will be unable to present any clues as to what can be attempted in order to 'rescue' the area.

During the 1980s there was a move to embrace the notion of 'community safety', rather than 'crime prevention', this move acknowledged the vital role of inter-agency co-operation in delivering effective crime reduction initiatives. Also implicit in this move was a recognition that 'Just as the incidence of crime can affect the whole community, so too its prevention is a task for the community'.[8] However, at the same time belief in the centrality of community in people's lives was waning in other quarters – note Margaret Thatcher's famous denunciation of society and emphasis on the individual – and within many local authorities an emphasis on community development was also waning. So community safety strategies have also suffered from a lack of connection with the communities to which they are to be applied. Existing community safety strategies have often failed to key into the very specific dynamics of an area. This process involves more than an analysis of local crime figures and trends and of indicators of economic and social deprivation, but should also entail gaining an understanding of the locality's social history, its position in relation to other areas of the city or region and its past history of community involvement. It should involve an understanding that relationships within an area are not static, that they have changed in the past and will do so again in the future. It should also acknowledge that the neighbourhood may lie somewhere on a particular trajectory of change which has contributed to its current position as a high or low crime area and that this position can greatly affect the ability of the area's residents to respond to local interventions.

Community safety, personal safety and the fear of crime – The research project

From 1994 to 1996 researchers based at the University of Salford and the University of Keele embarked on research into two similarly structured neighbourhoods in the same city in the North of England. The research set out to situate an understanding of the risk from and fear of crime in a comparative, urban context – to uncover how people who live and work in designated 'high-crime' areas manage their day to day lives and construct their own responses to 'risk of' and 'fear of' crime. The two areas chosen for the study were inner-city wards (to anonymise these places they have been named Oldtown and Bankhill) both of which were seen as areas of high deprivation, sharing many characteristics and indicators of poverty with other areas of British cities which might be said to be 'in crisis' Increasingly the research began to focus on the dynamics of what might be called 'community' within the two wards.

The research methodology utilised various data collection techniques including ethnographic field work as well as a more traditional survey of residents and organisations in both areas and a series of focus group discussions with local people and police officers. Although crime statistics for the two areas were collected, it was only in the last six months of the research that a detailed analysis of recorded crime statistics in both wards was attempted. In this respect then, it was not a crime-focused piece of work. The approach was very different to that outlined earlier as being typical of the crime audit – instead the methodology adopted placed primary importance on the lay perceptions of both the areas and its community make-up. The starting point for the research was neighbourhood, voluntary organisation and community. The study of these wards did include an analysis of the place which crime played in these localities but other aspects of living in the localities were allowed to form an equally important dimensions to the research.

The methodology and viewpoint adopted allowed some very interesting findings to emerge. The two research sites, although seemingly so similar when official indicators were chosen to measure their position within the city, and although geographically so close (they were less than two miles apart) actually exhibited very different responses to their situation. In the light of these findings it became clear that we were researching two very different areas, suggesting that crime prevention and community safety initiatives must be sensitive to these differences, involving the communities at very different levels and utilising quite clearly dissimilar techniques of intervention.

There were a number of examples of difference between Oldtown and Bankhill which lead to this conclusion – three of which are discussed below:

(1) Its residents' experience of crime
(2) The area's relationship to the city
(3) The area's trajectory of decline

Although discussed in three separate sections, it will become obvious to the reader that the three sections are closely linked to each other and inform each other's perspective.

(1) Its residents' experience of crime
Although the recorded crime statistics for both of these areas suggested a

similar experience of crime in both wards we soon found that this was not the case. The crime which took place in Oldtown was directed principally against businesses and new-built properties on the outskirts of the ward, or involved the driving and dumping of cars which had been stolen from elsewhere. So although residents might see crime taking place they were less often directly the victims of it themselves. A local criminal gang was known to operate from an estate in the heart of the ward. It operated under a code which was described to us as 'People don't take off their own'. Established residents of this area would tell us that they felt, in some way, protected by this gang's code and told us:

'It's safe for locals but not strangers in the area', and
'I've no real problems because I know the people and the area and grew up with the local villains and know local youths'.

This is not to say that all residents felt equally protected, and from all forms of crime, or that they wholeheartedly endorsed the activities of the gang, however they were aware that if they obeyed certain rules, especially that of not grassing, that they could possess a sense of immunity from certain crimes such as the theft of their property whilst on the estate and much petty crime and vandalism.

In Bankhill, however, crime did directly affect residents' lives on a daily basis. In this ward there was no sense that anyone was immune from crime and there was a feeling that the area's residents had been left unprotected and vulnerable. The threat of criminal victimisation hung over, and greatly affected, the lives of all those residents to whom we spoke during the research. It was felt that this threat came from others living in the same area or street. As one police officer described it:

"The people in this area have no trust even of their own sons".

Some community groups were forced to operate on a covert basis, only informing the neighbours whom they could trust of their planned meetings, and arranging venues outside of their area so that the existence of the group would not be discovered and jeopardised.

(2) The area's relationship to the city
Oldtown was considered to be an infamous trouble-spot within the city. This ward received a great deal of media attention especially after one night of disturbances in 1992 which came to be characterised in the popular imagination as a night of riots. Partly due to this local notoriety and partly due to prevailing conditions in the area, the ward had received much political attention. Estates Action money was secured to improve the physical fabric of the locality and a prestigious business and residential

development replaced the disused docklands. The area therefore stayed very much in the public eye, both as an area of regeneration and new possibilities and co-incidentally, as an area of decline and disorder.

The problems of Bankhill, on the other hand, went largely unnoticed and unremarked by the media. During 1992 similar disturbances to those in Oldtown were reported but did not receive the same prominence and attention. By 1994 however the area was beginning to gain a reputation as an area of high crime and disorder. It was included in a successful bid for Single Regeneration Budget funds in 1995 and work then commenced to try to reverse the area's decline.

In both areas community-led residents' groups were active in the locality. In Oldtown residents strove to rescue the reputation of their area, recognising that a positive image was necessary to attract business and residents back to the neighbourhood. In Bankhill local groups felt that they must fight to get the problems in their area recognised and onto the public and political agenda.

(3) The area's trajectory of decline
Oldtown was an area with a history which encompassed both disorder and difference. Its location near the city's docks gave it a reputation as a hard-working, hard-playing area of drinking and prostitution, but also as somewhat exotic – playing host as it did to visitors from all over the world. When the docks declined in the late 1970s and finally shut, the area came to be perceived as merely hard, somewhat removed from the rest of the city (not helped by its geographical isolation) but also as of the city, an important part of its once proud industrial history. The reputation of this area is therefore inextricably bound up with that of the city in which it is located – this may well add to the attention which it is given. The problems of the area are seen as very much bound up with the area's economic decline, which is long-standing and has been borne, therefore, throughout the 1980s and 1990s.

Bankhill, at the time of the research, was a once-proud area going rapidly downhill. This area of large Georgian and Victorian detached and semi-detached housing, alongside smaller terraced properties, had shifted from being a desirable place to live, in which a 2–3 bedroom terraced house would sell for over £30,000 in the housing boom of the late 1980s, to being an area of high crime, with large numbers of boarded-up, empty housing and heavily defended remaining properties by the start of the research in early 1994. In 1997 the houses in some parts of the ward are, to all intents and purposes, worthless. The only speculative interest in the area is from companies putting up cheap, new-build housing for sale on the periphery of the ward, or from landlords buying up some of the older three bedroomed housing for as little as £3,000 for a three bedroom property. The decline of this area, then, is associated with the slump of the 1990s, a brutal and rapid spiral of decline, over which the local residents had little control. The response of the residents in these neighbourhoods to their decline is quite different and illuminating. Oldtown is seen by many of its residents as an area which has declined, but stabilised, an area where the local people, who have stuck with it through the decline are now best placed to seek solutions and control the area's eventual destiny. In Bankhill, the residents are overwhelmed by what has happened, in the recent period, to both their investments and their sense of well-being. They look to the statutory authorities, such as the police and the local authority departments to guide them out of their malaise.

The experience of community in each neighbourhood

While recognising that the experience of 'community' is not universal within each of these areas, in the light of these findings we characterised the two areas quite differently – as a 'defended community' (Oldtown) and a 'frightened community' (Bankhill). In Oldtown – 'the defended community' there exists a perception of a negotiated stability and equilibrium and in this fiercely defended local area, crime too can be negotiated.

In Bankhill – 'the frightened community' – no such possibility of negotiation exists. In an area where movement in and out of the area is rapid, relationships are necessarily more heterogenous, fleeting and temporary. Many of the old relationships have been lost as those established residents who can do so, leave the neighbourhood in search of some stability and relief from constant fear of crime and acts of vandalism.

Different relationships of trust are found within the two areas. In Oldtown residents seek ways to manage their fears and anxieties, establishing relationships of trust where they can, hoping to find themselves 'on the inside' and thereby protected. In Bankhill there are few sustained relationships of trust – here crime is seen to come from within the community, and therefore alliances within the community to combat crime are more difficult to set up and maintain.

I hope that these case-studies have been able to illuminate some of the reasons why community safety strategies ignore community dynamics and relationships at their peril. It becomes increasingly obvious from these examples that there exist very different possibilities for intervention and participation in these two neighbourhoods. At a recent ESRC/LGA sponsored conference[9] the then opposition MP, and now Home Secretary, Jack Straw, suggested that national government might play a major part in helping to set local crime reduction targets. It is to be hoped that this will not be at the expense of locally-determined strategies which can key into local needs and concerns while developing strategies for change which are acutely sensitive to the locality in which they are to be applied.

Notes

1. This commitment had already been pledged by the then Opposition spokesman on crime – Jack Straw, at a Local Government Association (LGA) organised conference in March 1997 *Crime – the Local Solution*.
2. In 1996 the LGA and Local Government Management Board conducted a survey of local authority involvement in community safety work. Of the 71 per cent of local authorities which replied, just over one half had published policy statements on community safety or aims and objectives. These findings imply that the majority of local authorities had not yet written community safety strategies at this time.
3. The 1996 International Crime Victimisation Survey suggested that both the rate of and fear of crime was higher in England and Wales than in other parts of the industrialised world.
4. The research from which this paper has been written was funded by the Economic and Social Research Council's *Crime and Social Order* initiative. The research project was entitled *Community Safety, Personal Safety and the Fear of Crime*, Award no. L21025036. The researchers were Karen Evans (University of Salford and currently Community Safety Co-ordinator with the Moss Side Initiative within the city of Manchester, UK) and Sandra Walklate (University of Keele). They were assisted at different times by Penny Fraser (currently working for NACRO) and Linda Harvey (University of Salford).
5. See also Evans et al. (1996) and Evans (1997) for a consideration of the different ways in which community is experienced in these areas and how local relationships are experienced, intersect with one another and play a part in shaping local people's beliefs and behaviour.
6. See Home Office (1993).
7. For example racial and domestic violence, witness intimidation and the bullying of school children.
8. Scottish Office circular quoted by Bottoms (1990).
9. *Crime – the Local Solution*, op. cit. – March 1997.

Bibliography

Bottoms A. E. (1990) Crime Prevention Facing the 1990s in *Policing and Society*, Vol 1, No 1, pp 3–22.

European Union (1997) *Criminal Victimisation in Eleven Industrialised Countries, Key Findings from the 1996 International Crime Victimisation Survey*. Noordwjik, Netherlands.

Evans K. (1997) It's alright 'round here if you're local – 'community' in the inner-city in Hogget P. (ed.) *Contested Communities*. Bristol: Policy Press.

Evans K., Fraser P. and Walklate S. Whom can you trust? The politics of "grassing" on an inner city housing estate in *The Sociological Review*, Vol 44, No 3.

Home Office (1993) A Practical Guide to Crime Prevention for Local Partnerships.

LGMB/LGA (1997) *Crime – the local solution, current practice*. Report published by the Local Government Association and the Local Government Management Board for Crime – the Local Solution Conference: London, March.

CHAPTER 17

Monitoring, Measuring and Mapping Community Safety

Alexander Hirschfield and Kate Bowers

Introduction

The term 'community safety' has now firmly established itself in our vocabulary and is referred to frequently in discussions about the fear of crime and crime prevention strategies. There is, however, a broad distinction that can be drawn between 'community safety' and 'crime prevention'. The latter is primarily concerned with intervening in the processes and circumstances which lead to criminal events and associated forms of anti-social behaviour in order to reduce the likelihood of their occurrence. Thus in crime prevention the focus is on making it more difficult for offenders to commit their crimes either through target hardening or improvements in building design and street layouts or by introducing 'diversions' for those at risk of becoming offenders (e.g. vulnerable young people) in the form of special recreational, social and sporting activities. Crime prevention also addresses the vulnerability of victims of crime and seeks to reduce this vulnerability through changes to the lifestyle, behaviour and routine activities of those most at risk.

Community safety is more concerned with threats to the security and safety of the public which may result from criminal activities or other causes (e.g. deprivation, social exclusion, urban decay). The emphasis in community safety strategies is on effecting changes which bring about longer-term sustainable improvements in the social and physical environment (including economic regeneration, cultural renewal and associated programmes) which reduce threats to safety and the fear of crime and improve the overall quality of life for members of the community. The emphasis in community safety is on collaborative efforts to deliver sustainable crime reductions through partnership working and on taking action which involves and empowers the wider community. In this sense the approach goes far beyond situational crime prevention measures or offender-oriented programmes.

The community safety approach to crime reduction was given added impetus in 1997 by the publication of the Local Government Association's Manifesto *Crime the local Solution* (LGA 1997) and by the election of a new government committed to promoting community safety. The manifesto stressed how crime prevention in Britain had been *ad hoc*, incoherent and under-funded and made the case for a more strategic approach towards dealing with crime, the fear of crime and anti-social behaviour. It stressed the need to increase the community's confidence and willingness to report crime and recommended that strategies be produced for dealing with repeat victimisation, drug-related offences and other serious problems. Perhaps the single most important recommendation to come out of the manifesto for the monitoring, mapping and measurement of community safety was the proposed statutory duty for local authorities to prepare annual community safety plans in collaboration with other agencies. The annual plans would be informed by crime audits which would include a detailed picture of levels of crime within each local authority and their geographical distribution. The manifesto acknowledged that if this was to be feasible there would need to be more data sharing and that this would require amendments to the existing data protection legislation.

The new government has endorsed many of the recommendations put forward by the LGA and is expected to place upon local authorities and the police service a joint statutory duty to prepare annual community safety plans for their areas. The proposals will be published in the new Crime and Disorder Bill which is expected to receive the royal assent during the summer of 1998.

If local authorities, in collaboration with the police, are going to be required by law to undertake Crime and Disorder Audits and to produce annual community safety plans they are going to have to address a number of very practical questions. These include questions about what the audit should contain, the definition of 'relevant data', how those data might be acquired, how they should be analysed and presented, what can be achieved within the time available and, crucially, who within the organisation has the skills required to produce the audit. There are also other issues concerned with access to information and data sharing which will need to be resolved. Many local authorities are going to face difficulties especially where they have not had any previous experience in the handling and analysis of crime data or in the use of geographical information systems (GIS).

The rest of this chapter discusses some of the organisational and technical issues which underpin the use of information in monitoring, measuring and mapping community safety and illustrates some of these with examples of the innovative evaluation research carried out by the author for the Safer Merseyside Partnership.

General principles of evaluation and the role of information

Community safety initiatives can be diverse, not only in their overall aims, intended outcomes and means of implementation, but also, with respect to the types of input and level of resources going into them. Some might be problem-specific, for example, initiatives directed at combating auto crime or domestic burglaries, some territorially focused (e.g. schemes aimed at reducing crime on problem housing estates) and others preventative and diversionary (e.g. youth activity projects). Others may adopt a more strategic district-wide perspective (e.g. anti-drugs schemes).

This diversity has important implications for the design of an appropriate policy evaluation strategy within which policy monitoring and the mapping and analysis of crime and associated data will play a part. The key question in planning any evaluation is to arrive at a set of criteria which the investigator can use to judge the success of an initiative. While the diversity of the initiative effectively rules out the application of the same criteria to every scheme, there are number of general principles and tests which evaluators might apply. These include:

- the extent to which the aims, objectives and targets set for each initiative are achieved according to performance indicators established before each initiative started;

- some observation and assessment of planning, implementation and internal scheme monitoring processes which have been adopted;

- the effectiveness of inter-agency collaboration and partnership working;

- the strengths and weaknesses of the strategies and tactics adopted in individual schemes;

- the overall impact of the policy programme or project on crime reduction and the alleviation of the fear of crime;

- the extent to which the projects complement and reinforce anti crime initiatives sponsored through other policies, programmes and projects;

- the extent to which individual schemes have been responsible for redistributing or displacing crime into other areas.

Many practical issues need to be confronted in translating ideas about community safety into action and in reviewing their performance. These include the identification and assembly of relevant data and the application of appropriate techniques for identifying crime patterns and other threats to community safety in conjunction with the use of existing intelligence about the effectiveness of specific measures in developing suitable 'responses' to the identified problems.

Monitoring and mapping exercises can contribute to the formulation, implementation and review of community safety strategies in a number of ways. The main types of application include:

1. **Problem identification.** Establishing the most serious crimes, problems of anti-social behaviour within the area of interest and their geographical distribution.

2. **Strategy formulation.** Identifying appropriate action to tackle the problems. This will draw upon information generated from the crime data analysis about the nature of the problems in the area although information on potential solutions will come from elsewhere, in particular from evaluations and trials of specific crime prevention measures.

3. **Targeting.** Making decisions on how best to allocate resources; to areas, to properties, to vulnerable individuals or various combinations of these.

4. **Analysis of change.** Tracking changes in the victimisation of properties and individuals and in the clustering of crime and incidents of anti-social behaviour over time within and adjacent to those area in which strategies or programmes have been implemented. This would include the analysis of crime displacement.

5. **Broader evaluation of impacts.** Monitoring effects of policy upon intended beneficiaries and the wider community, assessment of achievement of aims and objectives, examination of inter-agency partnership working, scrutiny of succession strategies.

Each of these will require appropriate information. However, the definition of 'relevant information' has to be fairly broad in the context of community safety. Different types of information are required by policy makers, practitioners and evaluators at different stages in the decision making and implementation process. For example, information on calls to the police and recorded crime might be required initially to gain an insight into the nature, scale and geographical distribution of crime and anti-social behaviour (e.g. minor disorder, juvenile disturbances) throughout an area. These data might be augmented by primary data on the fear of crime and residents' attitudes generated from a questionnaire survey. This is the stage at which the nature and geographical location of the problems are defined so that practitioners at least know what they are faced with.

The next stage involves identifying appropriate strategies for tackling the identified problems. The type of information needed at this stage is of a very different nature. The requirement here is for information on 'what works' in crime prevention. In short, 'meta data' comprising examples of proven strategies and best practice in reducing crime (e.g. the most effective means of target hardening or social crime diversion) together with some indication of the prerequisites for success organisationally and the costs of implementation. The source of these data will not be the police but rather the results of case studies and evaluations carried out elsewhere. Once strategies have been formulated, resources need to be targeted and this requires information on where best to locate initiatives. Further information is then required to monitor performance over time and to evaluate the impact of the measures taken in reducing crime and the fear of crime in the community. It is at this stage that more up-to-date 'position statements' will need to be generated and comparisons made with baseline conditions.

At least this is is how it should work in theory. The reality is often very different. In practice, even seemingly straightforward questions are often the most difficult to answer. For example, most local authorities and community safety partnerships would find identifying the number and location of domestic dwellings which have been repeatedly burgled extremely difficult. This is because criminal justice information systems have not been designed to generate reports on the frequency with which particular individuals or specific addresses re-appear in the crime records within specified time periods. This would require either the use of unique property reference numbers and identity numbers for individuals or efficient and effective address matching software. The problems are further compounded by inconsistencies in the entry of address fields and other data items in police recording systems (Johnson et al. 1997). Yet this information is crucial, not only for identifying how to respond to problems such as repeat burglary and where to target limited resources, but also, for monitoring the impact of measures (e.g. target hardening) in reducing crime and possible side effects (e.g. displacement).

Monitoring the effectiveness of initiatives which seek to alter the behaviour of individuals (e.g. youth diversion programmes) can be an even greater challenge. The benefits of these programmes are less tangible and will not be seen within weeks, months or even years. Monitoring the impacts and effectiveness of these requires longitudinal data on individuals spanning a long period. This would need to include information about those individuals' personal circumstances, needs and aspirations and lifestyles as well as their involvement and contact with funded programmes aimed at improving their quality of life. This information is unlikely to be readily available. The only option is to assemble it through tracking individuals and their circumstances over time by means of longitudinal surveys. It is unlikely that many local authorities or partnerships will be engaged in this process.

Neither is the targeting of resources any more straightforward. Decisions have to be made on the criteria to be used (e.g. vulnerable areas, properties or people) and then appropriate methods have to be applied to identify those targets. In relation to target hardening of vulnerable domestic dwellings, vulnerable properties (e.g. those which have been repeatedly burgled within a year) might be eligible for assistance irrespective of who resides in them or, alternatively, the characteristics of the victims living in those properties might need to be taken into account. For example, extra weight might be given to repeatedly burgled dwellings which contain elderly people living alone or single parent families. Alternatively, only properties falling within certain areas (e.g. urban priority areas, disadvantaged neighbourhoods) might qualify. While analysis of individual crime records and the mapping of victimised dwellings might help with the targeting in terms of identifying properties which meet certain criteria and are located in priority areas, the initial choice as to who should be given priority remains a political decision and a question of policy.

However, the monitoring process needs to go further than this and to consider the performance of the strategies which have been adopted and their impact upon reported crime, the fear of crime and anti-social behaviour in the areas in question. Some understanding of the processes by which the knowledge gained from monitoring and evaluation exercises *is used* to modify objectives and change strategies is also important as this reflects the ability of an organisation, agency or partnership to learn from experience and thereby improve its effectiveness. After all if monitoring and mapping exercises are to be of any benefit it is imperative that their findings have some bearing upon the decision making process.

Assessing the impact of community safety strategies upon crime levels is fraught with problems. It is very easy to produce self-fulfilling prophecies – or to set targets which are very easy to achieve and are very visible in their achievement. For example, when seeking to reduce vandalism or repeat burglary against non-domestic dwellings, should the policy target all non-domestic premises (e.g. public buildings, commercial buildings and industrial buildings) or focus upon one type of property (e.g. schools)? Clearly, it is easier to demonstrate an impact by concentrating resources on *one* type of vulnerable non-residential building, for example, through implementing security measures and CCTV to reduce repeat vandalism and repeat burglary of schools. With a clear focus on one well defined objective it is easier to demonstrate success or achievements than if resources are spread thinly.

Availability of appropriate research skills

Not every organisation will be in a strong position to undertake effective monitoring, mapping and evaluation of their community safety strategies. A number of important questions need to be asked about the ability of local authorities and partnerships to undertake their own internal monitoring. For example:

- Do they have staff with the necessary technical and research skills available to undertake this role?

- Are appropriate data sharing arrangements in place between the police, local authorities and other agencies?

- Do the gatekeepers of relevant data (including the police) have the ability to respond to requests for information?

- Are the necessary analytical tools available (crime pattern analysis software, geographical information systems)?

The absence of skills, staffing and capability to undertake data analysis can present a problem. There is a real issue concerning the availability of 'people resources' to undertake this kind of work as well as the expense of information systems although the latter is less of a problem than in the past. Single-handed community safety officers are unlikely to be in a position to undertake monitoring and evaluation in-house. Nor are research units within local authorities, that is where they exist, necessarily geared up to do this work. An important issue is the amount of time which needs to be invested in assembling data bases and getting the information into the right format for mapping. Even when mapping, monitoring and evaluation activities are contracted out, the lack of expertise within local authorities and partnerships to *respond,* on a day-to-day basis, to the feedback from the evaluation team can present further problems. This is an area where there is a clear need for training i.e. in the interpretation of and response to monitoring and evaluation by practitioners. The difficulties are compounded where the responsibility for community safety initiatives falls to just one individual.

One way of addressing the skills shortage might be to involve local colleges and universities, especially those with applied social science departments (e.g. criminology, geography, planning) by providing data for research projects and for Ph.D. theses. They may well be able to provide valuable *independent* research and evaluation in which confidence can be placed.

If monitoring and evaluation can be combined with education, then quite a lot of work can be done at relatively modest cost. This can be handled by funding student placements or through sponsoring students doing higher research degrees. This model works well on Merseyside, where the Safer Merseyside Partnership currently sponsor Ph.D. and masters students based at the University of Liverpool.

Clearly, community safety strategies need some form of monitoring, mapping and evaluation capability to be able measure progress towards achieving objectives. An important starting point is to build up a comprehensive geographically-referenced data base on demography, social conditions, land use and crime risks which can be used for problem definition, resource targeting and policy evaluation. The most effective means of implementing this would be through the creation of a Geographical Information System (GIS). A GIS can best be described as a system of hardware, software and procedures designed to support the capture, management, manipulation, analysis, modeling and display of spatially referenced information. Such systems enable links to be established and relationships to be explored between data derived from different sources (e.g. calls to the police, crime reports, census variables, transport information and land use). They can be used in conjunction with grid-referenced crime data to undertake analyses which overcome the confounding effects inherent in the use of spatially aggregated data for pre-determined geographical boundaries (e.g. police beats). Such systems can also be used to identify geographic clusters of different types of incident or crime 'hot spots' and to relate these to the operational areas defined for various community safety programmes. Some of these uses are now described in the context of the monitoring and evaluation research undertaken on Merseyside by the University of Liverpool.

Case study: The Safer Merseyside Partnership evaluation.

The Urban Research and Policy Evaluation Regional Research Laboratory (URPERRL) at the University of Liverpool is currently evaluating the Safer Merseyside Partnership (SMP) Initiative; a nine-year community safety programme with core funding of £10 million through the Single Regeneration Budget Challenge Fund. The SMP is a collaborative venture bringing together Merseyside's five local authorities, the police service, the voluntary sector, the fire service, the passenger transport authority (Merseytravel) and the business community. A wide range of innovative approaches to crime reduction / prevention are covered. These include strategies aimed at reducing domestic burglary with a specific focus on repeat victimisation in the most disadvantaged areas, a small business security grants strategy, an action programme for young people, an alternatives to drugs programme, and an initiative aimed at improving personal security and safety on public transport. There is also a fire education programme. One of the objective's of the latter is to reduce the number of false malicious calls made to the fire brigade.

URPERRL's involvement with the SMP started in 1995 when the University was commissioned to produce baseline information on crime allegations to support the targeting of resources. During this period a range of data sets was brought together and stored within GIS software for use in mapping and data analysis. The data sets are shown in Figure 1. They include all telephone calls made to Merseyside Police since the beginning of 1992 (over 3 million by July 1997), geographically-coded anonymised recorded crime records (some to an accuracy of 1 metre), census indicators, boundaries, community facilities (e.g. all schools, pubs, night clubs and social meeting places) and infrastructure (i.e. the street network and major bus routes). The evaluation and research activities have also seen the creation of some new data sets. Examples include 'daytime', 'evening' and 'nighttime' population estimates for small areas (useful for identifying population fluctuations within town centres with distinct retailing, commercial and entertainment foci) and counts of repeatedly burgled domestic and non-domestic properties identified from the address of the offence.

Another important data set is the Super Profiles residential neighbourhood classification (Brown and Batey 1994, Batey and Brown 1995). This is a geodemographic classification which identifies similar types of residential neighbourhood in terms of their demographic socio-economic, ethnic and housing composition. Geodemographic classifications are generated using cluster analysis techniques to group together socially homogeneous areas on the basis of census data and other information. They are powerful discriminators of high, intermediate and low crime areas. In the case of Super Profiles, some 120 variables were used to collapse Britain's 146,000 enumeration districts (i.e. small areas with populations circa 500 persons) into 160 neighbourhood types. These were then re-grouped to form 40 'target markets' and 10 broader 'lifestyle' categories (see Appendix 1.). Pen picture descriptions of the demographic and social characteristics of the 10 clusters comprising the 'lifestyle' level of the classification are shown at the end of this chapter. It has been long recognised that certain types of residential neighbourhood are more criminogenic than others. The British Crime Survey (BCS) using the ACORN geodemographic classification showed that the areas of highest risk for residential burglary included the poorest council estates, multi-racial areas, and areas with a mixed social status and an over-representation of single people. Burglary rates in these areas were between two and three times the national average (Mayhew et al. 1993). In short, area classifications provide a better spatial framework than purely administrative units (e.g. electoral wards) which are unlikely to contain socially homogeneous populations.

Figure 1.   Data sets available for monitoring and evaluation on Merseyside

Command and control	Denominators	Recorded crime (ICJS)
• 600k Records p.a. • Grid reference • Date/time • Classification code • Crime property • Crime person • Disorder • Hoax calls/arsons	• Residential properties • Non-residential properties • All properties • Resident population • Daytime population • Evening population • Nighttime population	• 140k Offences p.a. • 60k Offenders p.a. • Category of offence • Day/time of offence • Age/sex/occupation of victim and offender • Victim/offence/offender location (1 metre resol'n)

1991 Census indicators	Super profile lifestyles neighbourhood typology
• Population age structure • Household composition • Housing tenure • Dwelling type • Housing conditions • Migration • Ethnicity • Car ownership • Unemployment • Social heterogeneity • Index of local conditions	1. Affluent professionals 2. Better-off older people 3. Settled sururbans 4. Better-off younger fams 5. Younger/mobile 6. Rural communities 7. Lower income older 8. Blue collar workers 9. Lower income h/holds 10. Lowest income h/holds

Boundaries	Community facilities	Infrastructure
• Census EDs • Wards • L.A. districts • Police beats • City Challenge • Estates Action • Objective 1 • SRB Areas	• Hospitals/clinics • Doctors' surgeries • Schools • Community centres • Youth clubs • Public houses • Restaurants • Night clubs • Police stations	• Motorways • A roads • B roads • C roads • Major bus routes • Bus stops • Place names • Residential areas

A large quantity of the data was supplied by the Merseyside Information Service (MIS) a public sector R and I unit to which the Merseyside Police Authority subscribes. Access to MIS also provided the partnership and the evaluation team at Liverpool University with a wealth of geo-coded data on properties (e.g. schools, pubs, social meeting places), the street network, administrative boundaries and land use which provided a framework for the mapping of crime incidents.

All of the information is arranged in a series of data modules or separate menus. Because the data are in a GIS, it is possible to select and combine items from any of the menus to produce maps and tables of varying complexity. For example, maps can be produced showing the location of disorder incidents on Saturday nights in relation to deprived areas, police beats, main roads, pubs and night clubs. The main uses of the GIS include:

- Plotting the location of victims, offences and offenders and measuring the physical distance between them.

- Data linkage (e.g. adding 'neighbourhood type' codes to each grid-referenced crime record).

- Data superimposition (e.g. relating crime incidents to police beat boundaries, the street network, residential neighbourhoods).

Use is also being made of software designed specifically for identifying crime patterns or 'hot spots' from a series of individual crime incidents input as a series of point locations. One such program is the Spatial and Temporal Analysis of Crime software (STAC) developed by the Illinois Criminal Justice Information Authority in 1994. This has now been fully integrated into the GIS developed for the evaluation (Hirschfield, Yarwood and Bowers 1997). Additional software applications have been developed by the evaluation team specifically for identifying the occurrence of repeat burglaries to residential and non-residential dwellings (Johnson et al. 1997) and for producing demographic, land use and crime risk profiles for areas of high crime (Hirschfield and Bowers 1997).

Fire safety

The first case study illustrates some of the analyses carried out for Merseyside Fire Brigade on hoax calls and cases of arson. Data bases were compiled comprising information on every hoax call made to the brigade over a nineteen month period (approximately 11,000 cases) and all arsons within one year (3,500 cases).

The overall aim of the work was to capture and analyse these data in order to assist the brigade target SMP funded programmes aimed at deterring persons involved in such behaviour, in particular, the "Learn not to Burn" campaign which was to be implemented in schools located in some of Merseyside's most deprived areas. A "Hoax Calls Kill" campaign targeting public telephone kiosks particularly popular with hoaxers with a poster campaign was also planned.

The data items recorded for each hoax call included the time and date of the call, the caller's telephone number which was logged automatically and the address of the alleged incident. The type of property or site which it was alleged was on fire was derived, by the evaluation team, from the address or location of the incident. Thus a classification distinguishing domestic dwellings, commercial premises, public buildings, vehicles and wasteland was derived. Although the addresses given by the hoaxers were not actual fire sites their locations were significant because they were the places to which fire engines were falsely diverted. This abuse of the service could have dire consequences for those in genuine distress. Where possible, postcodes were identified for the alleged addresses to enable the mapping of this 'pseudo geography' to be carried out.

The caller's telephone number was used to link into another data base containing the address and postcode of every public telephone kiosk on Merseyside. The addresses were used to generate a 100 metre grid reference for the kiosks so that they could be mapped.

Information on arsons was extracted from the official Home Office fire report form the FDR1. Data items included the full address of the incident, time and date of incident, property type, source of ignition, damage caused and number of casualties.

A comparison between hoax calls and arsons in terms of the types of site involved revealed that motor vehicles were particularly prone to arson but were very rarely the subject of hoax calls. In fact, only 1 per cent of hoax calls alleged fires in vehicles, although, the latter accounted for 43 per cent of all arsons. One implication which stems from this is that it would be fairly safe for a telephone operator to assume that a reported arson to a vehicle was not a hoax.

Results from an analysis of the hoax call data revealed that many telephone kiosks were being used repeatedly to make hoax calls. One kiosk was used to make 94 calls in the 19 month period and nine kiosks were identified each of which was used to make over 50 hoax calls during the period in question. The location of these kiosks and their frequency or use appear in Figure 2. The boundaries shown on the map are the Objective 5.1 Pathway Areas. These are the disadvantaged urban priority areas used by the SMP for the targeting of resources. A sizeable majority of the multiply used telephone kiosks fell within these areas which suggests that there is a strong correlation between the source of the hoaxes and social deprivation. These relationships were explored further by identifying the types of residential neighbourhood within which the kiosks used to make the hoax calls and the locations mentioned by the hoaxers were situated.

Figure 2.   Locations of Telephone Boxes Frequently Used for Hoax Calls to the Fire Brigade

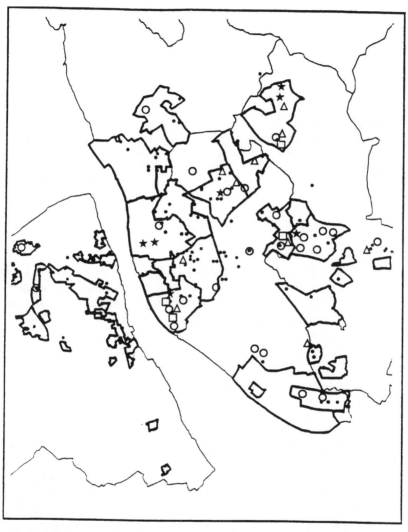

Hoax Calls	10-19	●	Boundaries of
	20-29	○	Merseyside Districts ———
	30-39	△	Objective 1 Areas ■■■
	40-49	□	
	50 and over	★	

Table 1   Distribution of hoax calls and arsons by type of residential neighbourhood on Merseyside

Super Profile Lifestyle	% Merseyside population	% Hoax kiosks (Origins)	% Hoax sites (Targets)	% Arsons
1. Affluent professionals	8.2	2.4	3.1	2.5
3. Better-off older people	8.3	3.7	2.7	3.3
3. Settled suburbans	14.4	8.0	4.7	6.7
4. Better-off younger people	14.5	9.3	7.7	8.0
5. Younger/mobile	1.9	7.4	4.1	5.5
6. Rural communities	0.1	0.0	0.2	0.3
7. Lower income older people	5.5	6.4	4.6	5.4
8. Blue collar workers	10.5	7.6	9.1	9.5
9. Lower income households	9.9	11.4	11.9	10.8
10. Lowest income households	26.7	44.0	51.8	48.0
Totals	1,394,854	1,178	1,228	2,400

The results appear in Table 1.

Significantly, 44 per cent of the kiosks and over 51 per cent of the locations of the alleged fires were in lowest income household areas as defined by the Super Profiles Geodemographic Classification. Almost half of all cases of arson were also located in these neighbourhoods. However, these areas, which had the highest levels of unemployment and social deprivation on Merseyside, accounted for only 26 per cent of Merseyside's population.

A resource targeting table was produced to present the hoax call data in a more digestible form. This appears as Table 2. The table revealed that 20 per cent of all the hoax calls were made from under 3 per cent of the kiosks on Merseyside which translated into just 33 kiosks. Thus by targeting just these 33 kiosks the brigade could effectively deal with one fifth of the problem.

The results from this and subsequent analyses which also take into consideration the peak times of the day and days of the week used to make hoax calls (i.e. time 'hot spots') are currently being examined by the fire brigade and will be used to pinpoint future covert surveillance operations aimed at apprehending the perpetrators. Maps are also being produced identifying those schools which are in close proximity to the multiply used kiosks. This will help with the targeting of educational programmes. The intelligence gathered as a result of these analyses is helping the fire service to impact upon a pernicious form of anti-social behaviour which wastes resources and puts lives at risk.

Table 2   Hoax calls resource targeting table

Calls per box	Boxes	Total calls	Cum No of boxes	Cum % of boxes	Cum No of calls	Cum % of calls
94	1	94	1	0.08	94	1.33
93	1	93	2	0.17	187	2.65
68	1	68	3	0.25	255	3.61
60	1	60	4	0.34	315	4.46
57	1	57	5	0.42	372	5.27
56	1	56	6	0.50	428	6.07
53	1	53	7	0.59	481	6.82
52	1	52	8	0.67	533	7.55
51	1	51	9	0.76	584	8.28
49	1	49	10	0.84	633	8.97
48	1	48	11	0.93	681	9.65
43	1	43	12	1.01	724	10.26
42	1	42	13	1.09	766	10.86
39	2	78	15	1.26	844	11.96
38	2	76	17	1.43	920	13.04
37	4	148	21	1.77	1068	15.14
36	1	36	22	1.85	1104	15.65
34	1	34	23	1.93	1138	16.13
33	1	33	24	2.02	1171	16.60
32	3	96	27	2.27	1267	17.96
30	2	60	29	2.44	1327	18.81
29	2	58	31	2.61	1385	19.63
28	2	56	33	2.78	1441	20.43
27	1	27	34	2.86	1468	20.81
26	3	78	37	3.11	1546	21.91
25	1	25	38	3.20	1571	22.27
24	5	120	43	3.62	1691	23.97
23	4	92	47	3.95	1783	25.27
22	8	176	55	4.63	1959	27.77
20	5	100	60	5.05	2059	29.18
19	8	152	68	5.72	2211	31.34
18	9	162	77	6.48	2373	33.64
17	10	170	87	7.32	2543	36.05
16	8	128	95	7.99	2671	37.86
15	8	120	103	8.66	2791	39.56
14	16	224	119	10.01	3015	42.74
13	12	156	131	11.02	3171	44.95
12	18	216	149	12.53	3387	48.01
11	22	242	171	14.38	3629	51.44
10	24	240	195	16.40	3869	54.84
9	38	342	233	19.60	4211	59.69
8	40	320	273	22.96	4531	64.22
7	42	294	315	26.49	4825	68.39
6	57	342	372	31.29	5167	73.24
5	79	395	451	37.93	5562	78.84
4	93	372	544	45.75	5934	84.11
3	132	396	676	56.85	6330	89.72
2	212	424	888	74.68	6754	95.73
1	301	301	1189	100.00	7055	100.00

Notes:
Cum = Cumulative   ☐ = Kiosks accounting for 20% of all hoax calls

Youth action programme

The second illustration of applications of monitoring and mapping community safety initiatives focuses upon the University's evaluation of the SMP's Youth Action Programme. The programme, which was launched in April 1996, funds twelve detached youth work projects which operate in some of the most disadvantaged areas of Merseyside. A common aim of all twelve projects, which are funded for a fixed period, has been to provide alternative programmes of activities which divert young people away from anti-social behaviour and crime. This aim is pursued through the projects in different ways. Some projects, for example, seek to achieve this through the use of organised events, sports activities and residential trips whilst others place greater emphasis on one-to-one work and involvement in training, education, art and environmental projects to enable young people to identify their own priorities. Other projects focus on a combination of preventative issue-based work around issues such as drugs, sex education and HIV (often with younger age groups) and general activities.

The projects operate by approaching young people where they happen to congregate using small teams of outreach workers operating in well-defined 'target areas' some large some very small. The detached teams undertake their own reconnaissance of the areas to establish where young people tend to gather and socialise prior to approaching them. Although this may provide them with a reasonable snapshot of the potential need for youth work within the confines of their operational areas, it does not give them a strategic longer-term picture of where juvenile disturbances and incidents of minor disorder (both perceived and actual) repeatedly occur. To fill this gap, the evaluation team has produced a series of maps for each project delineating juvenile disturbance 'hot spots' using information from the Merseyside Police command and control system and the STAC software. With over 220,000 geographically-referenced reports of juvenile disturbances contained within the GIS (i.e. every report between January 1992 and July 1997) it has been possible to generate fairly reliable statistics and maps for relatively small areas.

Figure 3 shows hot spots for 'youths causing annoyance' (YCA) in relation to Bus Route 20 which runs along the northern Liverpool corridor. This is also the operational area for the 'Youth on the Move' Project; one of the detached projects with a specific objective to reduce incidents of assault vandalism, and anti-social behaviour on public transport. The map, which shows only those hot spots which occur within close proximity to the route and the bus stops along it is being used by the project manager to focus the efforts of the detached youth work team. Additional information is being sought from the major bus operators about disturbances and incidents occurring on each bus route which have been logged by bus drivers. Once these data have been obtained they will be incorporated into the GIS and superimposed upon the command and control hot spot maps to generate a more comprehensive picture of potential problem locations within the corridor.

Figure 3.   Juvenile disturbance 'Hotspots' along Bus Route 20 in Liverpool

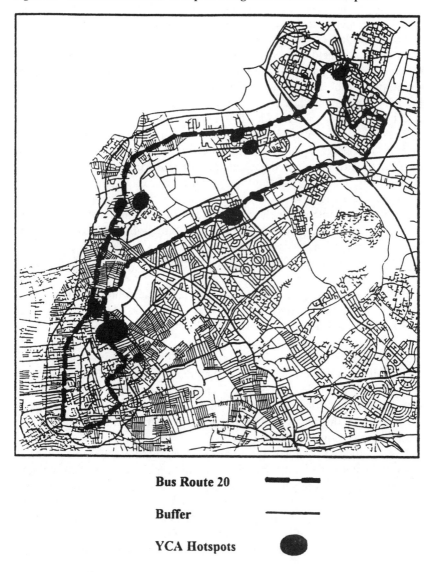

Bus Route 20

Buffer

YCA Hotspots

Although 'hot spot' maps are potentially useful for isolating clusters of crime or anti-social behaviour within relatively large areas, they do not provide any indication of where incidents occur within very small areas. To address this question the evaluation team has devised a method to enable the density and distribution of juvenile disturbances within these 'hot spots' to be identified. This has been achieved by producing maps which show the frequency with which specific locations have been identified as the site of a juvenile disturbance. The locations in question are small parcels of land which have been repreatedly referenced by the command and control system in respect of the incidents. Since the command and control system only pinpoints incidents to within an accuracy of 100 metres, the points which appear on the map are effectively 100 metre squares. Use of this technique, which has been named 'hot point' mapping, is illustrated in Figure 4. This shows 'hot points' for juvenile disturbances in relation to the street network in the Arundel Detached Youth Project area. The solid squares are specific sites within the area which have had between 12 and 58 juvenile disturbance reports within twelve months. Interestingly, when confronted with this map, detached youth workers in Arundel were able to explain why a number of the high volume incidents appear in isolation from the street network to the north east of the map. This was a cemetery where young people routinely congregate in the evenings and was an area which the team was about to target. The 'hot points' technique might usefully serve as a basis for mapping changes in the distribution of incidents over time and identifying displacement. This feasibility of this is currently being explored.

Both types of map have been used to assist detached youth workers identify where within their patches they should be concentrating their efforts. Feedback from the teams on the utility of the maps has been generally positive, although, their limitations, in particular the fact that they are unable to distinguish the number of juveniles involved in each alleged disturbance or their age and gender is acknowledged. The maps and statistics are being put into a local context through a series of 'site appraisals' (i.e. visiting the target areas rather than just mapping them) to get a feel for the particular landmarks, attractors and magnets which attract young people to those areas.

The production of maps and analysis of command and control data is just one element in a comprehensive evaluation methodology. This includes the assembly and analysis of data on the number of young people contacted by each project, the design and administration of a self assessment questionnaire to identify changes in the attitudes and behaviour of young people as a result of the initiative and face-to-face interviews with community police officers and other potential beneficiaries including the

Figure 4. Juvenile disturbance 'Hotspots' map for the Arundel Youth Action Area

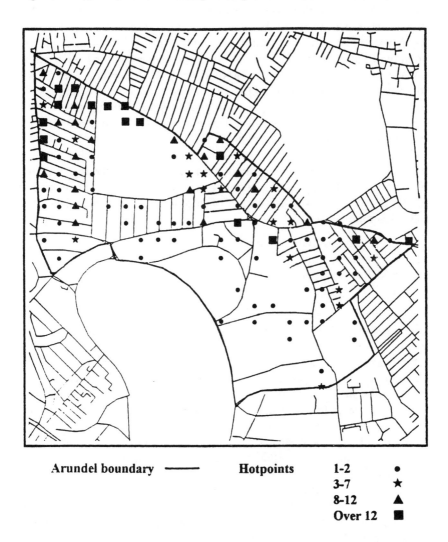

Arundel boundary ——— **Hotpoints** 1-2 •
3-7 ★
8-12 ▲
Over 12 ■

local business community and residents' groups. The general management of the projects, the extent of inter-agency working and collaboration and long term plans post funding, i.e. 'succession strategies', are also being considered.

Measuring contacts made with young people is particularly problematic.

However, data on contacts is essential because this is the population for whom detached youth work projects can make a difference. One of the difficulties is being able to distinguish the quality of the contacts made when compiling data for monitoring and evaluation purposes. Early attempts to quantify the number of young people engaged by the projects on Merseyside revealed the need to develop a systematic method of recording. When asked to quantify the contacts made with young people for an interim evaluation report one project stated 20, another with a similar budget and a roughly equivalent operational area stated 250 and a third equally resourced project claimed 1000!

The evaluation is breaking new ground by developing a best practice model for the assembly of information on the extent, nature and outcome of contacts made with young people through detached youth work. The model is effectively a classification of contacts which distinguishes the following four categories:

- Reconnaissance counts
- Casual contacts
- Closer encounters
- Participatory engagements

Reconnaissance counts are essentially estimates of the numbers of young people on the streets which are made by youth workers observing young people at a distance without establishing any contact. These estimates provide some indication of the number of young people who may be vulnerable (i.e. the potential population at risk). Although their number will be substantially smaller than the number of young people resident in the target area, they are, nevertheless, likely to provide a much more realistic denominator for calculating youth project participation rates for young people (i.e. those engaged by detached youth work per 1000 at risk) than young people in the residential population, many of whom will not be vulnerable.

Casual contacts are defined as young persons present when the first verbal contact or approach is made by youth workers to one or more young persons within the target area. This is the point at which the engagement process begins, although, some young people may never get beyond the casual contact stage. Closer encounters are more in-depth contacts between young people and youth workers and may be associated with the disclosure/confrontation of problems faced by young people. These also include direct approaches made by young people to youth workers. Finally, participatory engagements involve young people *doing things* that would not have happened without the active participation of both the youth worker(s) and the young people. They include the involvement of young people accessing services and facilities, participating in activities locally or away from the area (e.g. day trips) and participating in residentials.

This model for recording contacts is being adopted by all SMP-funded youth action initiatives. The monitoring data which it will generate should make it possible to draw some comparisons between the outputs delivered by different projects. It will also be possible to scrutinise the balance between casual contacts, closer encounters and participatory enagements for each project and to identify those projects where greater efforts are needed to transform more of the casual contacts into participatory ones.

The youth action programme evaluation demonstrates the need for and value of a multi-faceted approach to monitoring, measuring and mapping community safety, one which combines quantitative techniques with qualitative analysis to produce meaningful outputs for both youth workers and evaluators.

Conclusion

This chapter has examined some of the issues which need to be considered when embarking upon the monitoring and mapping of threats to community safety and the evaluation of preventative strategies. Although access to relevant data and information technology are essential elements in this process, equally important are analytical skills and the ability to understand and respond to the messages emanating from monitoring and evaluation exercises.

One way forward, especially since local authorities and the police are going to be required to prepare community safety plans, might be for guidance nationally on the core indicators which should comprise crime and disorder audits and on the monitoring methods/ systems which need to be implemented.

Whether or not this course is ever pursued there is an urgent need at this stage to produce a *position statement* of existing practice in the mapping, monitoring and evaluation area. There is a problem of duplication of effort and reinvention of the wheel in different parts of the country and a lack of communication. In particular, there is a lack of information about best practice in terms of defining data items, data structures and in the use of software packages. There are pools of expertise in different parts of the country. Northumbria Police, for example, have worked in the past with Newcastle University to develop crime pattern analysis systems. There are effective systems up and running in Wandsworth and Brent, Cleveland, North Yorkshire, Greater Manchester and elsewhere. There is a need to review all of this activity with a view towards producing a *good practice guide* to steer local authorities in the right direction so that they can produce community safety strategies that are informed by accurate assessments of the magnitude and manifestion of the problems with which they are faced.

References

Batey, P.W.J. and Brown, P.J.B. (1995) From Human Ecology to Customer Targeting: the Evolution of Geodemographics in P. Longley and G. Clarke (eds.), *GIS for Business and Service Planning.* Longman, London, 77–103.

Brown, P.J.B. and Batey, P.W.J. (1994) *The Design and Construction of a Geodemographic Targeting System: Super Profiles 1994*, URPERRL Working Paper 40, Department of Civic Design, University of Liverpool.

Hirschfield, A., and Bowers, K.J. (1997) The Development of a Social, Demographic and Land Use Profiler for Areas of High Crime in *British Journal of Criminology* 37 (1),103–120.

Hirschfield, A., Yarwood, D., and Bowers, K.J. (1997) *Crime Pattern Analysis, Spatial Targeting and GIS: The Development of New Approaches for use in Evaluating Community Safety Initiatives*, Paper presented to the conference on GIS for Health and Crime Data Analysis, Novotet Sheffield, May 1997.

Illinois Criminal Justice Information Authority (1994) What is STAC ? in *Stac News*, 2 (1) Winter 1994 p 12.

Johnson, S.D., Bowers, K., and Hirschfield, A. (1997) New Insights Into the Spatial and Temporal Distribution of Repeat Victimisation in *British Journal of Criminology* 37 (2), 224–241.

Local Government Association (1997) *Crime the Local Solution: Proposals for Community Safety and Crime Prevention.* LGA: London.

Mayhew, P., Maung, N.A. and Mirlees-Black, C. (1993) *The 1992 British Crime Survey*, Home Office Research Study 132, London: HMSO.

Appendix 1. Super Profile Lifestyle Pen Pictures
(including 1991 population and percentage of national population)

Lifestyle 1: Affluent professionals   Population: 1,977,551 [9.0%]

High income families with a lifestyle to match. Detached houses predominate, reflecting the professional status of their owners. Typically living in the stockbroker belts of the major cities, the affluent professional is likely to own two or more cars, which are top of the range, recent purchases, and are needed to pursue an active social and family life. Affluent Professionals have sophisticated tastes and aspirations. They eat out regularly, go to the theatre and opera and take an active interest in sports (such as, cricket, rugby union and golf). They are able to afford several expensive holidays every year. Financially aware, with a high disposable income, this group invests in both quoted and privatised companies. They are happy to use credit and charge cards and are likely to have private health insurance.

Lifestyle 2: Better-off older people   Population: 2,445,660 [11.2%]

Older than affluent professionals, possibly taking early retirement, better-off older people still retain a prosperous way of life. Their detached or semi-detached homes have now been purchased and most of their children have left home. This leaves money to spend or invest in the luxuries of life, such as a superior car. Better-off older people eat out regularly, take one or two holidays a year and enjoy playing golf and going to the theatre. They are financially aware and set aside some money for investment on the Stock Exchange and for private health insurance.

Lifestyle 3 : Settled suburbans   Population: 2,470,265 [11.3%]

These families are well established in their semi-detached suburban homes. The settled suburbans are employed in white collar and middle management positions. The presence of many part-time working wives ensures a fairly affluent lifestyle. For example, this group can afford to take one or two packaged holidays every year and purchase newer cars. They have taken advantage of government share offers in the past and are happy to use credit cards for their purchases.

Lifestyle 4: Better-off younger families   Population: 3,218,899 [14.7%]

Younger adults who have recently started a family, better-off younger families are middle management, white collar workers. Although there are two incomes, the mortgage on their home accounts for a large slice of their income. Having young children, and a relatively small amount of money for luxury purchases, means that better-off younger families rely on home based entertainment. Rather than going out they socialise at home and many watch sport on television, often on satellite or cable TV. They may have more than one car, which are often cheaper, older models.

Lifestyle 5: Younger mobile   Population: 2,262,828 [10.3%]

This cosmopolitan, multiracial group reside in areas of major cities which are undergoing gentrification but still retain a significant proportion of poorer quality housing. These young adults live in terraced houses or flats and have high levels of disposable income, which is spent on eating out, expensive holidays, keeping fit, going to pubs, concerts and the cinema. Close to where the action is, there is little need for a car, the bus, tube and train are preferred means of transport.

Lifestyle 6 : Rural communities   Population: 612,118 [2.8%]

Rural in nature, this group lives, works and plays in the countryside. Many live on farms or in tied cottages, which are concentrated in East Anglia, Scotland, Wales and the South West. Car ownership is high, given the distance to local facilities, and direct mail is widely utilised, reflecting the absence of retail outlets.

Lifestyle 7: Lower income older people   Population: 1,750,297 [8.0%]

An elderly group living in small possibly sheltered accommodation. Many have moved into retirement areas and there is a high proportion of lone single female pensioners. The lower income older people will live within their means, however limited this may be, with the key recreation activities being passive, such as the pub and television. They also prefer to shop at convenience stores in their own neighbourhood.

Lifestyle 8: Blue collar workers   Population: 3,358,632 [15.3%]

These more affluent blue collar workers live in terraces or semis. Many are middle aged or older and their children have left home. The blue collar workers work in traditional occupations and manufacturing industries, where unemployment levels have risen to a significant degree. Most are well settled in their homes, which are either purchased or still rented from the council.

Lifestyle 9: Lower income households   Population: 1,565,854 [7.2%]

Living in council estates, in reasonably good accommodation, unemployment is a key issue for these families. Most work is found in unskilled manufacturing jobs, if available, or failing that, on Government Schemes. The parochial nature of this group is emphasised by an unwillingness or inability to either move home or go on holiday.

Lifestyle 10: Lowest income households   Population: 2,225,250 [10.2%]

Single parent families, living in cramped, overcrowded flats is the everyday reality for this group which is composed of young adults with large numbers of young children. These are the underprivileged who move frequently in search of a break. However, with two and a half times the national rate of unemployment and with low qualifications, there seems little hope for the future. Many are on income support, and those who can find work are in low paid, unskilled jobs. There are very few cars and little chance of getting away on holidays.

CHAPTER 18

Delivering Multi-agency Partnerships in Community Safety

Adam Crawford

Crime and insecurity by their nature are multi-faceted both in their causes and effects. Traditionally, social responses to them have tended to be segmented and compartmentalised. The term 'community safety' has come to stand as a referent for an emerging approach to crime and disorder which (a) is local, (b) encompasses a broad focus upon wider social problems such as fear, anxieties and other quality of life issues, and (c) needs to be delivered through a 'partnership' approach drawing together a variety of organisations – in the public, voluntary and private sectors – as well as relevant community groups. The underlying justification for this lies in the belief that, as far as possible, social reactions to crime should reflect the nature of the phenomenon itself (Young 1992).

Of these three elements it is the concept of a 'multi-agency' or 'partnership' approach which is probably the most widely endorsed, and yet, has been the least considered. The present government's commitment to give local authorities statutory responsibility for organising community safety partnerships, has sharpened the need to address these issues. The advantages of multi-agency working are often rehearsed:

- it affords an holistic approach to crime;
- it is problem-oriented rather than bureaucracy-premised;
- it allows a systemisation and co-ordination of effort, expertise and information;
- it enables a pooling of resources.

And yet, the difficulties and pitfalls are seldom recognised or addressed. Achieving successful partnerships is by no means a straightforward or unproblematic task.

The aim of this chapter is deliberately critical. It is my contention that the absence of genuinely critical debate about the processes involved in delivering multi-agency partnerships in community safety only serves to impede practice. The development of good practice, with which to address and negotiate the conflicts which infuse partnership work, requires the recognition and exploration of the many unspoken problems that practitioners face and are implied by practice. Hence, this chapter will seek to introduce some research findings as to the social, organisational and interpersonal processes involved in community safety partnerships. It sets out to identify some of the problems associated with partnerships and to consider some of the vexed issues which often stymie good intentions. This critical starting point is deliberately chosen in order to begin a consideration of how best to manage inter-agency relations in community safety work. The intention, in focusing upon difficulties, is not to undermine or reject a partnership approach, but rather, to begin to highlight often ignored problems so as to refine good practice and identify positive strategies for negotiating conflicts. By knowing what does not work or is not appropriate in given circumstances we can help identify constructive ways of working.

Types of partnerships: inter-agency versus multi-agency work

In both the literature and practice the terms 'partnership', 'multi-agency', and 'inter-agency' are used interchangeably and with little precision as to their meaning (see Liddle and Gelsthorpe 1994). It is, however, worth beginning to draw attention to, and specify, the very real differences between conceptions of 'partnership' work (understood as a generic term). In this light, it is useful to make a conceptual distinction between two different 'ideal types' of partnerships in order to begin to question: what works best in which contexts? Hence, we can distinguish between, on the one hand, '*multi*-agency' relations and, on the other hand, '*inter*-agency' relations. These can be seen as two end points along a continuum:

- Multi-agency relations involve the coming together of various agencies, in relation to a given problem, without this significantly affecting or transforming the work that they do. The same tasks are conducted in co-operation with others.

- Inter-agency relations are those relations which interpenetrate and thus affect normal internal working practices of the agencies. They entail some degree of fusion and melding of relations between agencies. They involve collaboration and interdependence. For example, inter-agency work may impact upon the nature of mainstream service delivery within participating organisations. Often, new structures, identifiable units or forms of working arise.

Actual initiatives lie somewhere between these polar types. Whilst those which approximate more closely to the 'inter-agency' model offer greater rewards in collaborative activities, as we shall see, they also present more acute problems for the management of the conflicts to which inter-organisational relations give rise (see Crawford and Jones 1996). Importantly, both 'types' present participating agencies with different responsibilities, levels of involvement, and so on. What this conceptual distinction points us towards is the need for a greater clarity and specification by the parties as to the desirable form with which a given partnership model should accord.

Critical dynamics in partnership work

Partnerships which draw together diverse organisations and groups, by their very nature, embody two key structural dynamics. The first is the existence of often fundamental *conflicts over ideology, purpose and interests*. Deep structural conflicts exist between the parties that sit down together in partnerships. Criminal justice agencies have very different priorities and interests, as do other public sector organisations, voluntary bodies, the commercial sector and local community groups.

The second dynamic is the existence of *differential power relations between the partners*. The previously mentioned conflicts are overlain and exacerbated by very different access to resources (both human and material), claims to expertise and power relations. Together these dynamics can lead to or produce unhelpful strategies within partnership work:

1. **Conflict avoidance** may arise as a dominant mode of operation, whereby the parties seek to avoid conflict to such a degree that real issues are not confronted or addressed. This may be an understandable strategy in certain contexts (particularly in the earliest stages of an initiative's life) but leaves power differences unaddressed. Furthermore, real conflicts are often dispersed into other arenas, rather than being negotiated or resolved.

2. **A strategy of multiple aims** may arise whereby increasingly disparate aims or objectives are accorded to a particular partnership project. This is what we might prefer to call the 'Smörgasbord approach' in which something for everyone is placed upon the menu. In the process projects can find themselves signing up to such broad and sometimes confused aims, as to be almost meaningless. The danger is that in the attempt to appease all interests fundamental aims are not prioritised. This may lead to 'lowest common denominator' solutions and a lack of clarity and coherence. This also presents significant problems for evaluation as it is unclear which evaluation criteria should be prioritised.

3. **Informal or hidden relations** may arise often as a consequence of a

strategy of conflict avoidance. This can lead to decisions being taken outside of formal and public processes. Often, important decisions are taken elsewhere, behind the scenes and in private settings. Such 'shadow' relations are hard to monitor and present problems for accountability. This can be, and often is, justified in terms of 'getting things done'. However, it runs counter to the spirit of transparency and often reinforces the power of the more dominant partners and, at the same time, undermines the role of weaker partners.

Partnerships by their nature *blur the boundaries* between the roles and functions of incorporated organisations. This is particularly pertinent for initiatives which approximate more closely to an 'inter-agency' rather than 'multi-agency' type (as defined earlier). This can present difficulties for accountability and for the appropriate distribution of responsibilities. Hence, there is a need to maintain clarity of the divergent inputs and their collaborative objectives. Furthermore, this raises questions of autonomy for the parties which need to be addressed early on in the life of partnership agreement. How much autonomy is it necessary for each agency to lose for the sake of the corporate good? How much autonomy are agencies willing to lose? The answers to each of these questions will, in part, depend upon the type of partnership relations envisaged.

Hence, one of the key aspects of successful partnerships involves *establishing and sustaining trust relations* across agency boundaries. This is not easy particularly where there is a history of mistrust or misunderstanding. But it should be recognised that partnerships have a 'life-span', they need to develop and mature as circumstances change. As trust develops and partnerships become more established different ways of managing conflict may become more appropriate. A crucial element in establishing trust relations is making people aware of the limitations of their own and other agencies' contribution, so that they neither try to 'do it all' nor do they have unrealistic expectations of what others can deliver. There is a need for mutual respect for different types of contributions. In this regard, there is an important role for training in multi-agency relations and working dynamics which needs to be recognised, particularly in relation to designated staff performing link functions within partnership networks. Training can be one way of beginning to overcome the basis for misunderstandings and mistrust between agency workers.

Partnerships and the wider policy context

It needs to be recognised that that intra-organisational relations can affect and produce inter-organisational conflict. Often, conflicts and tensions within partner organisations can reproduce themselves in, or affect, inter-organisational relations. In other words, partnerships not only bring all the benefits offered by the inclusion of each partner, but are accompanied by the internal disputes and conflicts that sometimes rage within organisations. This can occur at an interpersonal as well as at a more structural level. For example, staff turnover, particularly of key link personnel or multi-agency co-ordinators, may undermine established trust relations or question the commitment of individuals or organisations to given partnerships.

More generally, recent government policy, in the form of 'new public management' reforms and the extensive use of internal performance indicators, has served to exacerbate this tension between inter-organisational and intra-organisational dynamics. 'New public management' reforms encourage an *intra*-organisational focus which pays little attention to managing *inter*-organisational networks (Rhodes 1996). In this context, there has been little attention given to negotiating shared purposes, particularly where there is no hierarchy of control. Hence, intra-organisational priorities can undermine, or run counter to, the needs of inter-organisational partnerships. The intra-organisational focus on outputs can make agencies concentrate their energies upon their core task and activities at the expense of peripheral ones. Community safety, by its very nature, is precisely one such peripheral function of diverse agencies. Perversely, 'new public management' reforms may actually serve to push government departments and public sector agencies further into prioritising their own introspective needs at the expense of collaborative and inter-organisational commitments.

One extreme but vivid example of the kind of undesirable consequences produced by an emphasis upon narrowly defined internal performance measurement is the growing use of exclusions from schools (cf. Isabelle Brodie in this volume). Current measurements of 'success' in terms of league tables of performance, together with funding criteria, give schools an incentive to exclude pupils needing more attention rather than to deal with the difficult behaviour within the school. The impact upon crime rates and community safety is all too obvious as exclusion from school often marks the first step in exclusion from society (Blyth and Milner 1993). An Audit Commission survey of 600 young people sentenced by the courts found that 40 per cent of persistent offenders and more than 30 per cent of transient offenders had been excluded from school at some point (Audit Commission 1996).

There is a further concern about the impact of the new-found emphasis within policy upon '*outputs*' as distinct from '*outcomes*'. 'Outputs' frequently refer to internally defined organisational goals over which organisations have considerable control and may depart significantly from 'outcomes' – the effects of an output or set of outputs upon the wider community. There is a danger that 'outputs' take precedence over 'outcomes' and that the gulf between the two may grow larger, so that social goals are eclipsed by organisational goals. This can result in a form of 'measure fixation' whereby more attention is given to the measure, not the service the measure is intended to signify. Concentration upon output measurement can create a form of 'tunnel vision' amongst managers which neglects the unquantifiable aspects of a service and which may marginalise long term thinking, so crucial to social crime prevention and community safety (see Tilley 1995). The involvement of lay people and forms of 'democratic input' can help mitigate these problems (Crawford 1997 and Usman Khan in this volume).

In many ways the focus of 'new public management' reforms is inappropriate for managing inter-organisational partnerships, and may serve to undermine them. The effective management of inter-organisational networks requires appropriate conditions in which joint and collaborative action can be sustained. This requires policies which foster reciprocity and interdependence between organisations, not insularity. The challenge for government is to enable partnerships and to seek out new forms of co-operation, rooted in inter-organisational trust.

Economic implications

There is a danger that funding is overly short term so that it restricts long term developments. If funding is 'pump-priming' as with the 'demonstration project' model, then there is a need to allow sufficient resources for a project to genuinely establish itself and 'get off the ground'. In the natural early life and development of most projects there is an initial period of 'learning' during which problems, pitfalls and hiccups are the norm, not the exception. To many fieldworkers who experience these realities it seems contradictory to remove funding at a time when projects are establishing themselves and should be moving beyond this initial developmental phase into producing valuable results.

The question of the relationship between designated crime prevention funding and wider mainstream social and criminal justice funding is a particularly vexed one which needs to be carefully considered. There is little point in setting up pilot or 'demonstration projects' if they collapse at the end of the funding period due to lack of mainstream support. We need to ask the question, is a partnership initiative a short term approach to a given problem? For example, is the perceived need limited to improving inter-organisational communication? Is it designed to get a project off the ground which will then be incorporated into mainstream service delivery? Hence, can the funding appropriately be withdrawn, or is its function a long-term collaborative one? If the latter, there is a need for durability in order to sustain activity. The lack of long term resources presents itself as the single biggest threat to the survival and enhancement of a partnership approach to community safety (c.f. Pitts in Ch. 19 of this volume).

The fact that community safety does not fit into any existing organisational 'box', but rather straddles and transcends organisational boundaries, accords to it certain pitfalls as well as its primary attraction and its significant potential. The danger is that local community safety initiatives are left to pick up the pieces that others shun. There is an ever-present danger that they are left to catch those who fall through the cracks between the concerns of established organisations and agencies. Often, this can extend far beyond community safety work. As a result, some schemes have to try hard not to be dragged into doing work which other agencies should be doing or for which those schemes were not established.

Furthermore, there is a genuine anxiety that the high degree of emphasis given to 'crime problems' within community safety may result in social policy, its direction and funding being redefined in terms of its implications for crime. One potential consequence of giving crime a central place in the construction of community safety and social order is that fundamental public issues may derive their importance in terms of their crimogenic qualities. The danger is that through a partnership focus to community safety, which wraps social and criminal policy in the same clothes, we may come to view unemployment, poor housing, homelessness, racism, failed educational facilities, the lack of youth leisure opportunities, and so on, as no longer important issues in themselves. Rather, their importance may become increasingly seen to derive from the belief that they lead to crime and disorder. The fact that they may do exactly that is no reason not to assert their importance in their own right. The fear is that social deficiencies are being redefined as 'crime problems' which need to be controlled and managed, rather than addressed in themselves. This would represent the ultimate 'criminalisation of social policy'. Hence, we need to ask the question: what is the appropriate relationship between multi-agency community safety activity and mainstream service delivery by partner organisations and groups? And furthermore, what are the implications for the transfer of resources between agencies if initiatives are not accommodated within mainstream activities?

Problems of accountability

Joint and negotiated decisions tie the parties into corporate policy and outcomes but often fail to identify lines of responsibility. Institutional complexity further obscures who is accountable to whom, and for what. In partnerships the problem of 'too many hands' presents itself, where so many people contribute that no one contribution can easily be identified: "If no one person can be held accountable after the event, then no one needs to behave responsibly beforehand" (Rhodes 1996: 663). Hence, accountability becomes a vexed but crucial issue in need of clarity.

Consultation, incorporation and representation are always problematic issues, particularly in crime prevention where there are overt dangers of the social exclusion of certain groups. The question is *how to get marginalised groups 'on side'?* particularly those with high representation within the criminal justice system. Some community safety groups appear to have addressed these issues in more constructive ways than have others. Notably, youth representation is a problem for many community safety initiatives. With the considerable emphasis upon 'youth at risk' in community safety strategies, there is a danger in constituting 'youth' as a problem. Consideration should be given to greater incorporation of youth interests onto multi-agency community safety bodies and greater consultation with youth groups in order that their voices can be heard as constructive and not merely as 'problematic'. However, this can be fraught with difficulties. Who do youth representatives actually represent? 'Youth' itself is not a homogenous social category.

As the Morgan Report concluded: "Any meaningful local structure for crime prevention must relate to the local democratic structure" (1991: 20). Community safety strategies require political legitimacy. And yet, the danger of majoritarianism and the capture of community safety as a 'political football', should challenge local authorities to look to, and experiment with, other forms of democratisation, not instead of, but as supplements to, traditional channels of representation. Some interesting developments in the UK include the use of local crime surveys and citizens juries to supplement traditional channels of democratic representation and to help inform local initiatives (see Stewart 1996; Crawford 1997). It is important to tap and facilitate local energies and commitments, not to duplicate or undermine them.

One important question often asked by practitioners about community safety partnerships is, what is the 'appropriate hierarchical level' within organisations at which partnership structures should be located? There is often the problem that decisions struck at a senior level need to be renegotiated at a lower level. In many instances, the implementation of inter-agency co-operation requires the, often ongoing, renegotiation of any such agreements at various different organisational levels. The perceptions, attitudes, and actions of 'ordinary' mainstream officers, therefore, are integral to an understanding of the way organisational change is fought over, negotiated, and resolved. Some practitioners complain that partnerships are set too high within organisational structures and have little relevance for front-line workers. Hence, we need to ask whether there should be multi-tiered partnership structures? If so, vertical communication between the structures becomes particularly important. The appropriate level for partnerships requires that they can gain the commitment of senior officers and simultaneously affect front-line workers and make them feel involved.

Finally, we need to be self-critical about the *rhetoric of partnerships*. There is a big gulf between the often-heard ideals of 'partnerships' and the reality of its practice. Many partnerships are better described as 'talking shops' or 'paper partnerships' (which exist merely for the purposes of satisfying funding requirements). This is not to denigrate those fine-sounding ideas but rather to ensure that they are translated into practice.

Conclusions

In order to return to our starting point, action must be local. Therefore, it would be wrong to prescribe a rigid model of partnership. They must reflect the locality, the nature of the problems to be addressed, the focus of the strategy, the make up of the constituent partners, and so on. Nevertheless, community safety does need to be set within the framework of a clear, overall community safety policy. In that light the following questions should be posed in relation to all community safety projects:

- Does the partnership have clear priorities and a sense of focus, which are reflected both in the corporate aims, their inter-relationship and the organisational structure given to the multi-agency approach?

- Is there clarity about the divergent inputs of the partners, their collaborative objectives and the distribution of responsibilities?

- Does the organisational structure enhance and facilitate the aims of the corporate strategy?

- Is there mutual respect for different types of contributions and the mutual recognition of different interests and values? If not, how can they best be fostered and sustained?

- Are conflicts addressed and managed in an open and constructive manner?

- Does the partnership structure successfully facilitate the commitment of senior officers and front-line workers and make them feel involved?

- Does the partnership have a long term goal or short term mission?

If the former, does the funding arrangement allow for long term planning? If the latter, who or what will progress the initial work undertaken after the demise of the partnership initiative?

- To whom are the partnerships accountable?

- Does government policy encourage conditions which will sustain joint and collaborative action?

Given the previous arguments, there is a clear need for evaluation of the processes as well as the outcomes of community safety partnerships. Outcomes will always be process dependent.

Achieving successful partnerships is by no means straightforward. One of the central challenges for those working in community safety in Britain will be to move beyond the mere co-ordination of diverse agencies and groups to establish collaborative and co-operative relations amongst the relevant parties at a local level. This will require the development and maintenance of appropriate conditions in which to build and sustain trust through openness and the mutual recognition of different interests. For a partnership approach to be translated beyond the level of rhetoric into vibrant practice in the field of community safety, practitioners and policy makers will need to face some challenging and reflexive questions. It is hoped that this chapter has begun to identify some of these issues.

Bibliography

Audit Commission (1996) *Misspent Youth: Young People and Crime*, London: Audit Commission.

Blyth E. and Milner J. (1993) Exclusion from School: A First Step in Exclusion from Society? in *Children and Society* 7(3), 255–68.

Crawford A. (1997) *The Local Governance of Crime: Appeals to Community and Partnerships*, Oxford: Clarendon.

Crawford A. and Jones M. (1996) Kirkholt Revisited: Some Reflections on the Transferability of Crime Prevention Initiatives in *Howard Journal*, 31(1), 21–39.

Liddle A. M. and Gelsthorpe L. R. (1994) *Inter-Agency Crime Prevention: Organising Local Delivery*, Crime Prevention Unit Series Paper 52, London: Home Office.

Morgan J. (1991) *Safer Communities: The Local Delivery of Crime Prevention Through the Partnership Approach*, Standing Conference on Crime Prevention, London: Home Office.

Rhodes (1996) The New Governance: Governing Without Government in *Political Studies*, 44, 652–67.

Stewart J. (1996) Innovation in Democratic Practice in Local Government in *Policy and Politics*, 24(1), 29–41.

Tilley N. (1995) *Thinking About Crime Prevention Performance Indicators*, Crime Prevention Unit Paper 157, London: Home Office.

Young J. (1992) Ten Points of Realism in Young J. and Matthews R. (eds.) *Rethinking Criminology: The Realist Debate*, London: Sage, 24–68.

CHAPTER 19

The French Social Prevention Initiative

John Pitts

Introduction

In line with the recommendations of the Audit Commission Report, (Misspent Youth 1996). and the Morgan Report (Safer Communities 1991), in 1998, the government will require local authorities to demonstrate how they intend to tackle community safety and, within this, how they plan to deal with youth crime. We can be assured that the resultant mission statements will be bold, and the inter-agency partnerships impressive, but what they will actually do with, to, or for children and young people in trouble remains uncertain.

This is because, until recently, the orthodox view in British youth justice circles has been that 'prevention' can seriously damage a young person's reputation and life-chances. The argument has been that, because 'prevention' concerns itself with largely irrelevant social and psychological factors, instead of focussing upon the offences committed by young people, it serves to 'widen the net of social control', thus drawing perfectly normal youngsters deeper into the youth justice system. In consequence, the focus of prevention in the UK in the 1980s and early to mid-1990s, has been largely 'correctional' in tone, and directed mainly at apprehended offenders. Meanwhile, the youth service, statutory and voluntary, has been seriously depleted by successive government cuts and community work has more or less withered on the vine.

In France, by contrast, there are a wealth of innovative preventive programmes, developed outside the judicial system under the auspices the Social Prevention Initiative (SPI) initiated by François Mitterand in 1983.

The origins of the social prevention initiative

Upon its election in 1981 the socialist administration of François Mitterand faced nation-wide riots in the multi-racial banlieue. Fearing that they might reach the proportions they had attained in Britain, Mitterand established the *été jeunes*, a 100,000-strong national summer playscheme, and a commission of town mayors under the chairmanship of Henri Bonnemaison (1983). The Bonnemaison commission was concerned with both the prevention of crime and those forms of 'social exclusion' which appeared to threaten social cohesion. Thus, in its report, the Commission argued that if youth crime and disorder in the *banlieues* were to be curbed, the solution must lie in a process of political incorporation, an expression of solidarity with the people who lived there (King 1989). Although evaluation has been uneven, the SPI undoubtedly made a significant impact upon youth crime in France. In 1981 in both Britain and France, approximately 3,500,000 offences were recorded by the police. By the end of the 1980s, the number of offences recorded in Britain was approaching 6,000,000. Meanwhile in France, between 1983 and 1986 there was a decline in recorded offences to around 3,000,000 from which the figure rose gradually to around 3.8 million by the end of the decade. In France, the fall in crime was most marked in those categories of offences most frequently committed by children and young people (King 1988). Moreover, whereas in Britain in the 1980s crime rose fastest in the poorest neighbourhoods, in France it was in the poorest neighbourhoods that the fall in crime was most marked (King 1988).

The structure of the Social Prevention Initiative

In her evaluation of the impact of the SPI, De Liege (1991) points to the importance of its political and administrative structure in the realisation of its goals. The National Council for the Prevention of Delinquency, chaired by the Prime Minister and attended by the majority of town mayors and senior civil servants from the ministries of Justice, Housing, Education, Health and Social Affairs was established in June 1983. The Council determined the relationship which should exist between central and local government, the structure of interprofessional and inter-agency co-operation at local level, the roles to be played by public professionals, the resources to be devoted to the discharge of these roles and the space for negotiation between elected officials, administrators and citizen groups. At regional level, Councils for the Prevention of Crime chaired by the chief civil servant (the *Commissaire de la Republique*) with the Chief Judicial Officer (the *Procureur de la Republique*) as the vice-chair, were established. At local level Communal Councils for the Prevention of Crime, chaired by the town mayors were created. Communal Councils monitored local youth crime patterns, established special working groups to deal with particular problems and targeted central government funds on these problems. In his evaluation of European youth crime prevention initiatives John Graham (1993) notes that:

"The main aim of the Communal Council is to reduce crime through improving the urban environment, reducing unemployment among the young, improving facilities for education and training, combating racial discrimination and encouraging the assimilation and integration of marginalised groups, particularly alienated youngsters and immigrants. To facilitate this process, a national network of Youth Centres, known as *Missions Locales* has been set up in more than 100 towns and cities. These centres try to bridge the transition between school and work for the unemployed and the unqualified (aged 16–25) by offering youth training and advice and assistance on matters such as improving literacy, managing financial affairs and finding accommodation. They also encourage young people, particularly the unemployed, to set up and run their own projects."

A major innovation in French social welfare practice was the creation of Crime Prevention Teams. These teams were composed of social workers and youth workers who had no formal links with, or accountability to the justice system. As Bill Walden Jones (1993) observes "although they do not have even an approximate equivalent in Britain they constitute the core of the SPI". Most towns in France with a population of more than 10,000 have a Crime Prevention Team. Often each worker assumes responsibility for a particular quartier. Teams are funded jointly by the state and the *Departements*, and employed and managed by charitable organisations under contract to the local authority. They are coordinated by a local steering committee. The team in *Bourg-les-Valence*, studied by Walden-Jones had four workers who served a population of 27,000. Each team member had a neighbourhood which could be covered easily on foot. Walden-Jones offers the following breakdown of a prevention team member's week:

Activity	% of time devoted to it
On the street	28
In the office	15
Meeting other social workers	12
Managing a homework project	9
Management meetings	9
In transit	9
Running activities	8
Meeting individuals	6
Meeting families	4

Teams undertake an analysis of local patterns of youth crime and disorder and the location of young people believed to be at risk in a variety of ways. On the basis of this analysis certain neighbourhoods or groups are targetted for intervention. One team identified a group of young drug users, hanging around the bus station, as their target. The agency gave the team 18 months in which to establish relationships with the targetted group and up to five years to locate and work with a broader network of around 300 drug-abusing young people in that part of the city.

The teams studied by Walden-Jones utilised a range of approaches to achieve their goal of shifting young people 'away from offending and disaffection, towards normal social behaviour and integration' Its work was carried out with the agreement of the young people, and never as a condition of a sentence or a magistrate's directive. Furthermore, it was normal for no information to be passed to other agencies or to the family without the young person's permission. Walden-Jones cites one of team's clients:

> "Other social workers sit behind a desk and call you in to give you a hard time", said one 16 year old, "it's [the prevention worker] who moves" ("C'est lui qui bouge"). "They're realistic about what you can and can't do. They know we're not intellectuals and can only do so much", said a 17 year old, "I only trust [the worker] apart from my own family".
>
> "But this loyalty was based on mutual respect: the prevention workers treated the young people much as they would adults and I saw no examples of patronising attitudes by workers".

Local initiatives

In 1993/4 Philip Smith and the author undertook a comparative study of the responses of local politicians and public professionals to youth crime and victimisation on the Dickens Estate in East London and the Flaubert Estate in the West of Paris (Pitts 1997). As the 1980s progressed the Dickens Estate, in common with many of the poorest neighbourhoods in England and Wales, experienced a decline in the numbers of adults engaged in primary sector employment. This was, in large part, an effect of the economic recession of the mid- and late 1980s which led to the closure or withdrawal of local businesses to the periphery of the city (McGahey 1986, Sullivan 1989, Hope 1994). By the end of the 1980s, this process was compounded by the exodus of many of the relatively prosperous, older tenants, with permanent jobs in the local economy, and their replacement by young single-parent families and families which had proved to be 'disruptive' or 'bad payers' on other estates in the borough. These factors had reduced the degree of social control to which young people on the estate were subject and limited drastically their opportunities to 'grow out of crime' (Rutherford 1986, Hagan 1993). Thus, those families most prone to victimisation and those most likely to victimise them were progressively thrown together on the estate, leading to a parallel rise in violent crime in general and racial violence in particular (Sampson and Phillips 1993). The period also witnessed the withdrawal of those youth service, social welfare and training agencies which, in a previous period, had contributed to the quality of communal life and social cohesion on the estate (Downes 1990).

Crime prevention on the Dickens Estate

David Downes (1990) has observed that employment schemes on the estate have, for their duration, been effective in diverting young people from crime, or minimising their involvement in it but, when these schemes terminated, their impact was quickly dissipated. This points up two key differences between the Dickens Estate and the Flaubert Estate. Crime prevention on the Dickens Estate has traditionally taken the form of time-limited projects, emanating from beyond the estate and unintegrated with the activities of the established local and central government and voluntary agencies operating there. Not only were they unintegrated at agency level, they rarely articulated with the plans and strategies of the local administration. Patterns of funding which increasingly promoted an arbitrary opportunism amongst local agencies and local politicians, dictated that those projects which were realised tended to come with fully-formed and non-negotiable 'targets', and unrealistic 'exit strategies' which required the under-funded local authority to make unrealistic commit-ments to future spending. This process had led to considerable cynicism amongst both professional and local residents, about the viability of developing a safer neighbourhood on a project-by-project basis; a feeling articulated most clearly by research participants who visited the Flaubert estate in Paris.

Social prevention on the Flaubert Estate

On the Flaubert Estate local employment policy aimed to offer local jobs on the estate to local people in order to reduce unemployment and reinforce community ties. A national youth and adult training agency *Association Jeunesse, Culture, Loisirs, Technique* (JCLT) was contracted by the *Maire* and the *Mission Locale* to offer youth and adult training and social and cultural activities on the estate. Professionals recognised that racism and its poor reputation often made it difficult to place people in employment beyond the estate but their emphasis on extended periods of training leading to nationally recognised qualifications meant that they had achieved some success in equipping residents for skilled, higher-paid, jobs in primary sector employment in the *Departement* and in Paris.

This policy was devised by the Town Council, the *Mission Locale* and the *Conseil de la Quartier* elected by local residents aged 16+ (Jazouli 1995). Local housing policy was developed in a similar way. It pursues social stability via a strategy of locating relatives of different generations in proximity to one another. The pursuit of this policy has, amongst other things, led to the construction of new, larger, low-rise flats on the Flaubert Estate. This is of particular interest when we note that the key issue in local elections and the 'space-specific ideology of race and nation' amongst some white residents of the Dickens Estate and its environs, concerned housing (Jackson and Penrose 1993, Cohen 1995). Beyond the ideology, in East London, as elsewhere, council house sales and a freeze on council housing revenues have generated a genuine shortage of accommodation which has served to exacerbate racial tensions in the area.

In addition to the relatively formal *Conseil de la Quartier* on the Flaubert estate, there was a womens organisation, the *Femmes Relais*, a network of Senegalese, North African, Kurdish, Iranian and Portuguese mothers, supported by *animateurs sociales* from the mayor's office who met regularly with representatives of the schools, the police, the local administration and relevant welfare agencies, to discuss problems affecting their children and devise new policies and strategies.

The other meeting point between the politicians and the people on the Flaubert Estate was *La Pagode*, a centre constructed by the Mayor's Office where young people met *animateurs sociale* to undertake the recreational, educational and political activities in which they were interested (Picard 1995). Over the three years it has been in existence the 500, or so, users have produced a regular newsletter, *Alors . . . Quoi de Neuf*, which discusses issues affecting the estate and the young people on it. About 60 young people attend monthly meetings at *La Pagode* with the mayor or his deputy at which these issues are discussed and policy options are considered.

It is evident from our study that the developments on the Flaubert estate flowed from the political possibilities created by the policies of 'Decentralisation', 'Deconcentration', 'Social Prevention' and the *Politique de la Ville* introduced by the Mitterand administration in the 1980s. By allowing space for political innovation at a local level, they created the ground for localised *nouvelle democratie*. This local political participation connected, via the town's Mayor, to the Crime Prevention Committee chaired by the Prime Minister of France of which the majority of French town mayors were members. This created a means, to influence the priorities of local officials, central government departments, the manner in which these departments co-operated at local level and the ways in which their resources were deployed in the attempt to realise shared goals which were, in part at least, formulated in consultation with local citizens. It also made it possible to institutionalise this activity, politically, administratively and professionally at national, regional and local levels and, apparently, to do so without too much bureaucratic stultification. Thus the SPI is a politically-driven system with a range of political, administrative, and professional feedback loops which ensure that there is a strong connection between policy, provision, professional practice and the needs, interests and wishes of the intended beneficiaries.

These structures have been central to the realisation of the developments on the Flaubert Estate but so too has been the congruence between the political values of the citizens and professionals engaged in them, and those articulated within French social policy. Grevot (1994) notes that the vocabulary of Mitterand's *Politique de la Ville* was derived in large part from the French social work profession, whose numbers were increased, and whose professional status and political influence was enhanced significantly, by the crucial role they played in the realisation of the *Politique de la Ville*.

English professionals under pressure

This stands in marked contrast with the, sometimes open, hostility with which social workers and other public professionals in Britain were regarded by central government in the 1980s and 1990s (Parton 1985, 1991, Cooper et al. 1995). Our London respondents in statutory and voluntary social welfare agencies were all concerned about the falling standard of the service they were able to provide but sceptical about the efficacy of grassroots or local political pressure to effect change upon those factors which generated the problems encountered by the children and young people for whom they were attempting to provide a service. They appeared to have reconciled themselves to the narrowing their professional focus, and the redefinition of their task as the efficient exercise of the statutory functions of their agencies, no more, and no less.

This inevitably meant that their scope for innovation and responsiveness to the 'public' was restricted. Asked to describe what role the local authority Social Services Department might play vis-à-vis the high level of assaults on Bengali school children on the estate, two senior officers of the authority observed, ironically, that at best, the victim might be made the subject of a child protection investigation and the perpetrators, if they were ever apprehended, could be required to pursue a correctional programme at the Youth Justice Centre.

Bureaucratic and resource pressures meant that a decision to cooperate with other agencies or professionals was often determined by whether, and to what extent, such co-operation would enable public professionals to discharge, or indeed displace completely, their primary tasks. Of all the agencies contacted during the research, only the police could anticipate a crime prevention initiative, which did not take the form of a new 'project' funded from elsewhere, which involved the development of new agency imperatives rather than the re-description of existing ones.

London respondents did not perceive any positive local or central government political leadership behind the changes they experienced and their actions were shaped, defensively, by the attempt to avoid attracting sanctions from local politicians if the agency 'fell down on the job' (i.e. failed to discharge its statutory responsibilities adequately). This anxiety was heightened during the research because a new administration with a mandate to centralise previously localised services was elected, raising the spectre of demotions and redundancies.

The changing role of French social welfare

The involvement of traditional welfare agencies in the SPI initiative precipitated a redefinition of the social work role and a refocussing of the social work task. This had led, in some cases, to the recruitment of new personnel with new skills and perspectives and the construction of new political alliances. In her study of the impact of social prevention and anti-exclusion policies on French social work, Crescey Cannan (1996) found that some social workers experienced involvement in collective action with neighbourhood groups difficult, preferring to play a more traditional role with individual service users. As a result, some *Departements* and *Communes* had grown impatient with professional social work's reluctance to grasp new roles and employed sociologists and geographers, whom they perceive to be more attuned to the goals of SPI.

Conclusion

Not since the American Poverty Programme of the 1960s has there been a governmental assault upon the problem of social cohesion on the scale of the French Social Prevention initiative of the 1980s. However, the French initiative emerged from a different political tradition, adopted a radically different political strategy and, in consequence, had a different effect upon the relationship between those on the social margins and the state. At the core of the political culture of both the USA and the UK is a notion of the state as a potentially antagonistic force which, unless it is rigorously controlled, may at any moment encroach upon the lives and abrogate the liberties of citizens. Thus 'freedom' consists in minimising the role of the state. In France, and many other Western European states, by contrast, the state is conceived as a potentially creative force, constituted by, and representative of the collective interest of its citizens. Although both of these views are idealisations, they open doors to quite different political possibilities for governments trying to fashion responses to the problems of crime and social cohesion.

Rather than circumventing the state apparatus, the task defined by Mitterand and Bonnemaison concerned the construction, and then the institutionalisation, of a new relationship between the political centre and the social margins. This was to be achieved through the reform and co-ordination of the relevant ministries and a devolution of state power which aimed to repoliticise, democratise and localise key areas of state activity and transform the practices of their agents. In consequence, for a time, the French initiative achieved the prize which had eluded the Kennedy-Johnson administrations, the construction of a political 'hotline' between the head of state and the ghetto.

The French initiative was borne of a recognition that economic globalisation and a burgeoning new technology had transformed class relations and that now, the key social division was between a contracting, relatively prosperous and skilled workforce and the growing body of usually young and often non-white people, who appeared to be permanently excluded from economic activity altogether (Donzelot and Roman 1991; Wilson 1987). This analysis marked an early recognition of the forces which were transforming advanced industrial societies throughout Europe and beyond. Its unique contribution was to devise new forms of social solidarity, and new routes to citizenship, to replace traditional but defunct, social and political structures rooted in the work place.

References

Audit Commission (1996) *Misspent Youth*, London, The Audit Commission

Bonnemaison (1983) *Face a la Delinquence: Prevention, Repression, Solidarite: Rapport a le Prime Ministre de la Commission Des Maires sur la Securite*, Paris, La Documentation Francaise, Bonnemaison

Cannan C. (1996) The Impact of Social Development and Anti-Exclusion Policies on the French Social Work Professions Social Work in Europe, Vol. 3. No. 2. pp 1–4

Cohen P. (1995) *Island Stories: Real and Imagined Communities in the East End*, London, Runnymede Trust

Cooper A., Hetherington R., Baistow K., Pitts J. and Spriggs A. (1995) *Positive Child Protection: a View From Abroad*, Lyme Regis, Russell House Publishing

De Liege M-P. (1991) Social Development and the Prevention of Crime in *France: a Challenge for Local Parties and Central Government*, Farrell M. and Heidensohn F. Crime in Europe London, Routledge

Donzelot J. and Roman J. (1991) Le Deplacement de la Question Social in Donzelot J. (ed.), *Face a l'Exclusion*, Paris, Editions Espirit

Downes D. (1990) *Public Violence on Two Estates*, London, Home Office (unpublished)

232

Graham J. (1993) *Crime Prevention Policies in Europe*, European Journal of Crime, Criminal Law and Criminal Justice, Vol.1. No.2.

Hagan J. (1993) *The Social Embededness of Crime and Unemployment*, Criminology, 31, pp 455–491

Hope T. (1994) Communities Crime and Inequality in England and Wales. Paper presented to the 1994 Cropwood Round Table Conference *Preventing Crime and Disorder* Sept. 14–15, Cambridge

Jackson P. and Penrose J. (1993) *Constructions of Race, Place and Nation*, London, University College

Jazouli A. (1995) *Une Saison en Banlieue*. Paris, Plon

King M. (1988) *How to Make Social Crime Prevention Work, the French Experience*, London, NACRO

McGahey R. (1986) Economic Conditions, Neighbourhood Organisation and Urban Crime in Reiss J. A. and Tonry M. *Communities and Crime*, Chicago, Chicago University Press

Morgan Report (1991) *Safer Communities: the Local Delivery of Crime Prevention Through the Partnership Approach*, London, the Home Office

Parton N. (1985) *The Politics of Child Abuse*, London, Macmillan

Parton N. (1991) *Governing the Family*, London, Macmillan

Picard P. (1995) *Mantes la Jolie, Carnet de Route D'un Maire de Banlieue 1977–1995*, Paris, Syros

Pitts J. (1997) Youth Crime, Social Change and Crime Control in Britain and France in the 1980s and 1990s in Jones H. *Towards a Classless Society*, London, Routledge

Rutherford A. (1986) *Growing Out of Crime*, Harmondsworth, Penguin

Sampson A. and Phillips C. (1995) *Reducing Repeat Racial Victimisation on an East London Estate*, Home Office Crime Detection and Prevention Paper 67, London, Home Office

Sullivan M. (1989) *Getting Paid, Youth, Crime and Work in the Inner City*, London, Cornell University Press

Walden-Jones B. (1993) *Crime and Citizenship: Preventing Youth Crime in France Through Social Integration*, London, NACRO

Wilson W. J. (1987) *The Truly Disadvantaged: the Inner City, the Underclass and Public Policy*, Chicago, University of Chicago Press